JUDAH'S SCEPTRE
AND
JOSEPH'S BIRTHRIGHT

AN ANALYSIS OF THE PROPHECIES
OF SCRIPTURE IN REGARD TO THE
ROYAL FAMILY OF JUDAH AND
THE MANY NATIONS OF ISRAEL

BY
REV. J. H. ALLEN

NINETEENTH EDITION

DESTINY PUBLISHERS
Merrimac, Massachusetts

"Listen, O isles, unto me, and harken, ye people from **far**;
* * thou art my servant, O Israel, in whom I will be glorified."
Isa. 49: 1-3.

"I am a father to Israel, and EPHRAIM is my first-born. * * Declare it in the isles afar off, and say, He that scattered Israel will gather him, and keep him, as a shepherd doth his flock." Jer. 31: 9, 10.

"Behold these (Israel in the isles) shall come from far, and lo, these from the north and from the west. The children which thou shalt have, *after thou hast lost the other*, shall say again in thine ears, The place is too strait (cramped) for me, give a place to me that I may dwell. Isa. 49: 12, 20.

EPHRAIM—ISRAEL IN THE ISLES.

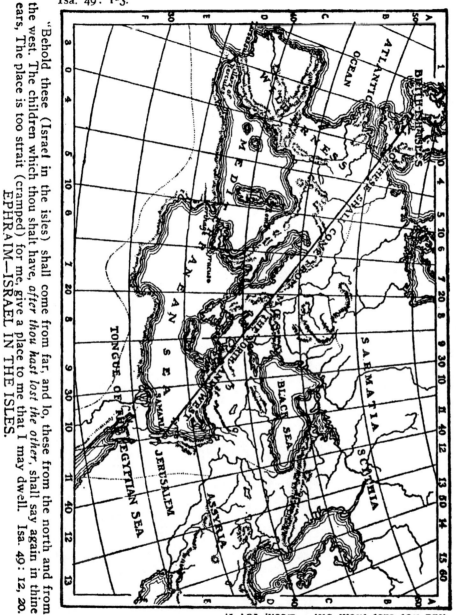

"I will save the house of JOSEPH, and I will bring them, for I will have mercy upon them; and they shall be as though I had not cast them off." Zech. 10: 1.

JUDAH'S SCEPTRE AND JOSEPH'S BIRTHRIGHT

Yours in Christ,— "The Truth."

J. H. Allen,

Author.

PREFACE.

Because of our connection with a certain school of Christian thought, we once held the erroneous opinion that most of the prophecies of the Old Testament were fulfilled, and that *its* present use was simply to feed the faith of devout men. Also, that any nourishment for faith which could be drawn from that source was not wholesome food for the soul, unless we were in possession of such an exalted type of spirituality that we would be able to rise above the somewhat prosy details of its histories, and find our soul-food in a surely accompanying spiritual influence, which, in its action upon us, was superior to the mere literalness of the subject matter.

We were also led to suppose that the unfulfilled prophecies of *"Moses and the prophets"* were of no special moment to Christianity, because the great momentous question, the coming of a Saviour, was settled forever. Consequently, when, perchance, we found some prophetic utterance therein, which we were forced to admit had not become a historic verity, and since this was the dispensation of the Spirit, we felt at liberty to give the reins to our somewhat vivid imagination, and let it run unchecked through the verdant and fruitful fields of speculation in search of some rare and deeply-spiritual truth which we might lay against that seeming rhetorical figure of Holy Writ.

But this roaming through those alluring fields always resulted in failure, for when those fanciful and random conjectures, no matter how lofty, were brought before our quickened conscience, they were soon condemned, because that judge who sits at the bar of our spiritual integrity not only revealed their insincerity, but also convinced us that they did not contain the real import, thought and purpose for which those words of God were written. Thus defeated, we could only bemoan our lack, not only of the mental power to grasp the true meaning of those holy words, but also the depth of spirituality which was supposed to be essential to the possession of that intense spiritual power which could pierce through the density of earthly things into the rarity of those which were heavenly. For the spiritual standards which we had erected for ourselves demanded the attainment of a soul life which would give us power to soar in the spirit into such rarefied heights of divine enlightenment that we could discern the graceful curves, the symmetrical outlines, the non-earthly shadows, the heavenly half-tones and the divine high-lights of that wonderful picture,—that spiritual masterpiece—which lay behind the coarseness of the letter.

These errors so blinded us, that, in our ignorance, we even considered that the twelve apostles, whom our Lord had chosen and enlightened, were in gross error when they understood Christ and the Scriptures to teach that there was to be a literal and visible kingdom of God on the earth with the Lord as king of all the earth when that day came. We assumed that their conception of the promised kingdom, when contrasted with our own, was carnal in the extreme, and that the superiority of our conception lay in the fact that it was free from all such mortal grossness. And we really thought that this spirit of moral groveling among the apostles had reached its climax, when James, who afterward became a martyr, and his brother John, he whom the Master loved, took their mother to Christ, and had her make a request of Him for them which they did not dare make for themselves.

But, thank God, such conceptions of divine truth were only our spiritual swaddling clothes, and the day dreams of spiritual babyhood. For, as we grew in grace, and became less presumptive, the Holy Ghost lifted the veil from our mind, and illuminated the following portion of the Saviour's reply to the request of the mother of James and John: "To sit on my right hand, and on my left, is not mine to give, but *it shall be given to them for whom it is prepared of my Father.*"

In this work we have followed the history of the two families, or kingdoms, into which the seed of Abraham were divided, through the intricate paths of their Biblical history, and the prophecies concerning them, which have thus far become history, down to the present day, without the loss of any single connecting link.

We have been moved by the Holy Spirit to thus write concerning the earthly history of God's chosen race, because so very little of it is known by the masses of our people, and yet it is the foundation upon which the entire structure of Christianity must rest. A knowledge of these earthly things not only renders the claims of Christianity impregnable, but they are also the basis upon which we must rest our faith for better things. For Jesus has said, "If I have told you of earthly things, and ye believe not, how shall ye believe, if I tell you of heavenly things?" The truth of this saying of our Lord has been demonstrated in our own ministry; for in the past seven years, during which time we have been able to demonstrate the special features of truth as set forth in this book—i. e., *the realization of the promises made to* ISRAEL, by THE PEOPLE OF ISRAEL—the Lord has used us to bring more skeptics to the light of his truth, than in all our previous ministry of twenty-one years. Also during this seven years, while we have seen the faith of some fail, the Lord has helped us to save the tottering faith of many. We are also sure, from the very reasons which are given, that the faith of those who have made shipwreck could not have failed, if they had known these things. Hence we have written this time concerning the *earthly things* which are the subjects of Divine inspiration, praying that God will use them to strengthen the faith of some, and to bring others into the faith in the inspiration of the Bible. But if there seems to be a demand for it we will write again, and then we will write on THE HEAVENLY THINGS.

CONTENTS

CONTENTS

PART THIRD

THE VEIL LIFTED FROM ABRAHAMIC NATIONS

PART FIRST.

THE BIRTHRIGHT; OR, THE PROMISE OF MANY NATIONS TO ABRAHAM.

"Behold, my covenant is with thee, and thou shalt be a father of *many nations*. Neither shall thy name any more be called Abram, but thy name shall be Abraham; for a father of *many nations* have I made thee. And I will make thee exceeding fruitful, and I will make *nations* of thee, and kings shall come out of thee."

CHAPTER I.

Although it is not generally known, it is nevertheless true that God made two covenants with Abraham, or, rather, that he made one with Abram and another with that same man after his name was changed to Abraham. This change of name was made that it might harmonize with the new character and the new order of things as they pertain to the covenant man.

The first, or Abram, covenant was made when the man was ninety years old; but the second, or Abraham, covenant was not made until this man was called upon to make the one great sacrifice of his life.

The text of the first of these covenants is as follows: "And when Abram was ninety years old and nine, the Lord appeared to Abram, and said unto him, I am the Almighty God; walk before me and be thou perfect. And I will make my covenant between me and thee, and will multiply thee exceedingly. And Abram fell on his face; and God talked with him, saying: As for me, behold my covenant is with thee, and thou shalt be a father of many nations. Neither shall thy name any more be called Abram, but thy name shall be Abraham; for a father of many nations have I made thee. And I will make thee exceeding fruitful, and I will make nations of thee, and kings shall come out of thee. And I will establish my covenant between me and thee and thy seed after thee in their generations for an everlasting covenant, to be a God unto thee, and to thy seed after thee. And I will give unto thee, and to thy seed after thee, the land wherein thou art a stranger, all the land of Canaan, for an everlasting possession; and I will be their God."—Gen. 17:1-8.

We see at once that the great feature of this covenant is a multiplicity of seed for a man that hitherto has been childless; and that this multitude of people are to become, not one great nation, not simply a plurality of nations, but a large plurality, i. e., "MANY NATIONS."

With the great majority of Bible students, and with most schools of Biblical thought, the fact that the Lord, when making this covenant, promised Abram that he should become *the father of more than one nation* is entirely overlooked. The general trend of the teaching is, that, of all the people who dwell upon the face of the earth, the Jewish people are distinctively the people, the one nation only, which is composed of the seed of Abraham; and that they, and they alone, are the chosen people of God whose national story makes up the great bulk of Biblical history and prophecy. But such cannot be the case, for if God has fulfilled the first promise which he made to the father of the Jewish people, he has made it possible for the people of some of the other nations of earth to stand side by side with that one, and with them to say: "We have Abraham to our father."

One special, and important, feature of this covenant is, that among this multitude of Abrahamic seed there is to be a royal, or kingly line; the posterity of which shall become the rulers of, at least, some of these nations which shall owe their origin to one common father. For the Lord not only promised Abraham that kings should come out of his loins, but when he reiterated the promises of his covenant to Sarai, the barren wife of Abraham, he said: "She shall be the mother of nations; kings of people (R. V., nations) shall be of her." And so her name was changed to Sarah, i. e., Princess, that she, too, might have a name which would be in harmony with her new character, for only a princess may be the mother of kings.

Another special feature of this covenant is, that there is a land consideration, which involves the land of Canaan in an everlasting bond—not only of ownership, but of possession. Evidently the everlasting possession of that land by its lawful heirs has not yet begun, for, at this writing, it is in the hands of the "Unspeakable Turk."

One other feature of this covenant is, that it is wholly unconditional. That is, the Lord has promised, irrespective of the moral or spiritual character of the people themselves, so to increase the posterity of the Abrahamic lineage, that, nationally, they shall become all that the covenant promises.

Centuries after the giving of this covenant, when the Abrahamic posterity were quite numerous, and while they were still together in one nation, the Lord made a covenant with them which was conditional; but they broke faith with him, and violated its specified conditions. Since it is true, that, in contracting or conditional covenants, there is both a party of the first and a party of the second part, and the law is, that, when either party breaks the conditions, the other is not held, or bound by them, hence when the covenant people broke their part of the contract, God was no longer bound, and said: "They continued not in my covenant, and I regarded them not." Thus that covenant was annulled. But in this covenant which we have under consideration, God has assumed all responsibility, and to his integrity alone must we look for its fulfillment. For while it is true that both God and Abraham are parties to this covenant, we well know who has pledged himself, and whose will it expresses, and whom to expect shall keep his word inviolate, and which will be to blame if this covenant goes by default.

The second covenant which God made with Abraham was not made until many years after the first, and was made at a time when Abraham had just offered his only son, who was the first of the promised many, as a sacrifice, in obedience to the command of him who produced that son, by his creative power, from that which was as good as dead, and as an expression of faith in the resurrective power of that same covenant-making God. It is recorded as follows: "And the angel of the Lord called unto Abraham the second time, and said, By myself have I sworn, saith the Lord, for because thou hast done this thing, and hast not withheld thy son, thine only son: that in blessing I will bless thee, and in multiplying I will multiply thy seed as the stars of the heaven, and as the sand which is upon the sea shore; and thy seed shall possess the gate of his enemies; and in thy seed shall all the nations of the earth be blessed; because thou hast obeyed my voice." Gen. 22: 16-18.

Before noticing the one great feature of this covenant, we wish to call your attention to some of the minor points; the first of which is, that it also is unconditional, "By myself have I sworn," is the declaration of the covenant maker; hence this covenant can neither be broken nor annulled, because, as in the first, God alone is the responsible party.

Another point is, that there is a repetition and confirmation of the multiplicity of children phase of the first covenant, to which is added the first detail as to what shall be a national characteristic of Isaac's multiplied seed in their relation to other nations, namely: "Thy seed shall possess the gate of his enemies."

The Lord usually gives himself two witnesses, or doubles his promises and prophecies, as in the case of Pharaoh when he had dreamed the same thing twice and Joseph told him the reason that the dream was doubled to him was because the thing which it signified was of God. So it was with this gate blessing. It was at a time, that, after consenting to accompany Abraham's servant and become the wife of Isaac, through whom must come this great multitude of people, this gate promise, together with that which pertains to the multiplicity of children, was given to Rebekah. It came as a parting blessing from her brothers, who, it seems, were imbued with the spirit of prophecy; for it is recorded that they blessed her, and said: "Thou art our sister, be thou the mother of thousands of millions, and let thy seed possess the gate of those that hate them."

But the one great special feature of this second covenant which God made with that one man, is most certainly couched in the following words: "In thy seed shall all the nations of the earth be blessed." It will take but little investigation to reveal the fact that this one phase of this last covenant is Messianic, and that it pertains especially to but one person. But, that the many to whom pertains the first covenant are involved in this, together with the one to whom it more especially pertains, and that the principal one of this covenant is involved, in the common bond of brotherhood, with the many of that first covenant, no one will deny.

We understand that at the time these words were uttered, it would have been impossible to give them the fullness of meaning which the Holy Spirit has given them, as interpreted in the New Testament, for it was under the illumination given to the Apostle Paul, that their full import bursts upon us. It was when contrasting the law covenant—the one which was annulled—with this only-son covenant that Paul is careful to say: "Now to Abraham were the promises made, even for his seed, He does not say, and to the *seeds,*" as concerning many, but as concerning one: "and to thy seed which is Christ."

We have here given the best translation, for clearness, that the text will allow. In it the Apostle makes no attempt to give an exact Old Testament quotation, but bases his argument on the strength of the subject noun being in the singular number. The subject with which he is dealing is the blessing that shall come upon all the Gentile nations through Abraham's sacrificed son, *the one seed*, who also was the Only Son of his

Divine Father, just as Isaac, the type, was the only son of his father when he was offered in sacrifice.

It is not only the words, but also the circumstances connected with the giving of these promises, which are prophetic. God had said to Abraham that the many nations which he had formerly promised him should come through Isaac, his only son, but afterward called upon him to sacrifice that son, who was the only one through whom that promise could be fulfilled. But Abraham knew that God had accomplished that which was equal to a creation, when, through him and Sarah, who were both as good as dead, Isaac had been produced; so, being strong in faith, he offered him up, "accounting that God was able to raise him up, even from the dead; from whence also he received him in a figure."

Could any analogy be more complete?

A Son of Promise, an only son, from whom so much is expected, sacrificed and accounted dead, then, in symbol, raised from the dead! And the two special reasons for this test, being, on the one hand, an encouragement to faith, and on the other, that the son might live to fulfill his God-ordered destiny. The prototype of this is another Son of Promise, an only Son, from whom so much—so very much—is promised and expected, sacrificed on the tree, dead. But that the two witnesses, the word and the symbol, of the promiser might not fail, the Divine Father, who gave back that other only son, raises from the dead his only Son, that he also might become the author and finisher of our faith, that he, too, might live and become all that was promised and expected of him, and thus fulfill his glorious destiny. We can ask no more, for both the lesser and the greater son, the type and prototype, are, "as concerning the flesh," sons of Abraham.

Throughout the world it is most generally known, and throughout Christendom it is universally known, that "the seed to whom the promise was made," did come; but it is not universally known, nor acknowledged throughout Christendom, that the many peoples are included in that same covenant with this *one* seed, without whom the entire structure of Christianity must fall, and that every argument for the Christ, from the covenant standpoint, must stand the crucial test of a numerous posterity from the loins of Abraham, or go down. And yet it is so.

True, the covenant with the people failed; true, the people sinned, and violated their obligations; true, the law was added, because of their transgressions, to bridge over, "till the (one) seed should come to whom the promise was made." But the argument in favor of the Messianic covenant against all this is, that "the covenant which was confirmed before of God in Christ, the law, which was four hundred and thirty years after, cannot disannul, that it should make the promise of none effect."

How could it? We, sirs, believe that it could not. All Christendom believes that it could not. And if it could not, neither can the promise concerning a multiplicity of children for Abraham be annulled.

For, with this same Messianic promise, there is a repetition of the metaphor of many seeds, as the stars of heaven and as the sands of the sea shore, together with the gate blessing; so we can just as reasonably expect that Christ could or would have failed, as to expect that the gate, the sand, and the star, promises shall have gone by default. But, at this late day in the history of the world, with the Divine light of prophecy shining upon well known facts, which once were only the subjects of prophetic utterances but are now the recorded facts of authentic history, we can say with a confidence, which is supported by the eternal Spirit, that neither have failed.

Elsewhere, when this same Apostle was making an effort to encourage the faith of believers in the faithfulness of God, he gives a word for word quotation from this same covenant promise, saying: "When God made promise to Abraham, because he could swear by no greater, he swore by himself, saying, Surely blessing I will bless thee, and multiplying I will multiply thee." This quotation, as you see, pertains to the multiplicity of seed, and not to the Messianic phase of the second covenant; but it proves to us that each individual feature of that covenant stands on the same secure foundation, and is just as sure of fulfillment as the other, for underneath every promise of that covenant there are two immutable things ;—God and his oath.

So, we are safe in saying that God has made two unconditional covenants with Abraham, and that, if he has been true to those covenants, then there are "many nations" in existence on this earth today, the people of which must have descended from Abraham and Sarah; and that these nations are in possession of the gates, or entrances, of their national enemies; unless it be that the time has not yet come for those promises to materialize.

The facts, in either case, are revealed, and, as we proceed, we shall see which of these is true; but thus far it is evident that one of these covenants is Messianic; that the other is multitudinous; that each is contained in the other; that in them there is no contracting party of the second part; and that both alike do stand on the integrity of God.

These are the days of skeptical indifferentism on the one hand, and of rampant infidelity on the other; of narrow sectarianism, worldly churchianity, and the blatant headiness of higher (?) criticism—Days "when Endor-ism is called *Spiritual*-ism," when Buddhism is sanctified by the name of Theo-sophia, i.e., Divine wisdom, and when pure faith and true spirituality are dubbed "Fanaticism."

Then surely, in such days as these, all who believe that the promises of God are never broken will be helped and encouraged when proof, full and abundant, shall be given that not only the promise concerning the many nations, but all the predictions of "Moses and the prophets," as they pertain either to the Christ or to the many-nationed people, have been, are being, or —on the strength of that which has been, and that which now is—shall yet be fulfilled.

CHAPTER II.

Since we are compelled to begin our search for light, concerning every phase of these themes, along the lines of Biblical history and prophecy, it will be well for us first to gather from those sources a few of the greater and more general facts. By so doing, we will find it to be a great help in our study of the more special features of the subjects, as it will enable us to place, with unerring certainty, each detail where it belongs.

It being true that the Lord included in the Abrahamic covenants a promise that the forthcoming children of promise should eventually develop into many nations, there are many other things that must follow as a consequent; one of which is, that for the accomplishment of this purpose, God must provide sufficient territory or scope of country, which shall become the home of each nation, for it is absolutely impossible that flourishing nations shall exist without national homes.

Pursuant to this thought, we know of no utterance in all the Word of God which furnishes a more general or comprehensive outlook than the following: "When the Most High divided to the nations their inheritance, when he separated the sons of Adam, he set the bounds of the people according to the number of the children of Israel. For the Lord's portion is his people; Jacob is the lot (cord, or line) of his inheritance." Deut. 32: 8, 9.

When Moses was commanded to write the above concerning the division of the earth's surface to the sons of Adam, only a very small portion of it was inhabited; nevertheless, in the mind of God every Island was set apart, and every continent divided. For the scope of the facts herein stated are world-wide, and embrace within their sweep the entire inhabited and inhabitable portion of the earth's surface. Also, those divisions were so arranged and subdivided, and the boundaries so set, that every nation, tongue, and people among the sons of Adam,—be they already in existence, or be they among the forthcoming nations,— had their national home allotted unto them.

Moreover, God always not only kept in mind that special country which he had promised should become the everlasting inheritance of the chosen race, but he also, when setting the territorial bounds for other nations, remembered Israel, and either restricted the boundaries of other nations, or enlarged those divisions of country intended for Israel, which will be needed by that immense multitude of people when they shall have fulfilled their appointed destiny of developing into many nations. For we must bear in mind that the posterity of Abraham are a natural seed, according to the flesh, and that each special nation of the many must have a place in which to dwell.

In addition to the fact that these Abrahamic nations are a fleshly seed, we must remember also that they are not necessarily a race of saints; for it is a notorious fact that some of that race have been, and others are now, just as wicked as that fallen son of the heavens would have them; but, on the other hand, that same race has furnished, and still is furnishing, men who are the grandest and best of earth.

When the time came for God to produce from the covenant man a son who should be the further progenitor of the covenant race, Abraham was anxious that Ishmael, his son by Hagar, the handmaid of Sarah, should be used for this purpose, and exclaimed, "O that Ishmael might live before thee!" To this earnest appeal the Lord was not indifferent, and promised that he would bless Ishmael. But on the subject of rejecting Ishmael as the covenant inheritor, and making his covenant with a son who should be a child of Sarah, as well as of Abraham, the Lord was inflexible. His word of promise was the insurmountable barrier, and so he said to Abraham: "Sarah thy wife shall bear thee a son indeed, and thou shalt call his name Isaac . . . and as for Ishmael, I have heard thee . . . twelve princes shall he beget, and I will make him a great nation. But my covenant will I establish with Isaac, which Sarah shall bear unto thee at this set time in the next year."

So Ishmael's posterity became alien before the legal line had any existence,—except that, on the authority and responsibility of creative faith, the Lord counts things that are not as if they were—for God had yet to create Isaac and bring forth life out of that which was as good as dead.

We have the record of another racial choice and rejection which was made before birth, that of Jacob and Esau, but before we discuss the question of race versus grace,—as involved in the caption of this chapter—relative to them, for it is over their case that the subject is argued in the New Testament, we wish to call your attention to the fact that after the death of Sarah, Abraham married a second wife whose name was Keturah, by whom he had a number of sons. These sons in time became the fathers of the Medes, Midianites, and other nations; but we can no more reckon these nations as a part of the promised many, than we can those which were formed by the posterity of Ishmael and Esau. Could we do so, our task would be an easy one and our story soon told; but we cannot do this, for the covenant nations must come only from Abraham and Sarah through their only son Isaac, whose posterity alone can be called, as they are called, "the Children of the Promise," in contradistinction to those who belong to the other families, and who are called "the Children of the Flesh."

This brings us to the question of race versus grace as understood by the New Testament Church, and explained by the Apostle Paul, who in his Epistle to the Romans says: "Neither, because they are the children of Abraham, are they all (racial) children, * * * but the children of the promise are counted for the seed." As he carries the argument still further, he makes this truth all the more apparent by declaring: "In Isaac shall thy seed be called," and then explains, as follows: "That is, they which are the children of the flesh, these are not the (national) children of God; but the children of the promise are counted for the seed. For this is the word of promise, at this time will I come, and Sarah shall have a son. And not only this; but when Rebecca also had conceived by one, even our father Isaac (for the children being not yet born, neither having done any good or evil, that the purpose of God according to election might stand, not of works, but of him that calleth): it was said unto her, the elder shall serve the younger. As it is written Jacob have I loved, but Esau have I hated. What shall we say then? Is there unrighteousness with God? God forbid!" Rom. 9: 7-14.

With this argument before us, it is clear that it is only the children of Isaac who are counted for the national seed of the covenant concerning the promised multitude, and that all this question of election as regards Jacob and Esau is purely racial and national. That is, one of these two nations which sprang from the same mater is the recipient of national promises, glories, honors, covenants, and service of which the other is not a partaker.

The argument is that when Rebecca, who we remember was to become the mother of thousands of millions, had conceived by Isaac, the father of the race, the result was that there were two nations, or nationalities, in the womb—not necessarily a nation, either of sinners or of saints. To convince us that the election was purely racial, Paul throws in the parenthetical clauses explaining that Jacob had done nothing good that he should deserve these covenant blessings. But he also just as assuredly affirms that Esau had done no evil that he should not have them, for the choice was made before they had the power to do good or evil, i.e., before they were born.

The King James version is a little unfortunate in its use of the word "hated," as herein used, for one meaning which is given to the original word is, "to love less," and when used in contrast to the word "love" as applied to Jacob, it will bear that simple meaning. The fact, which Paul states, is simply that God loved Jacob more and Esau less, or that he preferred one to the other, and that this preference for one excluded the other.

So Paul asks the question, "Is there unrighteousness with God?" and for a reply gives only that surprised exclamation, "God forbid!" He scouts the criminating thought that it could possibly be unrighteousness with God, that he should be pleased to choose the white race with which to work out his purpose, instead of the red, or copper-colored one; but makes the implication that there would have been unrighteousness, of a very grave character, with the Lord, if this election had been one of grace instead of race—that is, grace unto salvation for Jacob and his seed, and damnation, without any possible chance of grace, for Esau and his children.

Now for the facts concerning these contradistinctive appellations, "Children of the Flesh" and "Children of the Promise," as applied to the races which have Abraham for one common father.

(1) God, as we have shown, made a covenant with Abraham, in which it was promised that he should become the father of many nations, hence Abraham was the inheritor of a promise from God.

(2) Isaac, who was a natural son of Abraham and Sarah, according to the flesh, was not only the child of a special promise, but he was also the first child of the covenant promise.

(3) After the death of Abraham, God confirmed the original covenant promise to Isaac, the child of promise, as follows: "I will perform the oath which I swear unto Abraham thy father; and I will make thy seed to multiply as the stars of heaven, and I will give unto thy seed all these countries; and in thy seed shall all the nations of the earth be blessed." Hence Isaac also became the inheritor of a promise from the God of his father.

(4) The immediate posterity of Isaac, the promise-holder, were Jacob and Esau, the persons whom Paul uses in making his argument concerning the Lord's choice of race. Jacob, the younger of these two, who were twins, was chosen by the promise-maker, before they were born, to be the inheritor of the covenant promises. And so the Divine promiser reiterates those promises to him, as follows: "I am the Lord God of Abraham thy father, and the God of Isaac: the land whereon thou liest, to thee will I give it, and to thy seed: and thy seed shall be as the dust of the earth, and thou shalt spread abroad to the west, and to the east, and to the north, and to the south: and in thee and in thy seed shall all the families of the earth be blessed." Hence Jacob also received direct from the Lord the same covenant promises which had previously been given to his fathers.

(5) Since there can be no mistaking the purport of these covenant promises regarding a natural and multitudinous posterity for these promise-inheritors, and inasmuch as these promises were promised and re-promised, by the Divine promise-maker to the successive promise-holders, then, when that promised multi-

tude of people shall have materialized, it is they, and they only, who can be called "The Children of the Promise." And the only crucial test is that they be Abraham's seed who have descended from Isaac through Jacob.

Thus it is that the natural seed of Abraham, whose genealogical tree sprouts from the Jacob roots, are the children of the promise, and that others are not, although they also be the natural sons of Abraham, but, not having come through the family line of the promise-inheritors, they are "the Children of the Flesh" *only.* While to Israelites *only,* the seed of Abraham, Isaac, and Jacob, pertain the promises, the covenants, the adoption, the glory, the special service, the giving of the divine law, and through whom, as concerning the flesh, Christ came. But no such national glory, honor, dignity, and exaltation are promised to those other nations which sprang from that same father through Ishmael, Esau, and the sons of Keturah: no, not even such glory as comes from the least of these covenants promises and blessings.

Consequently, we can see why the Lord always declares himself to be the God of Abraham, Isaac, and Jacob, and not the God of Abraham, Ishmael, and Esau; and why it is that Paul's kinsmen according to the flesh are exclusively the children of the promise, for they are Israelities, to whom pertain the promises, etc. That is, they are the people who owe their existence to the fact that God was true to the promise which he made to Abraham, repeated to Isaac, and reiterated to Jacob, whose name was changed to Israel, and from whom come the elect people whose general racial name is Israel. Thus each individual member of the race is an Israelite, be he a good man or a bad one, and belongs to the elect or chosen people of God.

Therefore all this question of election between Jacob and Esau, which has caused so many unjust conceptions of God and his precious saving truth, is a question of Race, and not of Grace.

However, there is both an election of race and an election of grace, for Paul, when speaking of the seven thousand men who had not bowed the knee to Baal, declares that even now, "at this present time, also, there is a remnant according to the *election* of grace." But when he wrote regarding the attitude of a certain part of the elect race toward the election of grace, he says: "As concerning the gospel, they are enemies for your sakes; but as touching the *election*, they are beloved for the fathers' sakes." Here we find two elections, i. e., *the election of race and the election of grace.*

Touching the election of race, God could say, "And thou, Israel, art my servant whom I have chosen, the seed of Abraham my friend." But, when it was a question of individual service or relation to him, even among his chosen people, he could throw the responsibility on them, and say: "Choose ye this day whom ye will serve." Or when pressing the subject of eternal life to be accepted or rejected by each member of that elect race, God could say: "See, I have this day set before thee life and death," and then exhort them to "Choose life!"

If it is a question of race election, and the fidelity of the Divine promise is at stake, it can be asserted that the will of God, independent of the will of others, can cause certain conditions to obtain; "that the purpose of God according to election might stand"—not in the good or evil works, or unholy natures of unborn babes, "but of him that calleth."

When the call of God is of racial, or of national import, God can say: "Hearken unto me, O Jacob and Israel my called." But if it is a question of personal election to the grace of salvation, then faithful men of God may exhort other men, saying: "Give diligence to make your calling and election sure."

When it is race, it is, "Whom I (God) have chosen."

When it is grace, it is, "Whosoever will, may come and take the water of life freely."

When it is race, it is, "I have called thee by my name; thou art mine." In grace it is "Whosoever believeth," of whom the Lord says: "They are mine."

In grace it is, "Come."

In race it is fate, destiny, kismet.

One is a chosen *race,* and the other is a chosen *way.* The way is by faith that it might be of grace, but the choice of race is according to the predetermined and predestined purpose of God.

In race election it is generation, or born of the flesh.

In the election of grace it is regeneration, or born of the Spirit.

In grace it is, "Whosoever offereth praise glorifieth me;" but in race, it is, "This people have I formed for myself; *they* SHALL show forth my praise."

This declaration brings us to the consideration of the purpose, or object, which the Lord has in choosing, and forming a special race of men who, in spite of the wickedness of the great bulk of them, he calls his own chosen people, and whose national destiny he purposes to control.

Much of the manifest purpose of God touching this people is made known in that brief epitome given by the Apostle Paul, as quoted above, respecting the national honors of his own people. Figuratively speaking, every word in that resume of Israelitish history and the summing up of their honors weighs a ton. As we proceed with the story of Israel, it is our purpose to consider these facts in detail, but at this juncture we will take time only to say that, since the creation, no such opportunity, or such fitting cause, for national honor and greatness has ever come, or ever can come, to any other nation on the earth.

It would seem that their cup of glory was full to the overflow, when through them the Lord sent his word from Heaven, and spread it abroad over the face of the inhabited portions of the earth, and when God's word had been so fulfilled, and his purpose for them so fully accomplished that they could say: "Unto *us* a child is born, unto *us* a son is given; and the government shall be upon his shoulder; and his name shall be called Wonderful, Counselor, The mighty God, The everlasting Father, The Prince of Peace." *When they could say this*—then it would seem that their cup of national greatness and glory was overflowing, and that the supreme purpose of God for them had been reached. But it is our glad privilege to tell you that there is in God's word a declared purpose, which must yet be accomplished through that elect race, and until it shall be fulfilled, all that which is done is robbed of fully nine-tenths of its power and glory; since, outside the realm of faith, millions are today hopelessly drifting on the shoals of constantly increasing forms of unbelief, and with the great majority of men, the word of God must forever be regarded as a cunningly devised fable, unless God has some plan of vindication for it and himself.

Furthermore, the great love of God is misunderstood and despised; the blood of the atonement is trampled upon; Christ is still considered by the many a bastard, a fraud, and a failure. He is still put to an open shame in the house of his professed friends; shipwrecks of a one-time faith and a present professed faith in him are scattered everywhere. And so it is that God, his Word, and his Christ, must yet be fully vindicated. And they shall be, for God has promised it; and when this vindication shall have been accomplished, then, and not till then, will Israel have reached the supreme climax of greatness and glory of the purpose for which the Lord has chosen her.

Harken ye unbelieving ones! Harken to this!—

"Thus saith the Lord that created thee, O Jacob, and he that formed thee, O Israel, * * * ye are my witnesses, saith the Lord, and my servant whom I have chosen; that ye may know and believe me, and understand that I am He; before me there was no God formed, neither shall there be after me. I, even I, am the Lord; and beside me there is no Saviour. I have declared, and have saved, and I have showed, when there was no strange God among you: *therefore ye are my witnesses,* saith the Lord—that I am God."—Isa. 43: 1, 10-12.

Note this, *"That* YE *may know and believe* ME, *and understand that*—I AM HE."

God not only intends to use the Israelites for the purpose of convincing them that he is God, and the only God, but he also intends to use them to convince the rest of the world. For he says: "I will sanctify my great name, * * * *and the heathen shall* know that I am the Lord, saith the Lord God, when I shall be sanctified in you before their eyes."—Ezek. 36:23.

This is the great purpose for which the Lord has chosen Israel, and when this is accomplished, they shall have reached the acme of national glory.

If you ask, "Is the history of Israel, as a whole, a Divine work? we answer, yes. But if you ask, "Is that history designed as a preparation for the moral creation which Jesus Christ came to effect?" Our answer is, no; the law which the Lord gave to his people was intended to accomplish that purpose; but the history of Israel, together with prophecies concerning them, many of which must yet become history, is for the vindication of God.

CHAPTER III.

THE SCEPTRE AND THE BIRTHRIGHT.

Simply to show the fact that there is in Biblical history that which is styled the Sceptre, and also that there is a something which is designated as the Birthright, we quote the following: "The Sceptre shall not depart from Judah, etc."—Gen. 49: 10. "For Judah prevailed above his brethren, and of him comes the chief ruler (prince); but the Birthright is Joseph's."—1 Chron. 5:2.

That the Sceptre blessings, privileges, and promises pertain to Judah, from whom comes the royal family of Israel's race, is well known, and its import somewhat fully comprehended in the realm of light and knowledge as disseminated through Christendom. But that which is called the Birthright has not, in the past, been understood at all, and as yet is understood but by the few. And the very few who have written on themes which involved the Birthright have assumed that their readers were as wise as they, and have written concerning the Birthright without explaining what it was; hence, the reader is compelled to receive their use and application of the word without knowing it to be correct.

When we say that the word Birthright implies that which comes by right of birth, or as an inheritance, all will agree with us; but just what special inheritance is referred to as that which is declared, in the above text, to be the right of Joseph, few will understand until the matter is explained. Hence we give the following:

In the first covenant which the Lord made with Abraham, there are two distinct features, in so far as concerns his children; first, a multiplicity of seed, as involved in the following: "I will make thee exceeding fruitful, and I will make nations of thee;" second, a royal line, the promise of which is given as follows: "Kings shall come out of thee." Hence these covenant promises and blessings, which had been given him direct from the Lord, became the lawful heritage of Abraham.

This heritage which was given from God to a human being seems to have in it both a human and a divine right; the human right being that a son of the heritage-holder may succeed the father and become the lawful possessor of the inheritance; the divine right being that of choice among the legal posterity of the heritage-holder.

After this heritage was given, Isaac was the first heir in the line of succession, and he was also the one whom the Lord had chosen as the inheritor of that which had been given to his father. At the time of Abraham's death he was the father, not only of Isaac, but of six other lawful sons, who were the children of Keturah, his second wife. Notwithstanding this fact, the divine record declares that he gave all his possessions to Isaac, the son of Sarah. "Abraham gave all that he had unto Isaac."—Gen. 25:5.

Isaac became the heir because he was the first born among the lawful sons of Abraham; hence those possessions came to him as the right of the first-born, or by right of birth, i.e., as a Birthright. And, if Isaac was heir to all that Abraham had, then, aside from all else which may have come into his possession, he was most certainly heir of that God-given heritage, the covenants of promise which contained these two distinct features—a multitude of people and a royal line.

Esau, the son of Isaac and brother of Jacob, having been born first, for he was the elder of twins, was next in the line of succession, and being the elder or first-born, came into possession of the Birthright. Thus he had a birthright at his disposal, but instead of keeping it, and allowing it, in turn, to become the property of his first-born son, he undervalued it, and sold it to his brother Jacob, who, being the younger, could not have acquired it by right of birth.

The right of Esau to sell the birthright has never been questioned; his wisdom in selling it may well be questioned. The fact that Jacob, who became anxious to obtain that birthright, felt that he must not only make the purchase from Esau, its lawful owner, but also knew that he must deceive their father in order that he might secure from him the accompanying blessing, is proof positive that the Birthright was the lawful inheritance of Esau.

Moreover, when Jacob went in unto Isaac in the disguise which he and his mother had devised, he went with a lie on his lips, and said to his father, "I am Esau thy first born." But Isaac was distrustful; the hands felt all right, but the voice aroused suspicion. So the blind father asked, "Art thou my very son Esau?" Again Jacob answered in the affirmative.

What was he after? That which belonged to the first-born.

What did he get? That which belonged to the first-born.

He had not only bought it from the first-born himself, but also had deluded the father into bestowing upon him the blessing which made the purchase secure from the human side; for when Isaac found that Jacob had secured the blessing from him by subtility, he could not revoke it.

That word "blessing" seems to be the word which attaches itself to the receiver and inheritor of even these covenant promises which pertain wholly to earthly things. For God had said to Abraham "In blessing I will bless thee, and in multiplying I will multiply thee." It is also recorded that "God blessed Isaac * * * saying I will bless thee, * * * and I will make thy seed to multiply as the stars." Esau's sad cry was exceedingly bitter over his disappointment when he found that Jacob had supplanted him, but Isaac was compelled to say to him, "I have blessed him (Jacob) and he shall be blessed." So it is recorded: "And Isaac called Jacob and blessed him, and said unto him, Thou shalt not take a wife of the daughters of Canaan. Arise, go to Padan-aram, to the house of Bethuel, thy mother's father; and take thee a wife from thence of the daughters of Laban, thy mother's brother. And God Almighty bless thee, and make thee fruitful, and multiply thee, that thou mayst be a multitude of people; and I will give thee the blessing of Abraham, to thee and to thy seed with thee."—Gen. 28: 1-4.

Thus we see that this blessing, as given to Abraham, Isaac and Jacob, carries with it the promise of a numerous posterity; also, that the "blessing of Abraham" was given to Jacob by his father Isaac, who was the direct inheritor of the Abrahamic heritage; and that, while Isaac in fact gave it to Jacob, he intended it for Esau, his first-born son, to whom it belonged by right of birth. If it belonged to him because he was the first-born, then it was his "birthright." And since he sold his birthright to Jacob, who thus became its possessor, Jacob and not Esau must become the father of that promised multitude of people which is contained in the Birthright; i.e., the covenant promise to Abraham.

In truth Esau could justly say: "Is he not rightly named Jacob? (supplanter) for he hath supplanted me these two times: he took away my birthright; and, behold now he hath taken away my blessing."

Although Jacob had received from his father the much coveted blessing, which carried with it the inheritance of the Birthright promises, he was dissatisfied, and seemed to hold those blessings as insecure until they had been ratified to him directly by the blessing of God. Having secured them by fraud, he knew that he was holding them under the protest of both his father and his outraged brother.

So much from the human side. On the divine side, God intended that Jacob should have the birthright, for, as we have already shown, he chose Jacob in preference to Esau before they were born. Had Jacob trusted God, he would have placed him in possession of the birthright in a perfectly honorable way; but he, in distrust, took matters into his own hands, and gained possession of it by wicked conniving.

It was because of this that he had more trouble to secure the blessing of God upon his possession of this inheritance than had his predecessors, and though he wrestled for it with the angel all the night long, he did not secure it until he had first confessed his name—which was expressive of his character—to be Jacob, i.e., supplanter. Then it was that God bestowed the blessing, took away that reproachful name, and gave him a new and unstained one, even Israel: the meaning of which is: "As a prince thou hast prevailed with God."

The next legal inheritor of the Birthright was Reuben, the first-born son of Jacob and Leah, his first wife; but he, like Esau, lost it; and Joseph, the first-born son of Rachel, the second and best loved wife of Jacob, succeeded his father in the possession of it. But that we are right in saying that the first-born is the legal inheritor, is evident from the fact that Reuben, the first born son of Jacob, is declared to have been heir to the birthright. This is made clear in the Biblical account of the entertainment which was given by Joseph to his brethren, when they came into Egypt the second time to buy food and brought Benjamin with them; for when the feast was ready, and Joseph—who had not yet revealed to them the fact that he was their brother—gave the word, "Set on bread," it is said of the servants, who, it seems, had previously been instructed, that, "They sat before him the first-born ac-

cording to his *Birthright,* and the youngest according
to his *youth:* and the men marveled one at another."—
Gen. 43 : 33.

The fact that Reuben was the first born and possessor
of the Birthright, and the cause of his losing it, are set
forth in connection with the declaration that the Birthright had been given to Joseph, as follows: "Now the
sons of Reuben, (for he was the first-born; but forasmuch as he defiled his father's bed, his birthright was
given to the sons of Joseph the son of Israel: and the
genealogy [of Reuben's sons] is not to be reckoned
after the Birthright. For Judah prevailed above his
brethren, and of him is the chief ruler; but the *birthright* is Joseph's.) The sons of Reuben the first-born
of Israel were, etc."—I Chron. 5 : 1-3.

If our readers would know just why this act should
have caused Reuben to forfeit his birthright, they must
be able to read between the lines. We are only at liberty to say that, after that act, if either Reuben or his
probable first-born had come into possession of the
Israelitish birthright, the Lord could not have declared,
as he did concerning Israel, "I planted thee a noble
vine, wholly a right seed."

To Isaac and to Israel God had confirmed the
covenants of promise in their entirety, including in the
confirmation the promise of the land, a multiplicity of
seed, the *one* seed, or the Messianic covenant, and a
royal line; but you will note from the Scripture just
quoted, that the promise of a royal line, which, as the
sacred story proceeds, is clearly shown to contain the
Messianic covenant, had been separated from the

birthright, and given to Judah, the fourth son of Jacob and Leah, while the birthright fell to Joseph.

This individual separation of the Sceptre and the Birthright took place just previous to the death of Jacob, who had these blessings at his disposal. Not, however, as his own selfwill or human judgment might suggest, but only as God should direct; for the history of the people involved is a divine work from start to finish, and its ultimate object is the glory of God in the vindication of his word.

The call of Abraham and the giving of the promises to him were supernatural; for God had appeared unto and talked with him. The production of Isaac was also supernatural. No human possibility was there. But the possibility of faith was there, and it prevailed. The conception, and the birth of Jacob and Esau were also supernatural, for there were "two nations," two distinct races,—a white child and a red one—Caucassian and Arabic, in one womb; and the manner of their birth was so supernaturally manipulated, that, as they struggled in the womb, Jacob held Esau's heel, and thus they were born: the very manner of which, as we hope to show, is one of the most striking types in all the Word of God. And yet, none of these events are any more supernatural, nor attended with any greater manifest power of God, nor is his will any more clearly manifest in them, than is the transfer of the Sceptre, and the Birthright, by dying Jacob, to Judah and to Joseph.

At the time of Jacob's death, all Israel was in Egypt living in the land of Goshen. When it was reported to Joseph that his father was dying, he took with him his two sons, and hastened to the bedside of the dying patriarch. But when Joseph and his sons were ushered into the presence of the dying man, it appears that supernatural strength, from the one who had given him the name of Israel, was given him, for, although dying, it is recorded, that "He strengthened himself and sat up in the bed." Then discovering that Joseph was not alone he asked, "Who are these?" to which Joseph replied, saying, "They are my sons, whom God hath given me in this place," i. e., Egypt.

After Joseph had explained to Jacob, concerning his half-blood Egyptian boys,—Joseph had married an Egyptian woman—then Jacob proceeded to adopt them as his own legal sons; at which time he said: "And *now thy two sons* Ephraim and Manasseh, which were born unto thee in the land of Egypt before I came unto thee into Egypt, *are mine;* as Reuben and Simeon, they shall be mine." (Gen. 48:5.) But after the *adoption* was completed he said to Joseph, concerning the issue which should be begotten of him after them, "They shall be thine," but they "shall be called after their brethren in their inheritance." So it is that the tribal names of all the posterity of Joseph are dealt with, both from a historic and a prophetic standpoint, as Ephraim and Manasseh. Do not forget that, for upon it depends much of interest in that which is to follow.

It would appear that, at the time of the adoption or prior to it, the Holy Ghost had told Jacob that Ephraim was the one which had been chosen by the Lord as the inheritor of the birthright, or the blessing of the first born. For at that time, the name of Ephraim, the

younger, was mentioned before Manasseh, the older ; as
also the name of Reuben, who was the real first born,
is mentioned first when his name is coupled with that of
Simeon. But the transfer of the birthright from his
eldest to his younger son was not made known to Joseph until after he had presented his sons before Israel
for the promised blessing.

Jacob had said, "I will bless them." So when Joseph
brought them to him, and bowed himself with his face
to the earth, he held Ephraim in his right hand toward
Israel's left, and Manasseh in his left hand to the right
hand of Jacob. Joseph in his human calculation, was
managing so as to have Manasseh his first born get that
promised "blessing" which was in Jacob's right hand.
His thought was, "If I take Manasseh in my left hand,
that will bring him to the right of my father, so that,
even if he is blind, when he stretches forth his hands
to give the blessing, his right hand will rest on the head
of my first born son."

But no! Look! As Jacob reaches out his hands to lay
them in blessing upon those two heads, he being under
the inspiration of the Holy Ghost, is "guiding his
hands wittingly," i. e., knowingly, crosses them and lets
his right hand rest upon the head of Ephraim, the
younger brother. They were in this position when
"he blessed Joseph, and said, God, before whom my
fathers Abraham and Isaac did walk, the God which
fed me all my life long unto this day, the angel which
redeemed me from all evil, bless the lads; and let my
name (Israel) be named on them, and the name of my
fathers Abraham and Isaac, and let them grow into a

multitude in the midst of the earth.' These were the collective blessings which those two received; together they inherited the names of the racial fathers; together they are to grow into a multitude of people.

At this juncture Joseph noticed that Jacob's right hand was not resting on Manasseh's head, and wanted to remove it, but Jacob refused, saying "Not so."

"But," says the anxious Joseph, "You have your right hand on my younger son's head."

To this, Jacob replied, "I know it, my son, I know it."

How does Jacob know it? He is in a dying condition and blind. Ah, the Spirit—the Spirit of Prophecy—is upon him!

See what follows. Jacob does not remove his hands, nor change their position; but with his left hand still on Manasseh's head, and his right hand on Ephraim's head, he continues to prophesy; still the prophecies are no longer collective, but special and individual. Of Manasseh he declares, "He shall also become a people (nation) and he shall also be great; but truly his younger brother shall be greater than he, and his seed shall become a multitude of nations. And he blessed them that day, saying, In thee shall Israel bless, saying: God make thee as Ephraim and as Manasseh; and he set Ephraim before Manasseh." Gen. 48:19, 20.

So Ephraim was set before Manasseh, both nationally and tribally; but they were to grow together until they became a multitude of people in the midst of the earth. Eventually Manasseh was to become a separate nation, and as such was to be a great nation. But

Ephraim was to become a multitude of nations, or as some translate it, "a company of nations"; in either case this is a reiteration and confirmation of the promise made to Abraham.

In his tribal relations, also, Ephraim was placed before his elder brother, because he was elevated to the inheritance which was forfeited by Reuben, the first-born of Israel. This is why God declares "I am a father to Israel, and Ephraim is my first-born." Jer. 31 :9.

While the spirit of prophecy was still upon Jacob, he called all his sons together to tell them what their posterity should become "in the last days." Among other prophetic utterances, of which we shall speak later, was the following concerning Judah and the Sceptre: "The Sceptre shall not depart from Judah, nor a lawgiver from between his feet, until Shiloh come; and unto him shall the gathering of the people be." Gen. 49 :10.

Whatever else the Birthright may have contained, or if God ever did count those other blessings and promises as belonging to the Birthright, one thing is certain; that is, that when the Birthright passed into the possession of Joseph and his sons, it was stripped bare of all else, save the oft-repeated promises which pertain to a multiplicity of seed for Abraham, Isaac, and Jacob. Hence, when it was recorded in the Chronicles that the Birthright was Joseph's, it was understood that from the loins of Joseph's sons must come seed, posterity, people. Yea, multitudes, nations—"many nations," even races of people.

This is the crucial test. Since the promise of the fatherhood of many nations, which was given successively to Abraham and Jacob, was inherited and sold by Esau, then inherited and forfeited by Reuben, but finally given to Joseph and his two sons, and never revoked,—then, we say, that the crucial test, not only for the faithfulness of God, but also for the integrity of his Word, is that Joseph, through Ephraim and Manasseh, must of necessity become the father of those *many nations* which were promised to the fathers of Israel.

But the fact that Joseph must become the father of those promised nations is not only the crucial test of God and his Word, but it is also a test of the power and *worth* of FAITH; "By faith Jacob, when he was dying, blessed *both* the sons of Joseph." Heb. 11:21. What was that for which Jacob put forth faith when he blessed the sons of Joseph? It was that they should grow to be a multitude in the midst of the earth and eventually become that which the Birthright demanded: that is, a multitude of nations. It was this Birthright, the fatherhood of many nations, that Esau sold.

CHAPTER IV.

JACOB'S SEED DIVIDED INTO TWO KINGDOMS.

When Boaz took Ruth the Moabitess for a wife, the people who were assembled prayed for her, saying: "The Lord make thee like Rachel and like Leah, which two did build the house of Israel." The fact that these two women, as the wives of Jacob, were the builders of the house of Israel, would of necessity divide the immediate household of Jacob into two families. Hence the pertinency of the question: "Considerest thou not the two families which the Lord hath chosen?" (Jer. 33:24.)

Since the covenant promise of the Birthright was given to one of these two families, and that of the Sceptre to the other, it would be but natural—especially since one of these forthcoming blessings was to be so much superior to the other—for these families to keep somewhat apart, so as to keep their family distinctions intact. This they did, and yet they dwelt together for a number of centuries, apparently without any factions whatever.

Together, as one nation, they lived on in Goshen. Together the Sceptre and the Birthright families are pressed into bondage. Together the children of Rachel, of whom it was prophesied that there should be thousands of millions, and the children of Leah, the mother of coming royalty—royalty which, as the sequel proves, is not only the grandest and best that this world will

49

ever know, but also the most glorious that will ever be known in all the universe of God—together they bend their necks to the yoke, and their backs to the burdens. Together they serve those unjust taskmasters. Together their Lord, whose presence was with them, brought them out of that galling Egyptian servitude, out through the Red Sea, and into the wilderness. There, still together, they refreshed their spirits by drinking from that spiritual Rock which followed them; and there they refreshed their bodies with drink from that literal rock which, as we shall prove, they carried with them. Together they ate the same spiritual and temporal meat, albeit, at times, that temporal meat was angels' food which God sent down from one of their habitations.

Together they crossed the Jordan, marched around Jericho, drove out the Canaanites, and—*for a season only*—inhabited that promised land; in which they enjoyed the blessings and privileges of a theocratic government. But it is recorded that they lightly esteemed the Rock of their salvation, cried down the theocracy, and shouted over a man-archy. Refusing Him who had honored, protected and cherished them as a husband doth a wife, despising that Divine One who had followed them and led them, and nourished them, and fought for them, they demanded that like the nations around them, a man should be their king.

Then it was that there arose trouble, trouble which resulted in strifes and factions galore; for after the establishment of the monarchy only three kings—namely: Saul, David and Solomon—reigned over all Israel in one united kingdom.

After the death of Solomon, contingencies arose in Israel, which brought the two families that held the covenant blessings face to face with issues that resulted in a division of the nation, which placed both the families of Rachel and Leah—or more properly, Judah and Joseph, since they are the promise-holders—into positions to fulfill their God-appointed destinies.   And yet we shall find that the mills of God do grind—oh, so very slowly.

There is contained in the eleventh and twelfth chapters of the book of First Kings a record of the division of the tribes of Israel into two kingdoms, with a son of the royal family as king over one kingdom, and a son of the house of Joseph as king over the other and larger kingdom.

King Solomon had married strange wives, and because of them he had burnt incense, and sacrificed unto Moloch and other idols; and because of this, "The Lord said unto Solomon, Forasmuch as this is done of thee, and thou hast not kept my covenant and my statutes, which I have commanded thee, I will surely rend the kingdom from thee, and give it to thy servant.   Notwithstanding, in thy days I will not do it, for David thy father's sake; but I will rend it out of the hand of thy son.   Howbeit I will not rend away all the kingdom; but I will give one tribe to thy son for David my servant's sake, and for Jerusalem's sake which I have chosen."   1 Kings 11:11-13.

The twenty-sixth verse of the same chapter speaks of Jeroboam, the son of Nebat, an Ephrathite, Solomon's servant.   It is known that the word Ephrathite means Ephraimite.   The record further states—"And the man Jeroboam was a mighty man of valor: and Solomon seeing the young man that he was industrious, he made him ruler over all the charge of the house of Joseph." 1 Kings 11:28.

When the Birthright was transferred to the sons of Joseph, Ephraim, the younger, was set before Manasseh, the elder, and, aside from the fact of joint inheritance in the multitude of posterity, Ephraim seems to enjoy the special Birthright, or first-born distinctions. This is shown in several ways; but at present we will only call your attention to the fact that God says: "I am a father to Israel, and Ephraim is my first-born." Jer. 31:9.

We have in this man Jeroboam, a servant of Solomon's, an Ephraimite, who was ruler over all the Birthright family. God had told Solomon, that after his death he would give the kingdom to his servant, but, "not all." In harmony with these things we read:

"And it came to pass that at the time when Jeroboam went out of Jerusalem, that the prophet Ahijah, the Shilonite, found him in the way; and he had clad himself with a new garment; and the two were alone in the field. And Ahijah caught the new garment that was on him, and rent it in twelve pieces. And he said to Jeroboam, Take thee ten pieces: for thus saith the Lord, the God of Israel, Behold I will rend the kingdom out of the hand of Solomon, and will give ten tribes to thee. * * * Howbeit I will not take the whole kingdom out of his hand: * * * for David my servant's sake, whom I chose,—because he kept my commandments and my statutes. But I will take the kingdom out of his son's hand, and will give it unto thee, even ten tribes.   And unto his son will I give one tribe, that David my servant may have a light alway before me in Jerusalem, the city which I have chosen to put my name there.   And I will take thee, and thou shalt reign according to all that thy soul desireth, and thou shalt be king over Israel."

In this prophecy, there is made a promise to a son of the house of Joseph, that he shall reign over ten tribes, and be king over Israel.   Hence if Jeroboam ever received his promised kingdom, it must have been formed by a confederacy of ten of the tribes of Israel, and that ten-tribed kingdom or confederation must needs be called "ISRAEL," or the prophecy fails.

After this prophecy, which God gave to Ahijah to deliver to Jeroboam, was made public, Solomon became so jealous for himself and posterity that he undertook to kill Jeroboam; while he, in order to escape the wrath of Solomon, fled to Egypt and remained there until after the death of Solomon.   At the death of Solomon the royal succession fell to his son, Rehoboam, who, at the time of his accession, had gathered with all Israel at Shechem, the place where, for reasons which will be given later, Israel crowned her sovereigns.   But difficulties arose.   The people had grievances which they wanted adjusted, before they were willing to submit to the rule of this young sovereign.   Solomon had laid upon them an enormous tax for the building and furnishing of the temple and royal palaces. These were finished and furnished, but the taxes were not abated.   Also there was this taxation without representation by any in Israel, except from the royal tribe of Judah.   Still, in spite of the fact that a spirit of rebellion had possession of them because of these facts, they were willing to hold a consultation with Rehoboam, in hope that their condition might be bettered and amity might still prevail.   So they made Jeroboam their spokesman, and directed him to say to the young king; "Thy father made our yoke grievous; now, therefore, make thou the grievous service of thy father, and his heavy yoke which he put upon us, lighter, and we will serve thee."

His reply to this request was, "Depart yet for three days, then come again to me."   During this three days of grace, which he had asked, and they had granted, Rehoboam first consulted with the old men, asking them how they would advise him to answer the people. They gave him wholesome counsel, saying to him that if he would "Speak good words to them, then they will be thy servants forever."

Then he consulted with the young men, with whom he had grown up, asking them how they would advise him.   But their advice was hasty and hot-headed. They said, "Thus shalt thou say unto them, My little finger shall be thicker than my father's loins.   And now, whereas my father did lade you with a heavy yoke, I will add to your yoke: my father chastised you with whips, but I will chastise you with scorpions."

When the three days had expired, Jeroboam and the people came again to King Rehoboam, as he had appointed, to receive the answer to their request.   Then Rehoboam answered them roughly, forsaking the counsel of the old men, and adhering to the counsel which the young men in their pride and egotism had given, using their very words.

"Whips" and "scorpions!" How insulting! Surely in all the figures of speech there could not have been chosen any so hard for that "elect" people to swallow. But they did not swallow them; they rebelled. The command to the people was, "To your tents, O Israel!" The challenge to the royal house was, "Now, see to thy own house!"

Rehoboam's next move was to send Adoram, who had charge of the tribute, to collect the taxes then due. But instead of paying their taxes, the people stoned the man to death; and as soon as Rehoboam heard this, he fled in his chariot, and with all speed, to Jerusalem.

Then comes the following: "So Israel rebelled against the house of David unto this day. And it came to pass, when all Israel heard that Jeroboam was come again, that they sent and called him unto the congregation and made him king over all Israel. * * * And when Rehoboam was come to Jerusalem, he assembled all the house of Judah, with the tribe of Benjamin, an hundred and four score thousand men which were warriors, to fight against the house of Israel, to bring the kingdom again to Rehoboam, the son of Solomon. But the word of God came unto Shemaniah the man of God, saying, Speak unto Rehoboam, the son of Solomon, king of Judah, and unto all the house of Judah and Benjamin, and to the remnant of the people, saying, Thus saith the Lord, Ye shall not go up, nor fight against your brethren the children of Israel: return every man to his house; *for this thing is from me."* i. e., the division. I Kings 12: 19-24.

Well may the Lord say, "This thing is from me." In the division of that race into two kingdoms, he has fulfilled his word to Solomon concerning the rending of the kingdom out of the hand of his son, and giving it to his servant. Yet, in doing so, he remembered not only his oath to David, but also his word to Solomon, in that he did not rend away all the kingdom; for there was one tribe, that of Benjamin, left with the royal tribe.

Also the prophecy of Ahijah to Jeroboam was fulfilled, for he became king of the ten-tribed kingdom, which, by Divine appointment, retained the national name of Israel, while that of Judah was given to the other kingdom. Thus the titles "House of Israel," and the "House of Judah" are used to designate the two kingdoms, as they stand separated and in opposition to each other.

Moreover, since the Birthright tribes, Ephraim and Manasseh, went with the ten-tribed kingdom, and a scion of the house of Joseph, to whom pertains the Birthright, was king over that kingdom, and a son of the royal house of Judah, to whom pertains the Sceptre, was king over the other kingdom, which bears the name of the inheritor of the Sceptre, then, surely, the Sceptre and the Birthright were separated then and there. They were not only separated, but each became a nucleus around which either the one or the other, of all the seed of Abraham, Isaac, and Jacob, did gather. Thus the SCEPTRE and the BIRTHRIGHT families each became the head and representative of a distinct nation, or commonwealth. Each was then free to go forward, independent of the other, and fulfill its God-appointed destiny; one to fulfill the first covenant which the Lord made with their father Abraham, that of becoming many nations, and the other to fulfill the second covenant of bringing forth the Messiah.

The first thing recorded of Jeroboam, as king of Israel, is that he built the city of Shechem, in Mount Ephraim, and dwelt there.   This city was the first capital of that kingdom.   From there the king of Israel went out and built the city of Penuel, and seemed to prosper for a short season.   But Jeroboam fell to thinking that, if his subjects were allowed to continue going to Jerusalem to sacrifice unto the Lord, their hearts would turn again to Rehoboam, whose capital city it was, and they would then kill him, and go again to the kingdom of Judah.

Therefore he made two calves of gold, and said unto the people, "It is too much (trouble) for you to go to Jerusalem: behold thy gods, O Israel, which brought thee up out of the land of Egypt.   And he set one in Bethel, and one in Dan.   And this thing became a sin, for the people went to worship before the one (in Bethel), and even unto Dan.   And he made a house of high places, and made priests of the lowest of the people, which were not of the sons of Levi.

And Jeroboam ordained a feast in the eighth month, on the fifteenth day of the month, like unto the feast that is in Judah, and he offered upon the altar.   So did he in Bethel, sacrificing unto the calves that he had made: and he placed in Bethel the priests of the high places which he had made.   So he offered upon the altar which he had made in Bethel, on the fifteenth day of the eighth month, even in the month which he had devised in his own heart; and ordained a feast unto the Children of Israel, and he offered upon the altar and burnt incense." 1 Kings 12:28-33.

This was the great sin which was such a curse to the people. But we want you to note just how the Lord speaks of it. After the prophet whom he had sent out of Judah had proclaimed the doom of Jeroboam, he further adds: "The Lord shall smite Israel, as a reed is shaken in the water, and he shall root up Israel out of his good land, which he gave to their fathers, and shall scatter them beyond the river, because they have made their groves, provoking the Lord to anger. And he shall give Israel up because of the sins of Jeroboam, who did sin, and who made Israel to sin." 1 Kings 14:15, 16.

Dear reader, please note that it was Israel, and not Judah, over which Jeroboam reigned; that it was Israel, and not Judah, whom he caused to sin; that it was Israel the ten-tribed kingdom, and not Judah, the royal kingdom, that worshiped those two golden calves which Jeroboam the king of Israel had set up in his own territory, and not in the land of Judah; that it was Israel whom the Lord declared he would give up, root out of that land, and scatter beyond the river, because of this thing. For the people of the kingdom of Judah never did worship those golden calves; neither did they worship at Bethel, nor in Dan: they worshiped in Jerusalem. Later, the royal kingdom did go into idolatry; but it was Baalism, and not this special form of idolatry which had its origin in Jeroboam, for this was confined alone to Israel.

We find that the history of the two kingdoms is intermingled throughout the books of First and Second Kings, but never confounded. So that, with a little care and thoughtfulness on our part, there need be no confusion. For instance, it is recorded that, "The days which Jeroboam reigned were two-and-twenty years, and he slept with his fathers, and Nadab, his son, reigned in his stead." 1 Kings 14:20. But the very next verse tells us that, "Rehoboam, the son of Solomon, reigned in Judah. Rehoboam was forty years old when he began to reign, and he reigned seventeen years in Jerusalem." The two reigns began simultaneously. If Jeroboam's reign lasted for twenty-two years, and Rehoboam's only for seventeen years, then it must needs be that some other king or kings reigned for five years contemporaneously with Jeroboam, unless the kingdom of Judah had collapsed; but it had not. So the record declares, "Now, in the eighteenth year of Jeroboam, the son of Nabat, reigned Abijah over Judah. Three years reigned he in Jerusalem." 1 Kings 15:1. Seventeen years for Rehoboam and three for Abijah, are only twenty of Jeroboam's twenty-two years. So if the record be correct, we shall expect it to tell who ascended the throne of Judah in the twentieth year of Jeroboam's reign. This it does do, as follows: "And in the twentieth year of Jeroboam, king of Israel, reigned Asa over Judah." 1 Kings 15:9.

Now, if Asa lived and reigned more than two years, he lived to see the death of Jeroboam and the elevation of his successor. Hence, the record continues: "And Nadab, the son of Jeroboam, began to reign over Israel in the second year of Asa, king of Judah, and reigned over Israel two years. And he did evil in the sight of the Lord, and walked in the ways of his father, and in the sin wherewith he made Israel to sin."

Then follows a record of the fulfillment of the prophecy concerning the doom of Jeroboam, viz., the entire destruction of his family, at the hand of Baasha, of the house of Issachar, who reigned instead of Nadab son of Jeroboam. Hence it is recorded that "In the third year of Asa, king of Judah, began Baasha, the son of Ahijah, to reign over all Israel in Tirzah, twenty-and-four years. And he did evil in the sight of the Lord, and walked in the ways of Jeroboam, and in his sin wherewith he made Israel to sin." I Kings 15:33, 34.

We have brought you down to the contemporaneous reigns of Asa, the third king in Judah, and Baasha, the third king in Israel, not only to show that there need be no confusion in this intermingled history, but also for another purpose, which follows. You will notice that in the last quotation, the expression "all Israel" occurs, while in the twenty-second verse is the corresponding expression "all Judah." "Then King Asa made a proclamation throughout *all Judah*." These expressions, all Israel and all Judah, are undoubtedly used as contradistinctive titles of the two kingdoms into which the people were divided.

The expression "all Israel," as used in the above quotation, and with the same meaning in many other places in the Scriptures, has confused many students. They seem to think it means, or ought to mean, all the people who are the descendants of Israel, i. e., all Israelites; whereas it simply means, in this instance, and many others, all the country occupied by the ten tribes which formed the kingdom of Israel, just as the expression "all Judah," or "all Judæa"—the Greek form of the same term—is used to designate all of the country which was given to the tribes of Judah and Benjamin, they being the tribes which composed the kingdom of Judah. Jerusalem, the capital of the kingdom, was located in that portion allotted to Benjamin, and Judah's portion was the hill country south of Jerusalem.

CHAPTER V.

After the division which occurred among the seed of Abraham in the days of Jeroboam and Rehoboam, and before the two kingdoms had settled down to steady going, there arose several contingencies which we must understand, before we can intelligently follow their history any farther.

By consulting the eleventh chapter of Second Chronicles we find a brief recapitulation of the history of the revolt of the Ten Tribes, to which are added further details as to the result, a list of the cities which were built by Rehoboam for the defense of the kingdom of Judah, and the following:

"And he fortified the strongholds, and put captains in them, and stores of victuals, and of oil and wine. And in every several city he put shields and spears, and made them exceeding strong, having Judah and Benjamin on his side. And the priests and the Levites that were in all Israel (i. e., the territory of country occupied by the ten-tribed kingdom) resorted to him out of all their coasts. For the Levites left their suburbs and their possessions, and came to Judah and Jerusalem: for Jeroboam and his sons had cast them off from executing the priest's office unto the Lord: And he ordained him priests for the high places, and for the devils, and for the calves which he had made. And after them out of all the tribes of Israel such as set their

62

hearts to seek the Lord God of Israel came to Jerusalem, to sacrifice unto the Lord God of their fathers. So they strengthened the kingdom of Judah, and made Rehoboam, the son of Solomon, strong." 2 Chron. 11: 11-17.

These statements make it clear that, after Jeroboam, the king of Israel, had set up those golden calves, and made priests of the lowest of the people, he would not allow the Levites, whom the Lord had made the priestly tribe of the race, execute any priestly offices, or to conduct any services unto the Lord God of their fathers; and for this reason they returned to Rehoboam, who already, as is affirmed, had the tribes of Judah and Benjamin on his side. Thus the kingdom of Judah, for a while at least, was composed of three tribes, in addition to those scattered families out of all the rest of the tribes who would not forsake the worship of the God of Israel, and who would not worship the calves which Jeroboam had set up; but those people evidently lost their tribal relations and were assimilated into one of the three tribes of which the kingdom of Judah was composed, for in all the history and prophecy which concerns the three-tribed kingdom, there are no tribal names used, save only those of Judah, Benjamin and Levi.

Before we carry the history of these two kingdoms any farther, or leave the A B C of this matter, we deem it important to place before our readers an array of Scripture texts, in which both houses, kingdoms, nations, or families of Abraham's posterity, through the Isaac-Jacob line, are spoken of in the same passage in

such a way that the most simple minded cannot fail to
see that two distinct peoples are being considered.

We cannot, however, at this juncture, give the relative place of these Scriptures, as regards the history,
past, present and future, of these people under consideration.   We place these Scriptures before you, only to
show, at present, that ever after the division of the
people into two commonwealths, in the days of Rehoboam and Jeroboam, they were recognized in scriptural
history and prophecy as two kingdoms or nations.

For instance, take the following—"Behold the days
come, saith the Lord, that I will perform that good
thing which I have promised unto the house of Israel,
and to the house of Judah." Jer. 33:14.   Here the Lord
has promised to perform a certain, "good thing" for
"The house of Israel;" but he has just as assuredly
promised to perform that same certain "good thing" for
the house of Judah, as well as for Israel, for the house
of Judah is not included in the house of Israel, and vice
versa.

Take another, as follows: "And I will cause the captivity of Judah and the capitivity of Israel to return,
and will build them as at the first." Jer. 33:7.   Here
it is a question not only of "the captivity of Judah,"
but also "the captivity of Israel."   Neither is it a question only of the return of the captivity of Judah, for
there is promised also in the same sentence the return
of the captivity of Israel, i. e., a people who are not
included with "Judah."

Again, "For lo! the days come, saith the Lord, that I
will bring again the captivity of my people Israel and
Judah, saith the Lord: and I will cause them to return

to the land that I gave to their fathers, and they shall possess it. And these are the words that the Lord spake concerning Israel and concerning Judah." Jer. 30:3, 4. Here is something that concerns Judah; but it also concerns Israel; and the people whom it concerns are "my people Israel and Judah." So, if Judah, the Jews, are the people of the Lord, then the Lord has a people besides the Jews whom he calls Israel, and who are not counted among the Jews.

Still another: "For the children of Israel, and the children of Judah have only done evil before me from their youth." Jer. 32:30. You see that while speaking of the evildoing of his people, it was not sufficient for the Lord to speak of the children of Israel only, but the children of Judah must also be included, in order to embrace all who are under consideration.

In Jer. 13:11, we have indisputable proofs of the two houses, since the broadest generic terms possible are used. Here it is: "For as a girdle cleaveth to the loins of a man, so have I caused to cleave unto me *the whole house of Israel* and *the whole house of Judah,* saith the Lord; that they might be unto me for a people, and for a name, and for a praise, and for a glory; but they would not hear." This statement gives us to understand that "the whole house of Judah" are not all of the Lord's people, and that "the whole house of Israel" are not all of the Lord's people; but that it takes "the whole house of Israel" together with "the whole house of Judah" to make all of his chosen people.

It also proves that there is a people called "the whole house of Israel" of which "the whole house of Judah" is regarded as neither part nor parcel. True, they are

brethren, because they all are of the seed of Jacob.   As
such, they are Jacobites,—or, since Jacob's name was
changed to Israel his descendants may all be called
Israelites.   But it is a fact that the seed of Jacob have
been divided, by the will, the decree, and the direct intervention of God, into two kingdoms, or nations, one
of which, when politically considered, is called "the
whole house of Israel," "the children of Israel," "the
house of Israel," "all Israel," and "Israel"; while the
other nation is called "the whole house of Judah,"
"the house of Judah," "the children of Judah," "all
Judah," and "Judah," or "the Jews."

The name Jew is derived from, or rather is a corruption of, the name of Judah (Singular Ju-dah, or Jew-
dah; plural, Ju-dahs, or Jew-dahs; possessive, Ju-dah's,
or Jew-dah's; contracted, Jew, Jews and Jew's). Hence
it is that the names Jew and Jews are applied *only* to
the people who composed the kingdom of Judah. Also
it was their land *only* which was designated as "Judah"
and "all Judah," and which finally became known as
"Judea" and *"Jewry,"* "all Judea" and "ALL
JEWRY."

Indeed, long before the division took place, Moses,
while prophesying unto the seed of Jacob, cried out,
"Hear, Lord, the voice of Judah, and bring him unto
his people."   This can mean nothing else, except that
Judah was to be separated from his people, and finally,
if that prayer is ever answered, was to be brought back
to them.

But let us continue our array of texts in which both
houses are mentioned, almost in the same breath. "And
I saw, when for all the causes whereby backsliding

Israel committed adultery I had put her away, and given her a bill of divorce; yet her treacherous sister Judah, feared not, but went and played the harlot also." Jer. 3:8.

Here Israel and Judah are not the same;
They are only sisters, both in shame.

"And the Lord said unto me, That backsliding Israel hath justified herself more than treacherous Judah." Jer. 3:11.

Here Israel, in idolatry the adulterous,
Is justified more than Judah, the treacherous:

although God had said, "Though thou, Israel, play the harlot, yet let not Judah offend." Hosea 4:15. And he also said, "I will no more have mercy upon the house of Israel [that I should altogether pardon them— *Margin*]. But I will have mercy upon the house of Judah, and will save them by the Lord their God." Hosea 1:6, 7.

The name, "Jerusalem" is often used to designate the Jewish people because it was their chief city. When Jesus wept over the city and cried out "Jerusalem, Jerusalem, * * * how oft would I have gathered you as a hen gathereth her brood under her wing, but ye would not!" he did not mean the streets and buildings of the city, but the people; and not only the people dwelling within the walls, but the nation as well. For it was not only the Jewish capital—but it was their metropolis, their commercial center, their citadel, their royal city, their sanctuary and in every way the representative city of their nation.

This being true, we may expect that the name of the capital city of the ten-tribed kingdom would be used as a representative name and applied to that nation. Also, since the name of Judah was given as a national name for the Jewish people, because of the fact that it was one of the royal sons from the tribe of Judah who led the revolt when she became a separate nation, and the fact that her kings were of Judah's line, thus making the tribe of Judah the representative tribe, so we might expect the same thing with reference to the ten-tribed kingdom. Jeroboam reigned over Israel in Shechem twenty-two years, and was succeeded by Nadab, his son, who reigned two years. After this, Baasha conspired against him, killed him, and reigned in his stead; but he moved the capital to Tirzah, where he reigned for twenty-four years, and was followed by his son, Elah, who reigned in that city two years. Then he was conspired against by Zimri, who reigned only seven days, until he in turn was conspired against and died by burning the king's house down over his own head. Then Omri, who had conspired against Zimri and succeeded him to the throne, bought a hill from Shemar, on which he built the city of Samaria, which became the permanent capital of the kingdom of Israel. Hence the name of the chief city of Israel, Samaria, is often used, when referring to Israel, in the same representative way that Jerusalem is, in the case of the Jews.

For an example take the following: "Thy Calf, O Samaria, hath cast thee off; mine anger is kindled against them: how long will it be ere they attain to innocency? For from Israel was it also: the workman made it; therefore it is not God: but the Calf of Samaria shall be broken in pieces." Hosea 8:5, 6. Of course, the calf herein referred to is the calf worship instituted by Jeroboam, who caused Israel to sin, and since the calves were made by the workmen of Israel, they were not God. So we see that Samaria stands for Israel, whose capital it is, and whose own workmen had made the calf which they themselves worshiped.

But this nation has another name which stands for the whole, as well as that of Israel and Samaria. Look ye! "When I would have healed Israel, then the iniquity of Ephraim was discovered, and the wickedness of Samaria: for they commit falsehood." Hosea 7:1.

Thus we see that the name of Ephraim is used as a representative name for the northern kingdom, just as the name of Judah is used for the southern kingdom, and that the names Israel, Ephraim and Samaria are used as names of the ten-tribed kingdom in contradistinction to those of the three-tribed kingdom, which are Judah, Jerusalem, and the Jews.

On the very day on which Moses died, while he was reiterating and enlarging upon the prophecies which Jacob had given at the time of his death, he made a prophecy concerning the pre-eminence of Ephraim in Joseph-Israel, as follows: "Let the blessing come upon the head of Joseph, and upon the top of the head of him that was separated from his brethren. His glory is like the firstling of his bullock, and his horns are like the horns of unicorns: with them he shall push the people together to the ends of the earth: and they are the ten thousands of Ephraim, and they are the thousands of Manasseh."

With the name of Ephraim standing at the head of one of the two nations of Jacob, and the name of Judah at the head of the other, we can easily understand such expressions as the following: "O Ephraim, what shall I do unto thee? O Judah, what shall I do unto thee? For your goodness is as a morning cloud, and as the early dew it goeth away." Hosea 6:4.

Since both Judah, the fourth son of Jacob, and Ephraim, the second son of Joseph, had been dead for nearly one thousand years prior to the writing of these Scriptures which we have just given, we must know that these are national names, used to represent the national conditions of the two nations which are addressed.

So, also, is the following: "Therefore will I be unto Ephraim as a moth, and to the house of Judah as rottenness.   When Ephraim saw his sickness, and Judah saw his wound, then went Ephraim to the Assyrian, and sent to King Jared; yet he could not heal you of your wound.   For I will be unto Ephraim as a lion, and as a young lion to the house of Judah: I, even I, will tear and go away, and none shall rescue them.   I will go and return to my place, until they acknowledge their offence, and seek my face: in their affliction they will seek me early." Hosea 5: 12-15.

Before proceeding further with the history of these two kingdoms, there is one other point which must be settled once for all. This is that the people of God whom he distinctively calls "Israel," the heads of which are the birthright holders, unto whom was given that national name—it coming to them with the birthright at the time of the transfer of that inheritance—are not Jews, that the Holy Spirit has never, either in Biblical history or prophecy, called them Jews, and that they have never been called Jews except by uninformed historians and by unscriptural teachers of the Word of God.

Understand us: we do not say that the Jews are not Israelites; they belong to the posterity of Jacob, who was called Israel; hence they are all Israelites. But the great bulk of Israelites are not the Jews, just as the great bulk of Americans are not Californians, and yet all Californians are Americans; also, as in writing the history of America we must of necessity write the history of California, because California is a part of America; but we could write a history of California without writing a history of America.

So, in writing the history of Israel we must needs write the history of the Jews, *but we could write the history of the Jews and not write the history of Israel.* Or, in other words, in writing the history of the many nations we must write the history of the Jews, for, to say the least, they are one of those many nations; but in writing the history of the Jews, it would be utterly impossible to write the history of the many nations which were promised to the birthright people, whose national name is, in a special sense, Israel, and whose people are not Jews. Nationally speaking, they are brother nations, but not always very brotherly. But if we can keep track of the birthright nation, and if they ever have that birthright promise fulfilled to them, then, and only then, can we write the history of the many nations which the Lord God of Israel promised unto their fathers Abraham, Isaac, Jacob-Israel, Joseph, and Ephraim and Manasseh.

It will help us much in our study of this question, to know just when and under what circumstances the word Jew is first used in the canon of Sacred Scripture.

It was not until more than two hundred years after the revolt of the ten tribes from the house of David. It was at a time when Pekah, son of Remaliah, king of Israel, formed a federation with Rezin, king of Syria, and came up against Ahaz, king of Judah, to war for acquisition of territory. Notice how the prophet of God speaks of these three nations Israel, Syria and Judah. He declares: "And it came to pass in the days of Ahaz, the son of Jotham, the son of Uziah, king of Judah, that Rezin, the king of Syria, and Pekah, the son of Remaliah, king of Israel, went up toward Jerusalem to war against it (Jerusalem was the throne seat of Judah) but could not prevail against it. And it was told the house of David, saying, Syria is confederate with Ephraim." Isa. 7:1, 2. The prophet further explains, that "The head of Syria is Damascus, (Damascus was the capital of Syria) and the head of Damascus is Rezin (King of Syria) ; and within three-score-and-five (65) years shall Ephraim be broken that it be not a people. (*Marginal*—from being a people.) And the 'head of Ephraim is Samaria, and the head of Samaria is Remaliah's son." Isa. 7:8, 9. Remaliah's son was Pekah, king of Israel.

What Isaiah had to say concerning this war was for the purpose of making prophecies concerning the outcome. We must pass over the prophecies for the present, as our object now is to show the difference between the Jew and Israel and we have simply quoted sufficient for our purpose.

We now turn to the historic record of that war, and read: "In the seventeenth year (as king) of Pekah, the son of Remaliah, Ahaz, the son of Jotham, king of Judah, began to reign, and reigned sixteen years in Jerusalem. * * Then Rezin, king of Syria, and Pekah, son of Remaliah, king of Israel, came up to Jerusalem to war; and they besieged Ahaz (king of Judah), but could not overcome him. At that time Rezin, king of Syria, recovered Elath to Syria, *and drave the Jews from Elath;* and the Syrians dwell there unto this day. So Ahaz sent messengers to Tiglath-pileser, king of Assyria, saying, I am thy servant and thy son; come up and save me out of the hand of the king of Syria, *and out of the hand of the king of Israel,* which rise up against me." 2 Kings, 16: 1, 2, 5-7.

Here we have it clearly stated that in this war the besieging party is, "Pekah, the king of Israel," who is the "head of Samaria," which is the head of "Ephraim," together with another nation with whom they are confederate. And if we put it as Isaiah does concerning the other house, the besieged party was "Ahaz, king of Judah," head of "the Jews," whose head is "Jerusalem," the head of the house of David.

Do you see the point? The king of Judah, or the king of the Jews, was besieged in his capital, and wanted to form an alliance with the king of Assyria and, to secure him as an ally, even fawned upon the king of Assyria, saying "I am thy servant, thy son," and crying "Come up!" What for? *To save the JEWS from the hand of ISRAEL.*

Thus we see that the first time the word Jews is used in the history of the Abrahamic race is at a time when the Jews and Israel were at war with each other. Hence we ask, If the Jews were the besieged and Israel was with the besiegers, how can it be possible that the Jews and Israel are one and the same people?

According to the conclusion of the great number of our learned men, also some "higher (?) critics," we must needs conclude that the Jews were fighting their own shadow, which would be reducing the whole matter to an *argumentum ad absurdum.*

It is high time for the Christian world, yea, and all secular historians, too, "to awake out of sleep," take the advice of the learned Apostle Paul and "cease giving heed to Jewish fables" and quit telling the people that all Israelites are Jews. It is not true, never has been and never can be, for the difference between them is not only political and territorial but it is semiracial. For, although the inheritors of the Sceptre and the Birthright were sons of the same father, they were not sons of the same mother, and thus they were only half brothers. This, together with the fact that Leah is described as "tender-eyed" and Rachel was said to be "fair," would make some strong facial and physical distinctions in the posterity of the two families. But when we remember that Joseph married an Egyptian princess, thus blending the best Semitic blood with the royal blood of Egypt, and making the posterity of Joseph half-blood Egyptian, then we must know that while the children of Joseph are half Israelitish they are still three-fourths removed from the children of Judah. This alone would make great changes in their physique and largely eradicate all facial resemblances.

The fact that Ephraim and Manasseh, the sons of Joseph, who were the final inheritors of the Birthright, were half-blood Egyptians is that which made it necessary for Jacob to adopt them and make them fully his own, as Reuben and Simeon were his, before he could confer upon them the covenant Birthright. This is the adoption to which the Apostle Paul refers in his argument concerning the Children of the Promise versus the Children of the Flesh, as follows: "Israelites, *to whom pertaineth the adoption,* and the covenants, and the glory, and the giving of the law, and the service, and the promises; whose are the fathers, and of whom as concerning the flesh Christ came." Here Israelites as a whole, including both houses, are spoken of. Hence, to all who really believe, claim, or teach that the Jews ONLY are Israelites, and of all who believe that the word adoption, as used in this connection, can possibly have reference in any way to spiritual adoption we ask: When, how, or where did there ever occur an adoption, either spiritual or racial, among the Jews as a nation?

No answer required. Please reflect.

An eminent theological professor, who gives an exegesis of the Sunday-school lessons for the most prominent denominational papers in this country, began his exposition on "The Call of Abraham" as follows: "We come now to the third of the great landmarks of history, the call of Abraham. From being a universal history the record becomes national. Hereafter, we have to do with *one people, the Jews.* In the founder of the *Jewish nation* we find not a conqueror or a lawgiver but a saint." Yet it is fact that the term "Jews" is not used in writing the history of the Abrahamic people until *twelve hundred years* after the call of Abraham.

Another theological professor, of one of our largest training schools, defines "The Jews" as "A name given to all the descendants of Abraham." Ah!!! We ask—When?

Still another defines "The Jews": "A name given to the descendants of Abraham, who were divided into twelve tribes"; and yet it is a fact that in the Scriptures the name "Jews" was given only to those who dwelt in Jewry, which country was occupied by the tribes of Judah, Benjamin and Levi, and did not include Samaria, the home of the ten-tribed kingdom.

No; it is a fiction which has been foisted upon us by modern scholars, many of whom are presidents and professors of universities, colleges and theological seminaries, editors of religious and secular newspapers, doctors of divinity and church dignitaries, that the words "Jew" and "Jews" are equivalent to "Israel," "Israelites," "Israelitish," "Hebrew" and "Hebraic."

By not distinguishing Israel from Judah we have in the Bible a historical and prophetic chain which can never be linked together, and which sets all of the writers at variance with one another; for we cause Isaiah to question statements made by Jeremiah; set Joel, Amos, and Zephaniah against Zachariah; cause Jeremiah to convict Hosea of being a false prophet;

then make Ezekiel step in and contradict them both and many others in such a manner that one prophet is made to give the lie to the other.

We feel sorry for the so-called "Higher Critics," for they really do find trouble, but they cannot conceive that this trouble could, by any possible chance, arise because of their misconception of the subject matter; hence it must be in the style [*stylus*—a pen] or manner of the prophet. Thus if any of the prophets chance to reveal a mannerism at one time which is not so plainly manifest at another, then the exclamations,"Ah! Eureka! We've found it! *There are two of them!*" are heard to vibrate and revibrate throughout the ecclesiastical world.

Is it any wonder that skepticism is rampant, both in the church and out of it, since the common error of Christendom is to regard the Jews as the whole house of Israel? Is it any wonder that Tom Paine lost his soul while following the beaten path of this fallacy? For he did give the Bible up as a myth, and boldly states in his writings that he was led into infidelity because he saw that the Jews did not and never could verify the promises concerning Israel.

For it is true that God had declared, through Micah, of Israel, who was divorced and cast far off, that he would (at the proper time) make her a strong nation; while Judah was to become a remnant. Isaiah, Hosea, Jeremiah and the New Testament declare Israel to be lost; while both Jeremiah and Ezekiel affirm that Judah is well known. Hosea declares Israel to be as "the sands for multitude"; while Jeremiah insists that Judah is "few in number" and a remnant. Isaiah,

David, Micah, Jeremiah and others declare that Israel is the strongest war power on earth, never to be conquered by a Gentile power; and yet Jeremiah declares that Judah is "without might;" while Daniel bemoans and records the fact that the Jews will be conquered by a Gentile power. The entire line of prophets from Moses down declare Israel to be a continuous monarchy, whose sceptre is held by the seed of David; while Judah is to be "without government" of their own, but are to be ruled over. Hosea declares that "Israel shall ride" but "Judah shall plow."

Moses also declares that there shall come a time in the history of Israel (the ten tribes) when they also shall "be few in number," and yet it is prophesied concerning them that they shall obtain possession of "great possessions," inheriting and establishing (peopling) the desolate places of the earth, rule many heathen nations, have a great revenue, become the "mart of nations," hold the keys of commerce, be "exalted above their neighbors," and become "the chief of nations." But, on the other hand, Judah is to be "without geographical inheritance," "strangers in all countries," "howl for vexation of spirit," "leave their name for a curse," "be ashamed," and "cry for sorrow of heart" until the great day of Jezreel.

CHAPTER VI.

THE BROKEN BROTHERHOOD.

In the last chapter we gave much testimony from the Scripture showing that the ten-tribed kingdom is dealt with, both in history and prophecy—much of which is yet unfulfilled—as the house of Israel, and other titles, some of which you will find quite prominent in this chapter; while the three-tribed kingdom, which is composed of the Jewish people, is dealt with as the house of Judah and the Jews. If any of our readers are not yet satisfied on this point we promise that they shall still have abundant opportunity to become thoroughly convinced. Prof. C. A. L. Totten, of Yale University, says: "I can never be too thankful to the Almighty that in my youth he used the late Professor Wilson to show me the difference between the two houses. The very understanding of this difference is the KEY by which almost the entire Bible becomes intelligible, and I cannot state too strongly that the man who has not yet seen that Israel of the Scripture is totally distinct from the Jewish people, is yet in the very infancy, the mere alphabet, of Biblical study, and that to this day the meaning of seven-eighths of the Bible is shut to his understanding." This will become more and more apparent as we proceed with a few brief outlines of the histories of these two kingdoms.

Israel displeased the Lord by her idolatry, but it is quite evident that, for some time after the division,

Judah pleased him by her faithfulness; and it is also evident that, for a short period, fraternal relations existed between the two kingdoms. These evidences are found in the history of the war which occurred between Israel and Moab in the days of Jehoram, the son of Ahab, king of Israel, and of Jehoshaphat, king of Judah.

During the reign of Ahab he had conquered Moab, and the king of Moab paid him a revenue of one hundred thousand lambs and one hundred thousand rams, with the wool. But upon the ascension of Ahab's son to the throne of Israel the king of Moab rebelled against him; and so it is recorded that "King Jehoram went out of Samaria at that same time, and numbered all Israel." 2 Kings 3:6.

Here the expression "all Israel" has reference to all the region of country which was occupied by the ten tribes of which the kingdom of Israel was composed. Samaria was their capital city and the dwelling place of the king; but when the king of Moab rebelled against him it was but natural, and also good generalship, that he should want to know the fighting strength of the kingdom. So he made a tour throughout the realm that he might know just how many fighting men he had. But it seems that he returned fully satisfied that he did not have an army of sufficient strength to insure victory, for he sent a message to the king of Judah, saying:

"The king of Moab hath rebelled against me. Wilt thou go with me against Moab to battle?" To this the king of Judah replied in the affirmative, saying:

"I will go up: I am as thou art, and my people as thy people."

As a matter of course he could say, "My people are as thy people," for the people were brethren and subjects of brother nations, all being seed of Abraham, Isaac, and Jacob, the Children of the Promise. These two kings further decided, while holding a council of war, to go up by the way of the wilderness of Edom, and to ask the king of Edom to join with them against the Moabites. For the Edomites were also kinfolks of these two nations, they being the descendants of Esau, the brother of Jacob, whose name was changed to Edom after he sold his birthright.

The king of Edom consented to go with them, and thus the Children of the Flesh and the Children of the Promise made common cause, and went up together against the king of Moab. But when they had made a seven-days' journey they got into trouble, for there was no water for that great army of men and the beasts of burden which they were compelled to have with them.

At the beginning of the chapter which contains the history of this war concerning the king of Israel, we have the following: "Now Jehoram, the son of Ahab, began to reign over Israel in Samaria in the eighteenth year of Jehoshaphat, king of Judah, and he reigned twelve years. And wrought evil in the sight of the Lord, but not like his father and his mother; for he put away the image of Baal that his father had made. Nevertheless he cleaved unto the sins of Jeroboam, the son of Nebat, which made Israel to sin; he departed not therefrom."

But as soon as they were in trouble and the idolatrous king of Israel found there was no water, then
in startled fear he cried out, saying: "The Lord hath
brought us three kings out here to destroy us."

How quickly, when tortured with guilty fear, the
idolater knew there was a LORD who had power to
destroy them, or at least to destroy him, for he knew
that he deserved it, and only said "us three" because
of a spirit of guilty cowardice which hoped to shift
the responsibility, or, if failing in that, to insist that
others were fully as much to blame as he—which
is so often seen in frightened but impenitent men.
But it was not so with Jehoshaphat, the God-fearing
king of Judah, for he at once asked: "Is there not
here a prophet of the Lord that we may inquire of the
Lord by him?"

No doubt, the thought of Jehoshaphat in asking this
question was that by making inquiry of the Lord they
would receive such Divine instruction as would enable them to escape the threatened danger; for when
one of the servants of the king of Israel, upon hearing this inquiry, stepped forward and informed them
that Elisha the prophet was with the company the
king of Judah rejoiced and said: "The word of the
Lord is with him."

When Elisha was found and these three kings were
ushered into his presence he addressed himself to the
king of Israel, saying: "What have I to do with thee?
Get thee to the prophets of thy father and to the
prophets of thy mother." But to this the king, still
fearful, vouchsafed only the reply, "Nay: for the Lord

hath called these three kings together, to deliver them into the hand of Moab."

Then Elisha said: "As the Lord of Hosts liveth, before whom I stand, surely, were it not that I regard the presence of Jehoshaphat, the king of Judah, I would not look toward thee, nor see thee."

There are reasons given, and they are weighty ones, why the prophet of God should regard the king of Judah and emphasize the fact of his presence, in contrast to the king of Israel; for, through the prophet Hosea the Lord declares: "Ephraim compasseth me about with lies, and the house of Israel with deceit: but Judah yet ruleth with God, and is faithful with the saints."

Ah, yes; Judah is not only faithful among the saints, but she yet has power and ruling influence with God. Here are reasons, abundant, for that honorable distinction which was conferred upon Judah and her God-honoring king. It was because of them that the Lord sent water to that famishing army and gave them victory over the Moabites. But Israel and her king, although serving Jeroboam's calves, yet, in a time of trouble, when moved by guilty fear, admitted the power of the God of their fathers. Hence "lies and deceit" were in Ephraim-Israel, but faithfulness—as yet—among the Jewish people.

But there came a time when Judah was not among the faithful, and when she lost her power with God; and there also came a time when the fraternal relations were broken between these brother nations.

There are many instances of the severance of brotherly harmony between these nations, but the following instance, which occurred in the days of Amaziah, king of Judah, and Joash, king of Israel, not only reveals the broken ties but justifies the term Ephraim-Israel.

"Moreover, Amaziah gathered Judah together and made them captains over thousands and over hundreds, according to the houses of their fathers through all Judah and Benjamin (the Levites were priests, not warriors), and he numbered them from twenty years old and above, and found them three hundred thousand choice men, able to go forth to war, that could handle spear and shield. He hired an hundred thousand mighty men of valour out of Israel, for a hundred talents of silver. But there came a man of God to him, saying, 'O king, let not the army of Israel go with thee, for the Lord is not with Israel, to wit, all the children of Ephraim. But if thou wilt go and do it, to be strong for the battle, God shall make thee fall before the enemy; for God hath power to help and to cast down.'

"And Amaziah said unto the man of God, But what shall we do with the hundred talents which I have given to the army of Israel? And the man of God answered, The Lord is able to give thee much more than this. Then Amaziah separated them, to wit, the army that was come to him out of Ephraim, to go home again: wherefore their anger was greatly kindled against Judah, and they returned home in great anger. And   *   *   *   the soldiers of the army which Amaziah sent back, that they should not go with him to battle, fell upon the cities of Judah, from Samaria even to Beth-horon, and smote three thousand of them, and took much spoil."

Thus we see that the terms Israel and Ephraim are used interchangeably, for at one time we read "the army out of Israel," and at another, but concerning the same transaction, "the army that is come out of Ephraim." Also the man of God told the king of the Jews that, if he went into battle with the hundred thousand men that he had hired out of *Israel*, the Lord would defeat him, for God was not with *Israel*, to wit, Ephraim. And further, when the king of Judah sent the soldiers back home he sent them from the nation which the sacred history calls "the Jews" to that which is called "Israel."

There is one other point which must not be overlooked at this juncture; that is, that Ephraim is the representative of the house of Joseph; that Joseph represents the Birthright blessing, which carries with it the promise of a multitude of children, which was originally given to Abraham, Isaac and Jacob, and that it sometimes occurs that the name of Joseph, the father, instead of Ephraim, the son, is used when recording facts of history or prophecy concerning the ten-tribed kingdom. This does not often occur, but the following is an instance:

"And I will strengthen the house of Judah, and I will save the house of Joseph, and I will bring them again to place them; for I have mercy upon them: and they shall be as though I had not cast them off: for I am the Lord their God, and will hear them. And Ephraim shall be like a mighty man, and their heart shall rejoice as through wine." Zech. 10:6, 8.

This text clearly shows that the names of Ephraim and Joseph are titles of the ten-tribed kingdom, in con-

tradistinction from Judah and the Jews as titles of
the three-tribed kingdom.   And, since it is true that
Judah and Joseph are the inheritors of the two special
promises which pertain to the two covenants, we need
not be surprised at this, but should rather expect that
these two names would stand thus contrasted.   But all
the more should we expect this, when we see the
fact so clearly revealed in the history of the posterity
of these two men that the Birthright name and people
are representatives of one nation, and that Judah's
sceptre is swaying over the other.

But these facts are still more clearly brought out in
one of Ezekiel's prophecies, as follows: "Moreover,
thou son of man, take thee one stick and write upon
it, for Judah, and for the children of Israel his companions: then take another stick, and write upon it
for Joseph, the stick of Ephraim, and for all the
house of Israel, his companions.   And join them one
to another into one stick, and they shall become one
in thine hand.   And when the children of thy people
shall speak unto thee, saying, Wilt thou not shew us
what thou meanest by these? say unto them, Thus
saith the Lord God: Behold, I will take the stick of
Joseph, which is in the hand of Ephraim, and the tribes
of Israel his fellows, and will put them with him, even
with the stick of Judah and make them one in my hand.
And the sticks wherein thou writest shall be in thy hand
before their eyes. And say unto them, Thus saith the
Lord God: Behold I will take the children of Israel
from among the heathen, whither they be gone, and
will gather them on every side and bring them into
their own land.   And I will make them one nation

in the land upon the mountains of Israel; and one king shall be king to them all, and they shall be no more two nations, neither shall they be divided into two kingdoms any more at all. Neither shall they defile themselves any more with their idols, nor with their detestable things, nor with any of their transgressions: but I will save them out of all their dwelling-places, wherein they have sinned, and will cleanse them: so shall they be my people, and I will be their God."—Ezekiel, 37:15-23.

Many things will need to be explained before we can show the relative place in the history of these people of all the facts herein mentioned. But this much is clear:

(1) That there are two sticks, two nations, or kingdoms.

(2) That Judah, who inherited the sceptre and crown, has one of those sticks, kingdoms, or nations; while Joseph-Ephraim has the other.

(3) That Judah has with him as companions some of "the children of Israel," and that Ephraim has some of "the tribes of Israel," who are his fellows; and his companions.

(4) That when this prophecy was written they were divided; and that all the people belonging to the race had gathered, either to Judah or Joseph, or in other words, either to the Sceptre or to the Birthright.

(5) That at some future time they are again to be united, become one kingdom, and then remain so forever.

(6) That when they are thus united, one king shall be king over them all, and when this takes place the peo-

ple will have been so lifted up by Divine power and so enriched by grace that they will no more defile themselves, commit no transgressions, or in any way displease the Lord, but shall be his accepted people, and he shall be their God.

Evidently one of these sticks is the Sceptre and the other the Birthright; for these and the promises connected with each are of general interest to all the children of promise, but they are the exclusive property of the two men, Judah and Joseph, who are the special subjects of the prophecy, while the entire posterity of Jacob is the general subject. But this figure of the two sticks, or staffs, is used in another prophecy, which pertains to the two houses and which should be of profound interest to all.

Beginning in the midst of the seventh verse of the eleventh chapter of Zachariah, we have the following: "I took unto me two staves; the one I called Beauty, and the other I called Bands. * * * And I took my staff, even Beauty, and cut it asunder, that I might break my covenant which I had made with all the people. And it was broken in that day: and so the poor of the flock that waited upon me knew that it was the Word of the Lord. And I said unto them, If ye think good, give me my price; and if not, forbear. So they weighed for my price thirty pieces of silver.

"And the Lord said unto me, Cast it to the potter: a goodly price that I was priced at of them. And I took thirty pieces of silver and cast them to the potter in the house of the Lord. Then I cut asunder mine other staff, even Bands, that I might break the brother-hood between Israel and Judah." Zech. 11 : 7-14.

So Israel and Judah are the two sticks or staves which the Lord took unto himself. He first cut asunder one stick or staff called Beauty, i. e., ten-tribed Israel. Then, after a certain transaction in which their Lord was sold for thirty pieces of silver, he cut asunder his other staff, called Bands (i. e., Judah, the Jews), that he might break the brotherhood between Judah and Israel!

Just what a great and marvelously fulfilled truth is herein declared we are not yet prepared to explain. At this juncture we can only call your attention to the fact that Ezekiel's prophecy concerning the putting together of the two sticks could not have been fulfilled until after the transaction which concerns the thirty pieces of silver ; and that when it does take place it must be in harmony not only with those blessed results, which we have already mentioned, but also with that which is contained in the rest of that prophecy, a part of which is as follows:

"And they shall dwell in the land that I have given to Jacob my servant, wherein your fathers have dwelt ; and they shall dwell therein, even they, and their chil-dren, and their children's children forever: and my servant David shall be their prince forever.

"Moreover, I will make a covenant of peace with them; it shall be an everlasting covenant with them: and I will place them and multiply them, and will set my sanctuary in the midst of them for evermore."

The brotherhood is still broken, *but it shall be mended.*

CHAPTER VII.

EPHRAIM-SAMARIA-ISRAEL'S IDOLATRY.

"When I would have healed Israel, then the iniquity of Ephraim was discovered, and the wickedness of Samaria, for they commit falsehood." (Hosea 7:1.) Here the names of Israel, Ephraim, and Samaria, are used interchangeably for the one kingdom. It bears the name Ephraim, because it is the Birthright kingdom; that of Samaria, because that was the name of their capital city; and the name of Israel, for the reason that when dying Jacob, whose name had been changed to Israel, in bestowing the Birthright upon Joseph's two sons, said: "Let my name be named on them."

When the blessing of Him that dwelt in the bush came upon Joseph, he who was separated from his brethren, it is declared that his glory was the ten thousands of Ephraim and the thousands of Manasseh. Thus he received, in so far as tribal honor or glory is concerned, a double portion. So, at the time of the division of the land by lot, under the leadership of Joshua, we find the declaration that "there was also a lot for the tribe of Manasseh, for he was the first born of Joseph; but that "they gave no part unto the Levites in the land, save cities to dwell in," and the reason given for it is, "For the children of Joseph were two tribes, Manasseh and Ephraim." Josh. 14:4.

The fact is that Jacob adopted the two sons of Joseph gave them tribal headship, and thus made thirteen tribes in Jacob. And since Judah, Benjamin, and Levi were the tribal heads of the kingdom of Judah, there were still ten tribes for the Birthright kingdom, and the Lord's promise to the king of Israel stood fast.

The history of the kingdom of Israel, as opposed to that of the Jews, is full of the sin of Jeroboam and of her kings who walked in this sin. This sin was, in a special sense, the sin of that nation. It pertained exclusively to them, because it was born, bred, lived, and died among them; for no other nation took up with it, not even their brethren of the kingdom of Judah. It was the standing sin of the nation; to them it ever stood as an open door through which other forms of idolatry might enter, and through which they did enter. For, although it is said of Omri, the sixth king of Israel, that he wrought evil in the sight of the Lord in following the sin of Jeroboam, and also that he did worse than all that were before him, the Lord is compelled to say of Ahab, the son of Omri, that he did worse than his father; for it was he who introduced the worship of Baal among the Israelites. Following the introduction of Baalism, other idolatries were quickly introduced among them, and soon the cup of Israel's iniquity was full to the brim; the result of which was that she was cast out of the land.

Israel was not only cast out of that land, their God-given heritage and which—if God be true—must yet become their everlasting home; but she was cast off by the Lord and divorced from him, because of her harlotry in forsaking him, her lawful husband, for the worship of idols.

Before giving the details of the casting out and the casting off, we deem it advisable to give a complete list of Israel's dynasties, together with a list of all the kings who reigned over Israel from the time when the kingdom was taken from Solomon and given to Jeroboam, his servant, until they were finally driven out of the land, and also to give what the Scripture saith concerning the idolatry of each of these her kings.

So we place, in parallel columns, below, the name and number of the king, the number of the dynasty, and the length of time which each of the kings reigned, in one column ; and what is said concerning his idolatry in the other.

Idolatry.

I. DYNASTY.

1st King, Jeroboam.
Reigned 22 years.

"And Jeroboam said in his heart, Now shall the kingdom return to the house of David : if this people go up to do sacrifice in the house of the Lord at Jerusalem, then shall the heart of this people turn again unto their lord, even unto Rehoboam, king of Judah, and they shall kill me, and go again to Rehoboam, king of Judah, whereupon the king took counsel, and made two calves of gold, and said unto them, It is too much for you to go up to Jerusalem : behold thy gods, O Israel, which brought thee up out of the land of Egypt. And he set the one in Beth-el, and the other he put in Dan. And this thing became a sin, for the people went to worship." (1 Ki. 12: 26-30.)

"And he did evil in the sight of the Lord, and walked in the way of his father, and in his sin wherewith he made Israel to sin." (1 Ki. 15: 26.)

2nd King, Nadab. Reigned 2 years.

II. DYNASTY.

"And he did evil in the sight of the Lord, and walked in the way of Jeroboam, and in his sin wherewith he made Israel to sin." (1 Ki. 15: 34.)

3rd King, Baasha. Reigned 24 years.

"For all the sins of Baasha (Jeroboamism), and the sins of Elah his son, by which they sinned, and by which they made Israel to sin, etc." (1 Ki. 16:13.)

4th King, Elah. Reigned 2 years.

III. DYNASTY.

"And it came to pass, when Zimri saw that the city was taken, that he went into the palace of the king's house, and burnt the king's house over him with fire, and died, for his sins which he sinned in doing evil in the sight of the Lord, in walking in the way of Jeroboam, and in his sin which he did to make Israel to sin." (1 Ki. 16: 18, 19.)

5th King, Zimri. Reigned 1 week.

IV. DYNASTY.

"But Omri wrought evil in the eyes of the Lord, and did worse than all that were before him. For he walked in all the way of Jeroboam, the son of Nebat, and in his sin

6th King, Omri. Reigned 12 years.

wherewith he made Israel to sin, to provoke the Lord God of Israel to anger with their vanities." (1 Ki. 16: 25-26.)

"And Ahab, the son of Omri, did evil in the sight of the Lord above all that were before him. And it **7th King, Ahab.** came to pass, as if it had been a **Reigned 22 years.** light thing for him to walk in the sins of Jeroboam, the son of Nebat, that he took to wife Jezebel, the daughter of Ethbaal, king of the Zidonians, and went and served Baal, and worshiped him. And he reared up an altar for Baal in the house of Baal, which he had built in Samaria. And Ahab made a grove; and Ahab did more to provoke the Lord God of Israel than all the kings of Israel that were before him." (1 Ki. 16: 30-33.)

"And he did evil in the sight of the Lord, and walked in the way of his father, and in the way of his **8th King, Ahaziah.** mother, and in the way of Jeroboam, **Reigned 2 years.** the son of Nebat, who made Israel to sin: for he served Baal, and worshiped him, and provoked to anger the Lord God of Israel, according to all that his father had done." (1 Ki. 22:52, 53.)

9th King, Jehoram.
Reigned 12 years.

"And he wrought evil in the sight of the Lord; but not like his father, and like his mother; for he put away the image of Baal that his father had made. Nevertheless he cleaved unto the sins of Jeroboam, the son of Nebat, which made Israel to sin; he departed not therefrom." (2 Ki. 3:2, 3.)

V. DYNASTY.

10th King, Jehu.
Reigned 23 years.

"Howbeit from the sins of Jeroboam, the son of Nebat, who made Israel to sin, Jehu departed not from after them, to wit, the golden calves that were in Bethel and that were in Dan." (2 Ki. 10:29.)

11th King,
Jehoahaz.
Reigned 17 years.

"And he did that which was evil in the sight of the Lord, and followed the sins of Jeroboam, the son of Nebat, which made Israel to sin; he departed not therefrom." (2 Ki. 13:2.)

12th King, Joash.
Reigned 10 years.

"And he did that which was evil in the sight of the Lord; he departed not from all the sins of Jeroboam, the son of Nebat, who made Israel to sin; but he walked therein." (2 Ki. 13:11.)

13th King,
Jeroboam, the 2d.
(son of Joash).
Reigned 41 years.

"And he did that which was evil in the sight of the Lord: he departed not from all the sins of Jeroboam, the son of Nebat, who made Israel to sin." (2 Ki. 14:24.)

**14th King,
Zachariah.
Reigned 6 months.**

"And he did that which was evil in the sight of the Lord, as his father had done: he departed not from the sins of Jeroboam, the son of Nebat, who made Israel to sin." (2 Ki. 15: 9.)

**VI. DYNASTY.
15th King,
Shallum.
Reigned 1 month.**

(Sins of Shallum not recorded.)

VII. DYNASTY.

**16th King,
Menahem.
Reigned 10 years.**

"And he did that which was evil in the sight of the Lord: he departed not all of his days from the sins of Jeroboam, the son of Nebat, who made Israel to sin." (2 Ki. 15:18.)

**17th King,
Pekahiah.
Reigned 2 years.**

"And he did that which was evil in the sight of the Lord: and he departed not from the sins of Jeroboam, the son of Nebat, who made Israel to sin." (2 Ki. 15:24.)

VII. DYNASTY.

**18th King,
Pekah.
Reigned 20 years.**

"And he did that which was evil in the sight of the Lord: he departed not from the sins of Jeroboam, the son of Nebat, who made Israel to sin." (2 Ki. 15:28.)

**19th King,
Hoshea.
Reigned 22 years.**

"And he did that which was evil in the sight of the Lord, but not as the kings of Israel that were before him." (2 Ki. 17:2.)

After the introduction of Baalism and other idolatries, there were a few feeble attempts at reformation; but they were only partial, as we may readily see. Take, for instance, the case of Jehoram to which we referred in the last chapter; how it is written that "He wrought evil in the sight of the Lord, but not like his father and mother, for he put away the image of Baal that his father had made, nevertheless he cleaved unto the sins of Jeroboam, the son of Nebat, which made Israel to sin." It was this slight and hypocritical attempt to purify the worship of the people which so displeased the Lord, and which made Elisha the prophet give that scathing rebuke to Jehoram in the presence of his kinsman kings. For if he knew enough concerning the Lord God of his race to have his conscience troubled over Baal, he had sufficient light to have made a clean sweep of the whole thing, but he did not do it. And the sequel proves that he did not succeed in destroying Baalism from among his people, for they were soon back to it, and even went so far as to offer their own sons and daughters in living sacrifice to the idol of Baal.

It was to this kingdom, the people of which are Israelites and not Jews, that the Lord sent Elijah the prophet to make the fire test as to whether he or Baal be God. And when the Lord answered by fire, which not only consumed the sacrifice but the stones of the altar, the water in the ditch, and the very dust under the altar, it was these people who shouted loud and long: "The Lord, he is God! The Lord, he is God!" But they never forsook Jeroboam-ism, and soon relapsed into the worship of Baal worse than ever.

Finally the Lord raised up Jehu, who destroyed all the house of Ahab, and became the king of Israel. He, upon his ascension, "gathered the people together and said unto them, Ahab served Baal a little; Jehu shall serve him much. Now therefore call unto me all the prophets of Baal, all his priests; let none be wanting; for I have a great sacrifice to do for Baal; whosoever shall be wanting (lacking) he shall not live. But Jehu did it in subtlety, to the intent that he might destroy the worshipers of Baal." (2 Ki. 10: 19.)

His ruse worked like a charm; they all came, prophets, priests and all the worshipers, "so that there was not a man left that came not," and the house of Baal was full from one end to the other. Then he commanded his guards to destroy them, saying that the man who let one escape should pay the penalty with his own life. They did their work and did it well. So the record reads, "Thus Jehu did destroy Baal out of Israel." But, oh, note the very next words: "Howbeit, from the sins of Jeroboam, the son of Nebat, who made Israel to sin, Jehu departed not from them, to wit, the golden calves that were in Bethel and that were in Dan." (2 Kings, 10: 29.)

It was in regard to Israel, this same ten-tribed kingdom, that the Lord, through the prophet Hosea, said, "Israel slideth back as a backsliding heifer," and of whom he said, "I will heal their backslidings, I will love them freely"; and whom he exhorted, saying: "O Israel, return unto the Lord thy God!" But they would not. And yet at that same time the Lord declared that the Jews did have power with him, and that they were among the faithful saints.

In the face of all these facts can there be any further question as to the real meaning of the expression,

"Ephraim is joined to his idols"—Jeroboam's calves? Or need we be surprised, in the fact of these cold, hard facts, that the Lord should say, "Let him alone?"

No, surely no. The only surprise is that we should have been so stupid as to have tried to spiritualize Ephraim and his idols.

Since it is a well-known fact that the Jews also went into the worship of Baal, and that for this they were eventually carried away to Babylon, we deem it advisable that all may the more readily grasp other facts with which we shall yet deal, to give at this juncture a tabulated list of Judah's kings from the time God broke up the united kingdom,—for you will remember that he said, "This is of me"—until the Jewish people went into the Babylonish captivity.

KINGDOM OF JUDAH.
(Dynasty a continuation of David's house.)

1st King..........Rehoboam ....Reigned	17	years	
2nd " ....Abijah .... "	3	"	
3rd " ....Asa .... "	41	"	
4th " ....Jehosaphat .... "	25	"	
5th " ....Jehoram .... "	8	"	
6th " ....Ahaziah .... "	1	"	
7th " ....(Queen) Athaliah.... "	6	"	
8th " ....Jehoash .... "	40	"	
9th " ....Amaziah .... "	29	"	
10th " ....Azariah, or Uzziah... "	52	"	
11th " ....Jotham .... "	16	"	
12th " ....Ahaz .... "	16	"	
13th " ....Hezekiah .... "	29	"	
14th " ....Manassah .... "	55	"	
15th " ....Amon .... "	2	"	
16th " ....Josiah .... "	31	"	
17th " ....Jehoahaz .... "	3	mos.	
18th " ....Jehoiakim .... "	11	years	
19th " ....Jehoiachin .... "	3	mos.	
20th " ....Zedekiah .... "	11	years	

In this list we perceive that the same dynasty, which commenced when David was made king over the united tribes, continues throughout this entire list down to and including Zedekiah; while, in the previously given list of Israel's kings, you notice, there are no less than eight dynasties. The reason is obvious. Judah's kings are the God-given royal line, along which the swaying sceptre passed from father to son. For the Lord had promised this family that neither the sceptre nor a law-giver should depart from them until Shiloh should come. But such was not the case in the kingdom of Israel, hence feudalism prevailed among them.

CHAPTER VIII.

SAMARIA-ISRAEL CAST OUT AND CAST OFF.

Concerning the casting out of Israel, it is written: "And it came to pass in the fourth year of King Hezekiah (the king of Judah) which was the seventh year of Hosea, son of Elah, king of Israel, that Shalmaneser, king of Assyria, came up against Samaria and besieged it, and at the end of three years they took it; even in the sixth year of Hezekiah, that is, the ninth year of Hosea, king of Israel, Samaria was taken. And the king of Assyria did carry away Israel unto Assyria, and put them in Halah, and in Habor by the river of Gozan and in the cities of the Medes. Because they obeyed not the voice of the Lord their God, but transgressed his covenant, and all that Moses, the servant of the Lord, commanded, and would not hear them, nor do them." (2 Kings, 18:9-12.) "For the children of Israel walked in all the sins of Jeroboam which he did, they departed not from them; until the Lord removed Israel out of his sight (literally his fore-front regard, or fore-front favor; such as is expressed in other places by the use of the words face and countenance), as he had said by all his servants the prophets. So was Israel carried away out of their own land to Assyria unto this day. And the king of Assyria brought men from Babylon, and from Cuthah, and from Ava, and from Hamath, and from Sepharvaim, and placed them in the cities of Samaria instead of the children of Israel: and they possessed Samaria, and dwelt in the cities thereof."—(2 Kings 17: 23-24.)

If, as it is herein affirmed, the king of Assyria did take this ten-tribed kingdom *out of their own land*, which land is called Samaria, and then place another people there *instead of the children of Israel, then Samaria is the lawful home of those pre-Samaritans,* THE EGYPTO-ISRAELITES of the Ephraimitish or Birthright kingdom, while those mongrel post-Samaritans, who were gathered up from various places, were but strangers and foreigners in that portion of the Abrahamic land grant known as Samaria.

Following this record of the removal of Israel and the placing of these strangers in their former home, we have the following: "And so it was at the beginning of the dwelling there, that they feared not the Lord: therefore the Lord sent lions among them which slew some of them. Wherefore they spake to the king of Assyria, saying, The nations which thou hast removed and placed in the cities of Samaria, know not the manner of the God of the land: therefore he hath sent lions among them, and, behold, they slay them, because they know not the manner of the God of the land.

"Then the king of Assyria commanded, saying, Carry one of the priests whom ye brought from thence; and let him go and dwell there, and let him teach them the manner of the God of the land. Then one of the priests whom they carried away from Samaria came and dwelt in Bethel, and taught them how they should fear the Lord.

"Howbeit every nation made gods of their own, and put them in the houses of the high places which the (former) Samaritans (Israelites) had made, every nation in their cities wherein they dwelt; the men of Babylon made Succoth-benoth (an idol), and the men of Cuth made Nergalm (another idol), and the men of Hamath made Ashima (still another). And the Avites made Nibhaz and Tartak (still others), and the Sepharvites burnt their children in fire to Adrammelech and Anammelech, the gods of Sepharviam.

"So they feared the Lord and made unto themselves of the lowest of them priests of the high places, which sacrificed for them in the houses of the high places. They feared the Lord, and served their own gods, after the manner of nations (Joseph-Ephraim-Samaria-Israel *whom they carried away from thence*. Unto this day they do after the former manners." (2 Kings 17:25-34.)

Yes: "after the former manner" of idolatrous Isreal. Yes; after the former manner of Israel, who feared—was afraid of—the Lord, but served their own idol-gods. Yes; after the former manner of Israel, who built those same high places—the groves, temples and altars—and in them worshiped the works of their own hands. Yes; after the former manner of Israel, who rejected the priests of the Lord, and made priests of the lowest of the people. Yes; here is a perfect flower, produced from the pollen of example, and grown upon the plant of "after the former manner." Yes; here is a clear case of gathering thistles when they should have had figs. And yet that poor priest whom they sent back was not to blame, for he himself was one of the lowest of his race. The blame lay behind him—Israel!

The charge against the people of Israel is, "Surely as a wife treacherously departeth from her husband, so have ye dealt treacherously with me, O house of Israel, saith the Lord." (Jere. 3:20.) And the Lord cried out, "O Ephraim, thou hast committed whoredom. Israel is defiled." (Hosea 5:3.) Hosea is also used of the Lord to declare "Ephraim is smitten. * * My God shall cast them away, because they did not harken unto him." Thus the Lord declares, "I will love them no more;" but in the bitterness of his disappointment, for this is the same Lord that wept over Jerusalem, he cried out, "O Ephraim, how shall I give thee up?"

No! No! That loving One did not want to cast them off; but they forsook him; they would not have him to reign over them; they would no longer ask counsel of him after the judgment of Urim and Thummim, for the faithful but rejected One declares, "My people ask counsel at their stock (cattle, calves), and their staff (support or stay) declareth unto them: for the spirit of whoredom hath caused them to err, and they have gone a whoring from under their God." (Hosea 4:12.)

Still he cries after them, "Return, O backsliding Isreal, return! Return unto me and I will return unto you, for I am married unto you. I will heal your backslidings and love you freely." But they would not. Previous to this the Lord had said that he was a husband to Israel; but now, disappointed, he turns his heart more to the other kingdom—that of Judah—and says: "Though thou, Israel, play the harlot, yet let not Judah offend." (Hosea 4:15.) But as the story unfolds we find that Judah offended worse than Israel, and that one hundred and thirty years after the driving out of Israel they, too, were carried into captivity,—the captivity in Babylon.

Since "the head of Ephraim is Samaria," (Isa. 7:9) there need be no difficulty in understanding why the Lord should declare that "the inhabitants of Samaria shall fear because of the calves of Beth-aven." (Hosea 10:5.) Beth-aven is defined as "House of Vanities"; "vain emptiness." When Jeroboam set up the two calves for Israel to worship he set one in Bethel, which means "God's house;" and by worshiping those idols they turned the house of God into a house of vanity, or of vain, hollow, unsatisfactory emptiness. "Thus provoking the Lord God of Israel to anger (passionate suffering) by their vanities." Hence the wail of the prophet, "They trust in vanity and speak lies."

Let us note carefully, and we will get still clearer light concerning the calf question. "Israel hath cast off the thing that is good (God and his care): the enemy shall pursue him (because they had cast off the protection of God). They have set up kings, but not by me (their own, not the Lord's, choice): they have made princes (feudal princes, not of royal line), and I knew (Heb, yada, appoint, recognize) it not: of their silver and their gold have they made them (selves) idols (calves, etc.) that (as a result) they may be cut off.

"Thy calf (the cause), O Samaria, hath cast thee
off (the result): mine anger (long-suffering passion)
is kindled against them: how long will it be ere they
(Israel) attain to innocency? (i. e., lack of guilt
through the power of the calf to forgive, or take that
guilt away.)

"For from Israel was it also: The workmen made it,
therefore it is not God. But the calf of Samaria shall
be broken in pieces.

"For they have sown the wind, and they shall reap
the whirlwind: it hath left no standing corn (R. V.);
the bud shall yield no meal: if so be it yield, the
strangers (Post-Samaritans) shall swallow it up.

"Israel is swallowed up; now shall they be among
the Gentiles as a vessel wherein is no pleasure. For
they are gone up to Assyria a wild ass alone (without
God) by himself: Ephraim hath hired lovers *(Marginal reading: loves,* i. e., having no loving care from
the Lord, they hire some one to love them). Yea,
though they have hired (lovers) among the nations,
now will I gather them, and they shall begin to sorrow
in a little while (marginal reading) for the burden
of the king of princes.

"Because Ephraim hath made many altars to sin,
altars shall be to him a sin. I have written to him
the great things of my laws, but they were counted as
a strange thing. They sacrifice (other) flesh for the
sacrifices of mine offerings, and eat it; but the Lord
accepteth them not: now will he remember their iniquity, and visit their sins; they shall return to Egypt.
(Figurative to them of captivity and bondage). For
Israel hath forgotten his maker."

Isaiah fully explains the expression, "They shall begin to sorrow in a little while, for the burden of the King of Princes," in the following: "O Assyrian, the rod of mine anger, and the staff in their hand is mine indignation. I will send him against a hypocritical nation and against the people of my wrath will I give him a charge, to take the spoil and to take the prey and to tread them down like the mire of the streets. Howbeit he meaneth not so; but it is in his heart to destroy and cut off nations not a few. For he saith, Are not my princes altogether kings?" (Isa. 10: 5-8.)

This last expression was an Assyrian boast. The Assyrian king really expected to destroy Israel and cut them off, but the Word of God has gone forth that they shall never be destroyed. In order to punish them he allowed the Assyrian to "tread them down like mire of the streets." And further on he refers to the Egyptian bondage, and says that the Assyrian shall smite them with a rod and lift up his staff against them, "after the manner of Egypt."

It is high time for us, who live in the realm of faith, to throw off our lethargy, arouse ourselves from our God-dishonoring stupidity and ignorance and understand that the name Samaria has a prophetic significance, as well as a historic one. Yes, and that not only Samaria, but that the names of Ephraim, Joseph, Rachel, Judah, Jacob, Israel and many others have the same signification in the prophecies of the Bible that they have in its historic portions. That is, if the names Israel, Samaria, Ephraim, etc., are used in the history to designate the ten-tribed Egypto-Israelitish Birthright kingdom; then, when those names are used prophetically, surely the prophecy involved must refer to the same people. This is also true of the terms Judah and the Jews. True, the name Israel often includes the Jews, for, racially speaking, it is their national name; but it is used again and again and again when it has no reference whatever to the Jewish people.

In the thirty-first chapter of Jeremiah the Lord has made an unconditional promise to the Birthright nation. This promise is given in clear, definite and unmistakable language, which he declares they shall consider in the last days; and in which he uses the names of Jacob, Ephraim, Israel, and Samaria, together with the name of Rachel, the mother of the birthright family. It is in this prophecy that the Lord makes use of the expression, "I am a father to Israel, and Ephraim is my first born," in connection with which he says, "He that scattered Israel will gather him," and commands that this be told in the land where Ephraim is living in the last days. He also says to them, in this same promise, "Thou shalt yet plant vines upon the mountains of Samaria," and to this he further adds: "A great company shall return thither."

"Return thither."

"Where?"

To the place from which they came—SAMARIA!

"Who?"

Jacob-Rachel-Joseph-Ephraim-Samaria-Israel!!!

It is a well-known fact that the Jews went into the Babylonish captivity; but it is much more fully known that they returned from that captivity and dwelt, for a short season, in Judea, or Jewry. But, aside from that one priest who was brought back from among the captives of Israel, and who dwelt in Bethel, that he might teach those mongrel post-Samaritans the manner of the God of the land, there is not one word of history, sacred or profane, to show that any tribe, tribes, or remnants of tribes, of those pre-Samaritans, the children of Israel, who composed the northern kingdom, have ever returned to and dwelt in their former home.   That is, that portion of the land which the Lord God of heaven and earth promised to their fathers, and which is known in Biblical history as "Samaria," and "All Israel," in contradistinction from that which is known as "All Judea" and "Jewry," which was the home of the Jews.

In another chapter we have given the details of the Babylonian captivity of the Jews, but just at present we desire to call your attention to the fact that their captivity occurred in 588 B. C. (Usher's Chronology, which is not correct by more than eight years, but is sufficiently correct for our present purpose), and the first prophecy uttered concerning that captivity was 623 B. C. and the last one twenty-three years later, i. e., 600 B. C.   But the prophet Amos had prophesied concerning the captivity and return from captivity of the ten-tribed kingdom one hundred and sixty-four years prior to the first intimation that the Jews would ever go into captivity, and one hundred and ninety-nine years before they were carried away into captivity.

In writing concerning the captivity of the ten tribes the names which Amos used to designate them are, "Samaria," used four times; "Joseph," used three times; "Isaac," used twice; "Bethel," used five times, and "Israel," used seventeen times.

Amos is the only one of the prophets who applied the name of Isaac to either one of the two kingdoms. But there can be no possible doubt that Amos gives the name of Isaac to the ten-tribed kingdom. The first verse in the book of Amos reads: "The words of Amos, who was among the herdsmen of Tekoa, which he saw concerning Israel, in the days of Uzziah, king of Judah, and in the days of Jeroboam (this is Jeroboam the second) son of Joash, king of Israel. He uses the title of Isaac as follows: "And the high places (groves for worship) of Isaac shall be desolate, and the sanctuaries (Bethel and Dan) of Israel shall be laid waste, and I will rise up against the house of Jeroboam (king of ten-tribed Israel) with the sword. Then Amaziah, the priest of Bethel (the place where they went to worship the calf), sent to Jeroboam, king of Israel, saying, Amos hath conspired against thee in the midst of the house of Israel: the land is not able to bear all his words. For thus Amos saith, Jeroboam shall die by the sword, and Israel shall surely be led away captive out of their own land. Also Amaziah saith unto Amos, O thou seer, go flee away into the land of Judah (Jewry) and there eat bread, and prophesy there; but prophesy not again any more at Bethel: for it is the king's chapel." (Amos 7:9-15.)

In the days of Joshua, when the land of Canaan was divided by lot, Bethel fell to the house of Joseph. Thus we find it in possession of the Birthright kingdom and used as the chapel of this idolatrous king, for Jeroboam the first had polluted it with one of the calves.

While it is true that this people were taken to Assyria, and were given a promise that they shall eventually return, there is something else which must first occur; for the Lord has said of them that after they were cast out he would "sift the house of Israel among all nations, like as corn is sifted in a sieve, yet shall not the least grain fall upon the earth." (Amos 9:9.)

Then, after giving this prophecy concerning the sifting of the house of Israel among all nations, Amos prophesies concerning their return, as follows: "And I will bring again the captivity of my people of Israel, and they shall build the waste cities, and inhabit them; and they shall plant vineyards, and drink the wine thereof; they shall also make gardens, and eat the fruit of them. And I will plant them upon their land, and they shall no more be pulled up out of their land which I have given them, saith the Lord thy God." (Amos 9: 14, 15.)

But, in spite of the fact that this prophecy was written two centuries before the Jews were sent into captivity, while they were yet counted among the faithful saints, it having no application to them whatever, and that, when fulfilled, the people to whom it refers SHALL NO MORE BE PULLED UP out of their land—there are theory-bound men who are so determined that everything Israelitish shall be Jewish that they have the audacity to tell us that this prophecy was fulfilled when the Jews returned from the Babylonish captivity.

CHAPTER IX.

THE JEWS GO TO BABYLON AND RETURN.

The twenty-third chapter of Ezekiel contains a short story which seems somewhat veiled, but a knowledge of the two houses and their respective capitals lifts the veil and quickly sweeps it aside. It is of interest to us, or should be, and begins as follows: "There were two women, daughters of one mother, who committed adultery in their youth in Egypt, the names of whom were Aholah, the elder, and Aholibah, her sister, and they were mine, saith the Lord, and they bare sons and daughters." "Thus were their names; SAMARIA is Aholah (Israel), and JERUSALEM Aholibah (Judah)." Ezekiel 23:4. Then the story continues and tells how Aholah, the elder, played the harlot, and was followed into that sin by her sister Aholibah, who was more corrupt than Aholah had been. So God judged them "as women that break wedlock." Before the story is ended the history of Israel's captivity to the Assyrians is told, together with prophecies concerning the captivity of Judah in Babylon.

The Lord further says to the Jews: "And thine elder sister is Samaria (Israel), she and her daughters that dwell at thy left hand; and thy younger sister, that dwelleth at thy right hand, is Sodom and her daughters. Yet hast thou not walked after their ways, nor done after their abominations; but, as if it were a very

little thing, thou wast corrupted more than they in all
thy ways.   *   *   *   Neither hath Samaria (Israel) committed half of thy sins; but thou hast multiplied thine abominations more than they and hast justified (by comparison) thy sisters in all thine abominations which thou hast done.   Thou also, which hast
judged thy sisters, bear thine own shame for thy sins
that thou hast committed more abominable than they."
(Ezekiel 16:46-52.)

This is in harmony with the record of Judah, as
given by Jeremiah in the following: "And I saw, when
for all the causes whereby backsliding Israel committed adultery I had put her away, and given her a bill
of divorce; yet her treacherous sister Judah feared
not but went and played the harlot also.   *   *   *
And the Lord said unto me, The backsliding Israel
hath justified herself more than treacherous Judah."
(Jeremiah 3:8, 11.)

"And the Lord said, I will remove Judah also out
of my sight, as I have removed Israel, and will cast
off this city Jerusalem which I have chosen, and the
house of which I said, My name shall be there" (2
Kings 23:27).   So Jeremiah was commanded to stand
in the gate of the Lord's house and proclaim the word
of the Lord unto all the men of Judah, and among
other things say unto them: "But go ye now unto
my place, which is Shiloh (one of the cities of Joseph),
where I set my name at first, and see what I did to it
for the wickedness of my people Israel.   And now,
because ye have done all these works, saith the Lord,
and I spake unto you, rising up early and speaking, but
ye heard not; and I called you, but ye answered not.

Therefore will I do unto this house, which is called by my name, wherein ye trust, and unto the place which I gave to you and to your fathers, as I have done to Shiloh. And I will cast you out of my sight, as I have cast out all your brethren, even the whole seed of Ephraim." (Jeremiah 7:12-15.)

The above is the prophecy; the following is a part of the historic record of the fact after its fulfillment. "Thus Judah was carried away captive out of his own land. This is the people whom Nebuchadnezzar carried away captive in the seventh year (of his reign) three thousand Jews and three-and-twenty. In the eighteenth year of Nebuchadnezzar he carried away captive from Jerusalem eight hundred thirty-and-two persons. In the three-and-twentieth year of Nebuchadnezzar Nebuzar-adan, the captain of the guard carried away captive of the Jews seven hundred forty-and-five persons. All the persons were four thousand and six hundred." (Jeremiah 52:27-30.)

Thus doth Jeremiah teach, that it was the Jews, or the people composing the kingdom of Judah, who were carried into Babylon by Nebuchadnezzar; and in order to show that it was the Jewish people, and they only, who returned from that captivity, we cite the following: "Now these are the children of the province (Judea had been a province to Babylon twenty years before Nebuchadnezzar robbed and burned the temple, destroyed Jerusalem, and took the Jews to Babylon) that went up out of the captivity of those which had been carried away, whom Nebuchadnezzar, the king of Babylon, had carried away into Babylon, and came again unto Jerusalem, and Judah every one to his city." (Ezra 2 : 1.)

The books of Ezra and Nehemiah are the only books of the Bible which deal with the history of that return. Jeremiah had prophesied that the Jews should remain captives in the Chaldean Empire (Babylon was the capital of that empire) for seventy years. Just as the seventy years came to an end the empire was taken by the Medes and Persians, and it became known in history as the Medo-Persian empire.

Ezra begins his record as follows: "Now in the first year of Cyrus, King of Persia, that the word of the Lord by the mouth of Jeremiah might be fulfilled, the Lord stirred up the spirit of Cyrus, King of Persia, that he made a proclamation throughout all his kingdom, and put it also in writing, saying, 'Thus said Cyrus King of Persia, The Lord God of heaven hath given me all the kingdoms of the earth; and he hath charged me to build him an house at Jerusalem, which is in Judah. Who is there among you of all his people? His God be with him, and let him go up to Jerusalem, which is in Judah, and build the house of the Lord God of Israel (he is the God) which is in Jerusalem. And whosoever remaineth in any place (throughout the kingdom) where he sojourneth, let the men of his place keep him with silver and with gold and with goods and with beasts, besides the free will offering for the house of God that is in Jerusalem.'

"Then rose up the chief of the fathers of Judah and Benjamin, and the priests, and the Levites, with all them whose spirit God hath raised, to go up to build the house of the Lord which is in Jerusalem." (Ezra 1:1-5.)

Do you notice that it is only the men of the tribes of Judah, Benjamin, and Levi who are mentioned as responding to this call? Also you will remember that those three tribes are the three which compose the kingdom of Judah which went into the Babylonish captivity, the ten tribes having been carried away into the Assyrian captivity one hundred and thirty years prior to that.

Also notice that it was not all the fathers nor all of Judah, Benjamin, and Levi that rose up to this call, but the chief of the fathers, and all of the people in those tribes mentioned whose spirit the Lord had made willing. So these willing ones went to work, gathering together their silver, gold, goods, and other precious things. And Cyrus, the king, brought out of the house of one of the idols, where Nebuchadnezzar had put them, all of the vessels belonging to the house of the Lord, and through his treasurer "numbered them unto Sheshbazzar, the prince of Judah. And this is the number of them: Thirty charges of silver, nine and thirty knives. Thirty basins of gold, silver of a second sort four hundred and ten, and other vessels a thousand. All the vessels of gold and silver were five thousand and four hundred. All these did Sheshbazzar bring up with him of the captivity that were brought up from Babylon to Jerusalem." (Ezra 1:8-11.) Please notice that among these things mentioned as belonging to the house of God there is no mention of the Ark of the Covenant.   The reason is that the Ark was with the Birthright people.

Some presume to teach that the house of Israel returned to Palestine with the Jews when they came from Babylon.   When we get to that phase of our subject we will prove by both the Old and New Testaments that they did not.   But just here we need to say that in the books which deal with the history of this return there is not the slightest mention, direct or indirect, by inference or reference, of the other kingdom, or house, of Israel.

There is a mention of the army of Samaria by Nehemiah, but you will find that they belonged to the Post-Samaritans, who with others opposed and hindered the Jews in their work, until finally they forced them to cease work on the temple.   Here is the record: "But it came to pass, that when Sanballat heard that we builded the wall he was wroth, and took great indignation, and mocked the Jews.   And he spake before his brethren and the army of Samaria, and said, What do these feeble Jews?"   (Neh. 4: 1, 2.)   Again: "Now when the adversaries of Judah and Benjamin heard that the children of the captivity builded the temple unto the Lord God of Israel."   (Ezra 4: 1.)

Following these statements is the account of a prolonged persecution of the Jews by those mongrel nations of Post-Samaritans. They hired counselors, wrote letters of protest, resorted to trickery and hypocrisy. A letter of protest was written to Artaxerxes, king of Persia, which was signed by many, together with "the rest of the nations whom the noble Asnapar brought over and set in the cities of Samaria." This had the effect of stopping the work on the temple, and it did not begin again until during the second year of Darius, at which time these imported Samaritans again tried to hinder. The account of this is given by Josephus, as follows: "When the Samaritans, who were still enemies to the tribes of Judah and Benjamin, heard the sound of trumpets, they came running together, and desired to know what was the occasion of the tumult; and when they perceived that it was the Jews who had been carried captive to Babylon and were rebuilding the temple, they came to Zorobabel, and to Jeshua, and to the heads of the families, and desired that they would give them leave to build the temple with them, and to be partners with them in building it; for they said, "We worship your God, and especially pray to him, and are desirous of your religious settlement, and this ever since Shalmaneser, the king of Assyria, transplanted us out of Cuthah and Medea to this place." When they thus said, Zorobabel and Jeshua, the high priest, and the heads of the families of the Israelites, replied to them that, "it was impossible for them to permit them to be their partners, while they only had been appointed to build that temple at first by Cyrus, and now by Darius, although it was lawful for them to come and worship there if they pleased, and that they could allow them nothing but that in common with them, which was common to them with all other men, to come to their temple, and worship there."

"When the Cutheans heard this, for the Samaritans have that appellation, they had indignation at it, and persuaded the nations of Syria to desire the governors, in the same manner as they had done formerly in the days of Cyrus, and again in the days of Cambysses afterwards, to put a stop to the building of the temple, and to endeavor to delay and distract the Jews in their zeal about it."

This delayed matters for some time, but finally Darius ordered a search among the royal records, which resulted in the finding of the record of Cyrus concerning the restoration of the Jews, the building of the temple, and what the Lord commanded him in reference to them.   The contents of this proclamation is given by Josephus, as follows:

"Cyrus, the king, in the first year of his reign, commanded that the temple should be built in Jerusalem; and the altar in height should be three-score cubits, and its breadth of the same, with three edifices of polished stone, and one edifice of stone of their own country: and he ordained that the expenses of it should be paid out of the king's revenue.   He also commanded that the vessels which Nebuchadnezzar had pillaged out of the temple and carried to Babylon should be restored to the people of Jerusalem, and that the care of these things should belong to Sanadassar, the governor and president of Syria and Phœnicia, and to his associates, that they may not meddle with that place, but may permit the servants of God, the Jews and their rulers, to build the temple.   He also ordained that they should assist him in the work; and that they should pay to the Jews, out of the tribute of the country where they were governors, on account of the sacrifices, bulls and rams, and lambs and kids of goats, and fine flour, and oil, and wine, and all other things that the priests

should suggest to them; and that they should pray for
the preservation of the king, and of the Persians, and
for such as had transgressed any of these orders thus
sent to them, he commanded that they should be
caught, and hung upon a cross, and their substance
confiscated to the king's use. He also prayed to God
against them, that if any one attempted to hinder the
building of the temple, God would strike him dead,
and thereby restrain his wickedness."

Josephus also relates another trick of these Cuthean
Samaritans, as follows: "When Shalmanesar, the
king of Assyria, had it told him, that Hoshea, the king
of Israel, had sent privately to So, the king of Egypt,
desiring his assistance against him, he was very angry,
and made an expedition against Samaria, in the
seventh year of the reign of Hoshea; but when he was
not admitted into the city by the king, he besieged
Samaria three years, and took it by force in the ninth
year of the reign of Hoshea, and in the seventh year of
Hezekiah, king of Jerusalem, and quite demolished
the government of the Israelites, and transplanted all
the people into Medea and Persia, among whom he
took King Hoshea alive; and when he had removed
these people out of this their land, he transplanted
other nations out of Cutha, a place so called, (for there
is still a river of that name in Persia,) into Samaria,
and into the country of the Israelites. So the ten
tribes of the Israelites were removed, etc. * * *

But now the Cutheans who removed into Samaria,
(for that is the name they have been called by to this
time, because they were brought out of the country
called Cutha, which is a country of Persia, and there

is a river of the same name in it,) and are called in the Hebrew tongue Cutheans, but in the Greek tongue Samaritans. And when they see the Jews in prosperity they pretend that they arc changed, and allied to them, and call them kinsmen, as though they were derived from Joseph."

Our object in inserting these quotations is three-fold. First: to show that not only the sacred writers, but also the secular historian, and the rulers, both friendly and unfriendly, who had to do with those Israelites who went into and came out of the Babylonish captivity, called them Jews.

Second: to show how the bitter feeling was engendered among the Jews against those Cuthea-Samaritans, whom they called "Dogs," whom they never forgave, and with whom they never had any dealings. When Christ spoke to the woman of Samaria at the well, she was so surprised that her first words were, "How is it that thou, being a Jew, askest drink of me, a woman of Samaria? for the Jews have no dealings with the Samaritans."

Third: to show that neither Josephus, who writes on the "Antiquities of the Jews," nor their enemies, the Cuthea-Samaritans, ever confounds the ten-tribed Israelites with the Jewish Israelites.

Oh, how we do thank God that he made Josephus write concerning those imported nations in Samaria, who, because they were living in that land which had been the home of the Birthright kingdom, when they were seeking that which would be advantageous to them, would sidle up to the Jews, and claim kinship. "AS THOUGH THEY WERE DERIVED FROM

JOSEPH." What impudence! Think of the audacity of these imported mongrels claiming to be a portion of the Abrahamic birthright-holders. Is it much marvel that the Jews should dub such a race of fawners by the appropriate name of Dogs?

Both Ezra and Nehemiah, the Biblical historians of the return of the Jews from Babylon to Judea, give the genealogy of all who returned, a list of all the men who worked on the wall, a special list of all the priests who had married strange wives, and the exact number of individuals who returned. The aggregate of these is summed up as follows: "The whole congregation together was forty-and-two thousand three hundred and three-score, besides their servants and their maids, of whom there were seven thousand, three hundred thirty-seven." Ezra states that there were among these servants two hundred singing men and women, but Nehemiah puts the number of singers at two hundred and forty-five. This could easily have been the case by the time he got there, for the going up which was led by him was the second one, and did not take place until fourteen years and a half after that which was led by Ezra. And yet in the genealogical records of this "whole congregation" of forty-nine thousand eight hundred and ninety-seven Jews, there is not a tribal name mentioned except those of Judah, Benjamin and Levi

Please remember that it is the people of these three tribes who compose the mass of the kingdom of Judah, and who only are called Jews.

Josephus tells us of an epistle which was written by Xerxes, the son of Darius, at the time when the Jews

were getting ready to leave Babylon, and sent to Esdras (Ezra,) which was the cause of great rejoicing
among them. He speaks of the effect it had upon
them, as follows: "So he read the epistle at Babylon to
those Jews that went there, but he kept the epistle itself, and sent a copy of it to all those of his own nation
that were in Medea. And when these Jews had understood what piety the king had toward God, and
what kindness he had for Esdras, they were all greatly
pleased; nay, many of them took their effects with
them, and came to Babylon, as very desirous of going
down to Jerusalem; *but then* THE ENTIRE BODY
of THE PEOPLE of ISRAEL *remained in that country,* wherefore there are but two tribes in Asia and
Europe subject to the Romans, while THE TEN
TRIBES are beyond the Euphrates till now (A. D.
95), and are an immense multitude, and not to be estimated by numbers."

We note that First and Second Kings, the Chronicles, Josephus, Ezra and Nehemiah, all speak of the
kingdom of Judah at times, as "Judah and Benjamin." This is why Josephus says that there were only
two tribes under the power of the Romans.

The reason for this is supposed to be the fact that
the Levites were priests who served in the temple, and
did not count for anything when it came to the
political and fighting strength of the Jewish people,
for the Levites were undoubtedly with Judah and Benjamin, as a part of the Kingdom of Judah.

Furthermore, aside from the mention of the tribal
name of Ashur, as the name of the tribe to which

Anna, the prophetess belonged, there is not a tribal
name used in any historic portion of the new Testament, except the three tribal names of the Jewish people, i. e., Judah, Levi, and Benjamin. The ancestors
of Anna could easily have belonged to one of those
scattered families who returned out of Israel unto the
kingdom of Judah, because they would not serve Jeroboam's calves.

CHAPTER X.

JOSEPH-ISRAEL LOST.

In spite of all the facts to the contrary, there is a class of teachers who without one word of historic proof insist upon teaching that the Egypto-Israelites returned with the Jews. Here is the argument of a commentator who has written two commentaries on "The Revelation." He is a good man and has a pure heart; but in so far as this subject is concerned, he certainly has not informed himself. He first asks the question: "Were not the ten tribes lost after the deportation of Shalmanezar, as none but Judah and Benjamin returned in the Exodus of Nehemiah?" And answers it thus: "There is a general misapprehension and delusion on that subject. As the ten tribes were carried into captivity a hundred and thirty-four years before Judah and Benjamin; yet doubtless many of the ten tribes returned with them to Palestine. So the ten tribes were not lost, but they simply lost their tribe-hood, as they did not return in their organized tribes, but as individuals. Hence all of this hue and cry about the lost tribes, ransacking all the world to find them, and writing vast volumes, is a piece of twaddle and nonsense."

Thus with one presumptive wave of the hand he attempts to sweep from before our eyes the most important subject, so far as the vindication of the Word of God is concerned, that has ever made an appeal to a Bible-loving people for an honest hearing.

This same commentator speaks of "The Exodus of Nehemiah," and of the number that returned "under Nehemiah," as though there were but one Exodus from Babylon. Whereas there were two, the first and largest being under Ezra, while that of Nehemiah was fourteen years later, and was composed of those Jews "which were left" of the Babylonish captivity, who did not go up with the first or Ezra exodus.

He further says: "The ten tribes had been in the Chaldean Empire two hundred years at the time of the Exodus." But it is written "that Israel was taken into Assyria, and placed in the regions of the rivers Hilah and Habor," a region of country more than five hundred miles from Babylon. To us it seems an insult to the integrity of God for any man to presume that the ten tribes ever saw Babylon.

This commentator still further says: "Of course they were but a fraction of Judah and Benjamin" which returned. But God says: "All the men of Judah and Benjamin gathered themselves together unto Jerusalem, and EVERY ONE unto his city." Is there any question here as to which we shall believe? None whatever; but, since our brother says that only a fraction of Judah and Benjamin returned, we would ask: Where are the remaining fractions from which that fraction was taken? And since he tells us that doubtless many of the ten tribes returned with that fraction, we would ask: Where is the whole number from which the "many" came? And, without waiting for an answer, we will hasten to say that when this man was driven to use the "doubtless" argument, he had evidently lost something, and that the people in question are lost, at least to him.

When the Lord had determined to give Israel a bill of divorce, he called Hosea to prophesy against her, and, in order to have a perfect type of her adulterous condition, made him take a wife of whoredoms and bear children of whoredoms because the people of "the land had committed great whoredoms, departing from the Lord."

As the wife of the prophet bore children, the Lord took the privilege of naming them, and in each name uttered a prophecy.

When the first daughter was born, "God said unto him, Call her name Lo-ruhamah (which means, not having obtained mercy), for I will no more have mercy upon the house of Israel; but I will utterly take them away. But I will have mercy upon the house of Judah." (Hosea 1 : 6, 7.)

"Now when she (the prophet's wife) had weaned Lo-ruhamah, she conceived and bare a son. Then said God, Call his name Lo-ammi (which means, not my people), for ye are not my people, and I will not be your God. Yet the number of the children of Israel shall be as the sands of the sea, which cannot be measured nor numbered—and it shall come to pass that in the place where it was said unto them Ye are not my people, there it shall be said unto them, Ye are the sons of the Living God." (Hosea 1 : 8-10.) Beloved, do you catch the wonderful meaning to all this? Look! The name of the newborn son is Lo-ammi, for God refuses any longer to be the God of that people among whom the child is born; he casts them off and forsakes them.

"*Yet*"—O do you see the immutability of the promise of the covenant-making and covenant-keeping Jehovah, who after making an unconditional promise must keep it, even if some conditions do change? God has said it. He cannot lie; with him there is "no variableness nor shadow of turning." He has promised Abraham, Isaac and Jacob, that their seed shall become "many nations." "I will make thy seed to multiply as the stars of heaven." "I will make thee fruitful and multiply thee." "Thy seed shall be as the dust of the earth, and thou shalt spread abroad to the west, and to the east, and to the north, and to the south." And then he told Joseph that all these promises should be fulfilled in his sons, at that same time making Ephraim his first-born. Then in due time he separated the Sceptre and the Birthright, causing all the tribes to gather under the one or the other, making two kingdoms of the entire Abrahamic posterity, saying, "This thing is of me."

But now "Ephraim-Israel is joined to his idols." "They are not my people," "I will not be their God," "I cast them out"; and "*yet*," in spite of this, and although driven from home by their enemies, "yet the number of the children of Israel shall be as the sands of the sea, which cannot be numbered." This language proves that, although cast off, they must still increase and fulfill their God-appointed destiny by growing into a multitude of people in the midst of the earth, and in due time become a great nation or a company of nations. Also, the words which immediately follow these show that, while in that cast-out condition, and while developing into their destiny as regards multiplicity, they will become lost, so lost that they themselves will not know who they are. For it shall come to pass that, in the place where they go, they will be told that they are not the people of God, that they are not Jacob's seed, that they are not Israel, as at the time of the casting off they knew themselves to be. And when they are told that they are not the people of God they shall have so forgotten their origin, that they will believe it. This being the case, they certainly will be LOST, at least to themselves, and will need some one to prove to them that they are the descendants of God's chosen people. So, when the time comes, the Lord has said that those persons shall be there, and shall say unto them: "Ye are the sons of the Living God."

While Israel was true to the Lord, she was likened to a delicate and comely woman, and the Lord called her his wife; but when she became an idolatrous nation, she was called a harlot, and the Lord treated her as a woman who had broken wedlock, by giving her a bill of divorce. After the Lord has "cast her out of his sight," and allowed her to be carried away into the Assyrian captivity, she is spoken of in prophecy as "forsaken," a woman in "widowhood," "a wife of youth," "refused," "barren" and "desolate."

But the Lord made a promise of redemption to that same desolate one, saying: "Thou shalt forget the shame of thy youth and shalt not remember the reproach of thy widowhood any more. For thy Maker is thy husband (once more), the Lord of Hosts is his name; and thy Redeemer the Holy One of Israel; the God of the whole earth shall be called. For the Lord hath called thee as a woman forsaken and grieved in spirit, and a wife of youth, when thou wast refused, saith thy God. For a small moment have I forsaken thee, but with great mercies will I gather thee." (Isa. 54:4-7.)

You will also find by consulting this same chapter that, while barren, forsaken, and desolate, this same woman was to become the mother of more children than while married, or, in other words, Israel was to increase while cast out more than before. This is exactly what the prophet Hosea has declared in the prophecy which we have been considering.

The Lord further uses Hosea to teach that Israel would become lost after being cast out in the following: "For she said: I will go after my lovers ('Israel is swallowed up: now shall they be among the Gentiles as a vessel wherein is no pleasure, for they are gone up to Assyria, a wild ass alone by himself: Ephraim hath hired lovers'), that give me my bread and my water, my wool and my flax, mine oil and my drink. *Therefore, behold, I will hedge up thy way with thorns, and make a wall, that* SHE SHALL NOT FIND HER PATHS." (Hosea 8:8, 9; 2:5, 6.)

To show that the Scriptures, which we have just quoted, refer to Israel, aside from the Jews, we call your attention to the opening words of the chapter in which the non-parenthetical, or enclosing text appears, which is as follows: "Say ye unto your brethren Ammi, and to your sisters, Ruhamah. Plead with your mother, plead! for she is not my wife, neither am I her husband."

When God gave to Israel the name of Lo-ammi, or not my people, it was because he had cast them off, and they were no longer his people. For when the Lord gives a name to a person, or a nation, he names them in harmony with their character or condition. But while it is true that Israel was not at that time the people of God, it is true that Judah was then ruling with him, and was counted among the faithful; hence, they were Ammi, or the people of God.

Also when God gave to Israel the name of Lo-ruhamah, the meaning of which is, not having obtained mercy, he did so because that name was characteristic of his attitude toward them, at that time, for he declared that he would no longer have mercy upon them, but would cast them out. But at that same time he said, "I will have mercy upon the house of Judah." So, if Israel was Lo-ruhamah, the one not having obtained mercy, then Judah was Ruhamah, the one which obtained mercy. For that word "Lo" is the Hebrew negative, and, in the Scriptures under consideration, the words Ammi, Lo-ammi, Ruhamah, and Lo-ruhamah are Hebrew words which are transferred, but not translated.

These things being true, it is clear that the brethren Ammi, and their sisters Ruhamah, who are exhorted to plead, are the Jews and Jewesses of the kingdom of Judah. It is they who are exhorted to plead with their mother, i. e., to plead with that out from which they came, namely: THE KINGDOM OF ISRAEL.

Yes, Israel, she of whom the Lord hath said: "She is not my wife, neither am I her husband;" she, the woman of whoredom: she, the woman who had broken wedlock; she, who had run after hired lovers; she, who asked counsel of cattle and stone images; she, who was joined to Jeroboam's calves, and of whom, after she was sent adrift, the Lord said that he would hedge up her way, and make a wall, "that she shall not find her paths," i. e., lost.

The Lord further declares, "When Ephraim spake trembling he exalted himself in Israel; but when he offended in Baal he died. And now they sin more and more, and have made them molten images of their silver, and idols according to their own understanding, all of it the work of craftsmen; they say of them, Let the men who sacrifice *kiss the calves*. Therefore they shall be as the morning cloud, and as the early dew that passeth away, as the chaff that is driven with the whirlwind out of the floor, and as the smoke out of the chimney." (Hosea 13: 1-3.)

After the smoke out of a chimney has disappeared, after the sun has risen and scattered the morning cloud, after the dew has been drawn from leaf and blade, and passed away—if we were to ask you to *hunt* that scattered cloud, to *search* for that smoke, and *find* again that dew, we are certain you would be willing to admit that they were lost. This is certainly what the Lord intends us to understand concerning the kingdom known as Israel, for subsequent to this, and yet prior to the time when the Jews went into the Babylonian captivity, he declares, through Jeremiah the prophet, "My people have been lost sheep."

Ezekiel not only corroborates these prophets, but he visited Israel about twelve years before Nebuchadnezzar destroyed Jerusalem and took the Jews to Babylon. He says, "As I was among the captives by the river of Chebar, the heavens were opened, and I saw visions of God." (Ezek. 1:1.) You will find by consulting the map that this river Chebar is in the same region of country with Habor, Halah and the river Gozan, where the Israelites were deported by Shalmaneser, king of Assyria. In fact, the rivers Gozan and Halah empty into the Chebar, which, in turn, empties into the Euphrates. Chebar, Chabor, Habor, Kebah and Heber are only different forms of the same word.

Ezekiel continues and says, "Then I came to them of the captivity at Tel-abib, that dwelt by the river of Chebar, and I sat where they sat, and remained there astonished among them seven days. And it came to pass at the end of seven days, that the Lord came unto me, saying, Son of man, I have made thee a watchman unto the house of Israel." (Ezek. 3:15, 17.) Then after speaking of many who should be destroyed by sword, famine and pestilence because of their abominations, how that he would scatter their bones round about the altars of their idols, he says: "Yet will I leave a remnant, that ye may have some that shall escape the sword among the nations, when he shall be scattered through the countries. And they that escape of you shall *remember me among the nations* whither they shall be carried." (Ezek. 6:8, 9.)

Again, the offended God of Israel uses Ezekiel to declare, "I will scatter thee among the heathen and *disperse thee* in the countries, and will"—What? Destroy them? No, but—*"consume thy filthiness out of thee."* (Ezek. 22:15.) After this, the Lord declares this dispersion to have been accomplished, saying: "I scattered them among the heathen and they were dispersed through the countries: * * * and when they entered into the heathen, whither they went, they profaned my holy name, when they said to them, These are the people of the Lord, and are gone forth out of his land. But I had pity for mine holy name, which the house of Israel had profaned among the heathen, whither they went. Therefore say unto the house of Israel, Thus saith the Lord God, I do not this for your sakes, O house of Israel, but for mine holy name's sake, which ye have profaned among the heathen, whither ye went. And I will sanctify my great name, * * * and the heathen shall know that I am the Lord God, when I shall be sanctified in you before their eyes. For I will take you from among the heathen, and gather you *out of all countries,* and bring you into your own land." (Ezek. 36:19-24.)

The Jews were taken into Babylon and returned from thence; but the house of Israel, as herein stated, was scattered throughout all countries. But for the vindication of his holy name, he declared that he should yet be sanctified in the eyes of all nations, by saving Israel and bringing them back to their own land. When this takes place, Israel shall come *out from all countries.*

In two of these quotations they are called, "The dispersed." This will enable us to understand Zeph.

3:10—"From beyond the rivers of Ethiopia, my suppliants, even the *daughter of my dispersed,* shall bring mine offering."

Since we understand that "the dispersed" are the ten tribes, which composed the Birthright kingdom, we comprehend the grave import of the question asked by the chief man of Judah in the following: "When the Pharisees heard that the people murmured such things concerning him; and the Pharisees and the chief priests sent officers to take him. Then Jesus said unto them, Yet a little while am I with you, and then I go unto him that sent me. Ye shall seek me and shall not find me: and where I am, thither ye cannot come. Then said the Jews among themselves, Whither will he go that we cannot find him? "Will he go unto the dispersed among the Gentiles?" (John 7: 32-35.)

This very question reveals the fact that the Jews knew that the ten tribes were dispersed among the nations, and that they did not know where they were; hence, that they could not go to them. They also comprehended the fact that, if this man called Christ should prove to be the long-expected Messiah, he did know where the lost people were, and could go to them. It is also an admission, from the chief men of Judah, that a portion of the race were lost.

Isaac Leeser, an eminent Jewish scholar, who translated the Hebrew Scriptures for the English speaking Jews, says in his great work, "The Jewish Religion," Vol. I, page 256: "Let us observe that by this return of the captives (from Babylon) the Israelitish nation was not restored; since the ten tribes, who had formerly composed the kingdom of Israel, were yet left in banishment; and to this day the researches of travelers and wise men have not been able to trace their fate."

Micah, also, falls into exact line with the rest of the prophets, for through him the Lord declares: "I will surely assemble, O Jacob, all of thee; I will surely gather the remnant of Israel; I will put them together as the sheep of Bozrah, as the flock in the midst of their fold, they shall make great noise by reason of the multitude of men. The breaker is come up before them: they have broken up, and passed through the gate, and are gone out by it; and their king shall pass before them, and the Lord on the head of them." (Micah 2:12, 13.)

The reason the Lord says that he will assemble and put them together is, that, prior to the time when Shalmaneser took the main body of the kingdom of Israel into Assyria, it seems that a former king (Tiglath-Pileser) had taken the Reubenites, the Gadites, a portion of Naphtali, and one of the half tribes of Manasseh, "And brought them unto Halah, and Habor and Hara, and to the river Gozan." Later, the rest of the ten tribes were brought to this same region.

As we have already noted, the last that Josephus knew concerning the ten tribes, is that they were beyond the river Euphrates. This river rises at the foot of Mount Ararat, up in the Caucasian Pass, between the Black and Caspian seas. Israel, making a great noise because of the multitude, went out through this pass, or gate, or entrance.

What is meant by the *king passing on before them* is explained later.

CHAPTER XI.

If it could be proved that Israel returned with Judah from the Babylonish captivity, it would only prove that her prophetic history was not fulfilled, and that those prophets which both Jews and Christians have reecived as the true prophets of God, are but lying prophets. For Jeremiah also has given utterance to prophetic sayings which are in full accord with those of the prophets already quoted, and which cover the same ground, but give additional facts. As in the following:

"Therefore will I cast you out of this land, into a land that ye know not, neither ye nor your fathers, and there shall ye serve other gods day and night; where I will not show you favor. Therefore, behold, the days come, saith the Lord, that it shall no more be said, The Lord liveth, that brought up the children of Israel out of the land of Egypt; but, The Lord liveth, that brought the children of Israel from the land of the north, and from all the lands whither he had driven them: and I will bring them again unto their land that I gave unto their fathers.

"Behold I will send for many fishers, saith the Lord, and they shall fish for them; and after I will send many hunters, and they shall hunt them from every mountain, and from every hill, and from out of the holes of the rocks. For mine eyes are upon all their ways: they are not hid from my face, neither is their iniquity hid from mine eyes. And first I will recompense their iniquity and their sin double; because they have defiled my land, they have filled mine inheritance with the carcasses of their detestable and abominable things. O Lord, my strength and my fortress, and my refuge in the day of affliction, the Gentiles shall come unto thee from the ends of the earth, and shall say, Surely our fathers have inherited lies, vanity, and things wherein there is no profit. Shall a man make gods unto himself, and they are no gods? Therefore, behold, I will this once cause them to know. I will cause them to know mine hand and my might; and they shall know that thy name is the Lord." (Jer. 16: 13-21.)

We have given the above quotation in full and at length, because, as a prophecy, it contains the facts of the casting out and return of Israel, together with a brief epitome of their history while thus cast out. Let us notice them:

(1) "I will cast you out of this land." We know that they were taken into Assyria.

(2) "Into a land that ye know not." They were not to remain in Assyria.

(3) "Neither ye nor your fathers." A land unknown to the entire race, and as they were among the most, if not the most, civilized nations on the earth, we are safe in saying that it was to be a long way from their home; that they were to move on through the nations until they came into unknown regions, into the uninhabited, unexplored wilderness beyond the pales of civilization.

(4) "And there shall ye serve other gods day and night." They can then and there get their fill of idolatry.

(5) "I will not show you favor," i. e., not ease their punishment, until, as he says, he has first recompensed "their iniquity and their sin double; because they have defiled my land, they have filled mine inheritance with the carcasses of their detestable and abominable things," i. e., Jeroboam's calves, Ahab's image of Baal, Moloch, etc.

(6) When he says that he will not show them favor, the context proves that he means for a certain season or period. For he says, I will bring them again into their land, i. e., the Samaritan portion of Palestine.

(7) "I will send for many (Hebrew, *rab*—abundant, enough, plenteous, a multitude) fishers." Jesus said to his disciples, "I will make you fishers of men." He came to his own tribal house, Judah, but his own received him not, and then he said unto them: "Your house is left unto you desolate." But he said to his fishers, "Go to the lost sheep of the HOUSE of Israel." Six hundred and thirty years prior to this, one hundred and twenty years after Israel had been cast out, and before the house of Judah were taken to Babylon, God had said through the mouth of Jeremiah, "My people hath been lost sheep: their shepherds (their priests, who were of the lowest type of the people) have caused them to go astray, they have turned them away on the mountains; they have gone from mountain to hill (wandering), they have forgotten their resting place," i. e., their home.

(8) "And they shall fish them." These gospel fishers of men are successful. Lost Israel takes the bait and is fished. Hallelujah!

All this is in harmony with the prophetic history of Israel, as read by the other prophets. For when Hosea is being used to prophesy concerning Israel being hedged in with walls and thorns, and losing her paths, the Lord further adds, "Behold I will allure her, and *bring her into the wilderness,* and speak comfortably (marginal reading: speak friendly to her heart) unto her. And it shall be in that day saith the Lord that thou shalt call me Ishi (my husband) and shall call me no more Baali (my master). For I will take the names of Baalim (plural of Baal) out of her mouth, and they shall no more be remembered by their names." (Hosea 2: 14, 16, 17.) Is it any wonder that this same prophet declares, "Ephraim shall say, What have I to do any more with idols?" (Hosea 14: 8.)

Concerning this fact of Israel's receiving the gospel while cast out: "Thus saith the Lord, The people which were left of the sword found *grace* in the wilderness; even Israel." (Jer. 31: 2.) The law came by Moses, but *grace* and truth came by Jesus Christ. Hence the lost sheep of the house of Israel receive the gospel blessings because of the fishers which are sent to them.

(9) "And after (that) I will send for many hunters, and they shall hunt them." The violent protest of our brother, from whose commentary we quoted on a former occasion, is prima-facie evidence that this prophecy concerning the hunting for them has been, and is being, fulfilled; it is as follows: "Hence, all of

this hue and cry about the lost tribes, ransacking all the world to find them, and writing vast volumes, is a piece of twaddle and nonsense. Thousands of people are now studying (Glory to God!) great books (Thank God for them!) which claim to identify the 'lost tribes.'" Amen! and amen! For God says: "They shall hunt for them."

Another of those who object to so much hunting, Rawlinson, has unwittingly proved this prophecy to have been fulfilled, for he says: "They (the ten tribes) have been found a hundred times in a hundred different localities." This proves that the Lord, in order that his word of truth might be fulfilled, has, to say the least, raised up one hundred hunters. Had Prof. Rawlinson said, "They were supposed to have been found a hundred times in a hundred different localities," we could not doubt that his statement was true. For it is true that thousands are studying, and writing, and ransacking the world, to find the lost tribes of Israel; and the prophecy concerning the hunters and the hunted, stands vindicated, albeit many have hunted in vain.

Otherwise, we are forced to the conclusion that one of the holy men who was moved by the Holy Ghost to write the Bible was jesting, when he wrote concerning a corps of men who should become hunters of that which was not lost. And since God has furnished the hunters,—for it is by reading his Word that they become inspired to hunt,—we would be forced to conclude that he would play, or juggle, with the credulity of the human race.

(10)   It is evident from the declaration, "They are not hid from my face," that the people in question were hid from others.   Else, why should the Lord say that they were not hid from him?

"If they were not hid from the Lord, who were they hid from?"

We answer—THE HUNTERS.

(11)   The nineteenth verse relates to Gentiles who shall come unto the Lord, from the ends of the earth. The Hebrew word *(Goy)* which is here translated Gentiles, is often translated, nations, people, tribes, and, far away people.   God had told Israel that he would cast them afar off, and in Jer. 1:10 this same Hebrew word is translated nations.   In Jer. 31:9, while speaking to Joseph-Ephraim-Samaria-Israel, the Lord says: "I am a father to Israel, and Ephraim is my first-born.   Hear the word of the Lord, O ye nations *(Goy)*, and declare it in the isles afar off, and say, He that scattered Israel will gather him."

(12)   And in this prophecy which we are considering, we are told that these nations shall yet come "from the ends of the earth," and say: "Surely our fathers have inherited lies."

How so?

Do not forget, Hosea has prophesied concerning the same people, saying that in the place where it shall be said unto them, "Ye are Lo-ammi, or not the people of God," there it shall be said unto them "Ammi," or "Ye are the sons of the living God."   These people shall return to their home and to their Lord, who will be there about the time they get there.   And they shall say: " We have inherited lies, for we have been told that we were not the seed of Abraham, but now we know that we, too, have Abraham as our father."

(13) Then, saith the Lord, "I will cause them to know mine hand, and my might; and they shall know that my name is the Lord, i. e., Jehovah.

So we find that while Israel was taken into Assyria they were not to stay there, but were to wander into an unknown country, called the wilderness; and that eventually, when they have fulfilled their destiny by becoming "many nations," the head of the nations is in the isles of the sea, and that the Lord is to gather them from there. So it is evident that the school of teachers, who say that Israel returned with Judah from Babylon, do not know where the Birthright kingdom is, thus making it quite clear that they are *lost* even to those who say that there is no lost Israel.

The above facts are in harmony with still other authentic history as contained in the apocryphal book of Ezra, i. e., Esdras. Mind you, we do not assert that this book is inspired, although there are thousands who, with ourselves, believe it is. But we give it simply as corroborative history. Esdras had seen a vision in which there were two companies, one a warlike and the other a peaceful company. The declared explanation of the peaceful company is as follows: "Whereas thou sawest that he gathered another peaceful company, those are the ten tribes, which were carried away prisoners out of their own land in the time of Hosea, the king whom Shalmanesar, the king of Assyria, led away captive; and he carried them away so they came into another land. But they took counsel among themselves, that they would leave the multitude of the heathen, and go forth into a further country, *where never mankind dwelt,* that they might keep their statutes, which they never kept in their own land. And they entered into Euphrates by the narrow passage (the gate) of the river. For the Most High then showed signs for them, and held still the flood till they were passed over, for through that country there was a great way to go, namely, a year and a half. And the same region is called Asaareth (Margin: *Ararath,* same as *Ararat* or *Armenia,* which are only different forms of the same word). Then they dwelt there until the latter time; and now when they shall begin to come, the Highest shall stay the springs of the streams again, that they may go through: therefore sawest thou the multitude with peace." (2 Esdras 13:39-47.)

Every statement made in this extract is corroborated by unquestioned canonical writings, as we have shown, except one; and Isaiah settles that one as follows: "The Lord shall utterly destroy the tongue of the Egyptian sea; and with his mighty wind shall he shake his hand over the river, and shall smite it in the seven streams, and make men go over dry shod. And there shall be an highway for the remnant of his people which shall be left from Assyria,—like as it was in the day that he came up out of the land of Egypt." (Isa. 11:15, 16.)

Mind you, he does not say that they shall come from Assyria; he is speaking of the remnant of his people which are *left* from Assyria, i. e., the Assyrian captivity. The tongue of the Egyptian sea is not en route from either Babylon or Assyria. The tongue of the

Egyptian sea is a tongue of the Red sea, and the river with seven streams, mouths, or delta, is the river Nile, which waters Egypt; and these are in a direction from Palestine which is diametrically opposite to that of Assyria and Babylon.

After all, it is not so much a question of the lost ten tribes, for some out of all the tribes returned to the kingdom of Judah, in the days of Rehoboam, the first king of Judah. This is no doubt the reason that the Jews, upon their return from Babylon, offered the twelve bullocks for all Israel, as a burnt offering unto the Lord. But it is a question of the lost house of Joseph, that is, *THE LOST BIRTHRIGHT*. The Jews, although denationalized and scattered everywhere, have never been lost; but, as foretold, they have always been so *"well known"* that they have become a "by-word"; consequently, they have never been hunted for. But there is a prophecy in the Psalms concerning a people by the name of *Israel,* who are spoken of as the hidden people of the Lord, and whom he is called upon to defend from their enemies. Of these it is declared: "They have taken crafty counsel against *thy people* and consulted against *THY HIDDEN ONES.* They have said, come, and let us cut them off from being a nation; that the name ISRAEL may be no more in remembrance." (Psa. 83:3, 4.)

Hence, there is a people who bear the name of Israel, which, as we have learned, is the name of the birthright nation, which if it is not now hid, has in the past been hid from all except the Omnipotent One.

PART SECOND.

THE SCEPTRE; OR, THE PROMISE OF A PERPETUATED HOUSE, THRONE, AND KINGDOM TO DAVID.

"OUGHT ye not to know that the Lord God of Israel gave the kingdom over Israel to David for ever, even to him and to his sons by a covenant if salt?"

CHAPTER I.

THE SCEPTRE, AND THE DAVIDIC COVENANT.

There is no question, with those who have followed us thus far, that the Birthright people have been cast out into an unknown and far-away country, which, when they entered, was an uninhabited and unexplored wilderness. While Israel has been exploring, pioneering and settling this wilderness, the Lord has so hedged up their way that they can find neither the paths by which they came nor the place from whence they came.

Although lost, in so far as their national identity is concerned, they are in the place where the Lord has said they shall find grace, and where he has promised to speak comforting words to their hearts—in the wilderness.

There we will leave them to fulfill their appointed destiny of becoming a multitude of nations, while we follow the history of the Scepter, and learn what the Word of the Lord has revealed concerning his present and its future. For, if God has been true to his word, and unless the faith of Abraham, Isaac and Jacob has become of no effect, then the Scepter, as well as the Birthright, has not only a present existence, but a glorious future.

When God made the covenant with Abram in which he made him (prospectively) the father of many nations, thereby changing his name to Abraham, he gave

the promise,—"Kings shall come out of thee." Also,
when the promise concerning the multiplicity of nations was reiterated to his wife, whose former name
was Sarai, but now Sarah, or princess, it was said,—
"Kings of nations shall be of her" (R. V.). Thus by
the choice or election of God were they made, not only
the progenitors of a race which was to develop into
"many nations," which were to spread abroad to the
North, South, East and West, but also *a royal family.*
This, of course, includes a Sceptre—the emblem and
sign of royalty.

These promised blessings, given by the Lord and
confirmed to Abraham by an oath, were received by
him in faith, and counted as though they were already
in existence,—for the simple reason that, when a thing
is promised by the Lord and received by any one in
faith, that thing must eventually materialize, because
faith is the God-given force or power which will and
must eventually bring promised things into existence.
Hence both "the Birthright" and "the Sceptre" blessing
passed from Abraham to Isaac as a real inheritance;
while he in turn bestowed them upon Jacob, who so
much desired them and considered them so surely to
exist already that he was willing to strike bargains
for them, or even resort to fraudulent measures to get
possession of them.

At the death of Jacob these two covenant blessings—
the Birthright and the Sceptre—were separated, the
Birthright falling to one of his sons and the Sceptre to
another one of them, as we have heretofore fully explained. When Jacob, at the time of his death, while
acting under the direction of the Holy Spirit, gave the

Sceptre blessing to *Judah* and his lineage, the prophecy which he gave with it was,—"The sceptre shall not depart from Judah, nor a lawgiver from between his feet, until Shiloh come; and unto him shall the gathering of the people be." (Gen. 49:10.)

After the Abrahamic people had cried down the Divine Theocracy, rejected the Lord as their king, and insisted on having a human king, they chose Saul. Although Saul was not of the royal line, but a Benjamite, he was permitted to reign, for the Lord had determined to give the people the desire of their hearts. But after the downfall of that haughty Benjamite, David, a son of the royal family, was enthroned, and to him were reiterated the promises concerning the royal family, which had been emphasized to Judah by his dying father when he bestowed on him the covenant blessing of royal fatherhood.

When the Sceptre covenant was confirmed to David, the Lord gave the message through Nathan the prophet in these words: "When thy days be fulfilled, and thou shalt sleep with thy fathers, I will set up thy seed after thee which shall proceed out of thy bowels, and I will establish his kingdom. He shall build an house for my name, and I will establish the throne of his kingdom *forever*. I will be his father, and he shall be my son. If he commit iniquity, I will chasten him with the rod of men. But my mercy shall not depart from him, as I took it from Saul, whom I put away before thee. And thy house and thy kingdom shall be established forever before thee: *Thy throne shall be established forever."* (2 Sam. 7:12-16.)

David was so impressed with the magnitude of this prophecy and with the period of time which it covered that he went in and sat before the Lord, pondering over it, until in wonderment he exclaimed: "Who am I, O Lord God, and what is my house that thou hast brought me hitherto? And this was yet a small thing in thy sight, O Lord God (i. e., the present power, glory and prestige of David's house, throne and kingdom): but thou hast spoken also of thy servant's house for a great while to come. And is this the manner of man, O Lord God?" (2 Sam. 7:18, 19.) No. It is not the manner of man to prophesy concerning things *"for a great while to come."* But it is the manner of God. Yes, and it is the manner of God to make good that which he has spoken. David understood this; so he prayed—"And now, O Lord God, the word that thou hast spoken concerning thy servant, and concerning his house, establish it forever, and do as thou hast said."

If it be possible that there can be such power put into written words as shall yet come from that voice which shall sound the seven thunders, we pray that it may be put into those which record the above facts; and thus compel our readers to see that it is not the spiritual throne, the spiritual sceptre, the spiritual house, nor the heavenly kingdom, which are therein spoken of, but that it is the literal throne, the earthly kingdom, and the lineal house of the Judo-Davidic family which are the subjects of this prophecy; and *that all these are to endure* FOREVER.

There is also in this prophecy a note of warning to David's successor, which is given in the following:

"If he commit iniquity I will chasten him with the rod of men." It is not at all presumable that the ruler, sitting on the spiritual throne, and holding the sceptre over the heavenly kingdom, would commit iniquity; hence no such a threat could have been given with reference to him. But when it is applied to Solomon, the immediate successor of his father David, and to others of the royal line, it is altogether another question, for many of them were as wicked as men ever get to be.

Further, this prophecy was to go into effect when David's "days were fulfilled," and when the son who should be set up after him would build a house for God. Solomon, who was "set up" after David, did build a house to the Lord, viz., the temple at Jerusalem. But the Messiah has never, as yet, built any such house. Before the temple was built, and when Solomon was giving orders to Hiram concerning the material for its construction, he said: "Behold, I purpose to build an house unto the name of the Lord my God, as the Lord spake unto David my father, saying, Thy son whom I will *set upon thy throne in thy room* he shall build an house unto my name." (I Kings, 5:5.)

Also, when the temple was finished, Solomon, standing before the altar of the Lord, in the presence of all the congregation of Israel, and with uplifted hands spread toward heaven, in that wonderful prayer at the dedication of the temple, said: "The Lord hath performed his word that he spake; and I am risen up in the room of David my father, and sit on the throne of Israel, as the Lord promised, and have built an house for the name of the Lord God of Israel. * * * There is no God like thee, in heaven above, or on earth beneath, who *keepest covenant* and mercy with thy servant, * * * who hast kept with thy servant David my father *that which thou promisedst* him; thou speakest also with thy mouth, and *hast fulfilled it with thine hand,* as it is this day. Therefore now, Lord God of Israel, keep with thy servant David my father that thou promisedst him, saying: There shall not fail thee a man in my sight to sit on the throne of Israel." (1 Kings, 8:20-25.)

By this prayer we see that Solomon understood that the throne, the kingdom, and the lineal house of David should stand forever.

Solomon not only understood it this way, but declared it before all the congregation of Israel, so that the entire nation should be fully aware of the fact. This was so thoroughly known in Israel and acknowledged by her prophets that, at the time of the division of the race into two kingdoms in the days of Rehoboam and Jeroboam, Abijah, in his zeal that the lineal rights of the royal family might not be ignored, stood upon a mountain in Ephraim and cried out: "Hear me, thou Jeroboam and all Israel. Ought ye not to know that the Lord God of Israel gave the kingdom over Israel to David *forever* and to his sons (not son,— not one, but many) by a covenant of salt?" (13:5.) The marginal reading is, "a perpetual covenant."

The eighty-ninth Psalm contains much light regarding the covenant under consideration, which the Lord made with David and his sons, concerning the perpetuity of his throne, *scepter,* kingdom, and his posterity. In it the Lord declares: "I have made a covenant with my chosen, I have sworn unto David my servant, saying, Thy seed will I establish forever, and build up thy throne to all generations." Not a few, not some, not even *many*, but *"ALL* generations."

Continuing, he says: "My mercy will I keep for him *forevermore,* and my covenant shall stand fast with him. His seed also will I make to endure forever, and his throne as the days of heaven. If his children forsake my law, and walk not in my judgments; if they break my statutes, and keep not my commandments: then will I visit their transgressions with the rod, and their iniquity with stripes. Nevertheless, my lovingkindness will I not utterly take from him nor suffer my faithfulness to fail. My covenant will I not break, nor alter the thing that has gone out of my lips."

Surely it is not possible to break the force of these words. The proposition could not be stated in stronger terms. The Lord simply will not break his covenant; he will not change, nor modify, nor in any way or for any reason alter, the thing that he has spoken, even if the children of David do forsake his law and break every commandment in his statute book. If they do break his law, he will chastise and punish with "the rod" and "with stripes," but he will not suffer his faithfulness to fail.

The covenant is unconditional. It *"shall stand fast,"* no matter how often they are visited with rod and stripe for their transgressions. No matter how severe the punishment, the fact remains that the throne, the sceptre, the kingdom and the seed, must endure *forevermore.*

The fact that in this confirmation of the Davidic covenant the Lord uses the expressions, "his children," "they" and "their," all in the plural form, is proof that this covenant does not have reference to the spiritual reign of his son Jesus Christ in the hearts of Christians. Furthermore, it could not be possible that Jesus Christ,—he of whom the prophet Isaiah wrote saying, "Unto us a child is born, unto us a son is given," whose "name shall be called Wonderful, Counsellor, The Mighty God, The Everlasting Father, The Prince of Peace,"—we say it is not possible for this Prince of Peace, who is The Mighty God, to break his own commandments, forsake his own law, or disregard his own statutes, and then punish himself for his own wickedness. No, these warnings do not apply to the Immortal One, but to the frail mortal sons of David, of whom Solomon was the first, and whom the Lord punished for his wickedness,—as we may learn by referring to the eleventh chapter of 1 Kings, where we read as follows: "And the Lord was angry with Solomon, because his heart was turned from the Lord God of Israel, which had appeared unto him twice, and had commanded him concerning this thing, that he should not go after other gods, *but he kept not that which the Lord commanded.* Wherefore the Lord said unto Solomon: Forasmuch as this is done of thee, and thou hast not kept my covenant and my statutes, which I have commanded thee, I will surely rend the kingdom from thee, and I will give unto thy servant. Notwithstanding, in thy days I will not do it, for David thy father's sake; but will rend it out of the hand of thy son. Howbeit, I will not rend away all the kingdom; but will give one tribe to thy son for David my servant's sake." (1 Kings 11:9-13.)

Please notice how perfectly the facts agree, in every detail, with the declared purpose of God. Solomon, the seed of David, who was set up after him, who sat on the throne in the room of his father, who built and dedicated the house of the Lord, did forsake his God and refuse to obey his commandments. If God is true to his word, he must punish any of the children of David who thus forsake his law. So, as a punishment to Solomon, he purposes to take the greatness and power of the kingdom away from that son, who, as Solomon hopes, shall inherit the throne, crown, sceptre and kingdom, in all its glory. But no; the Lord purposes to take away the greater part of the national strength and power of the kingdom and give it to one of the servants of Solomon instead of the royal heir.

But while the Lord is declaring unto Solomon the punishment which he purposes to visit upon him for his disobedience, he is careful to say: "Howbeit, I will not rend away *all* the kingdom; but will give one tribe to thy son."

Why not "rend away all the kingdom?"

The Divine reply is, "For David my servant's sake."

Why for David's sake?

Because the Lord gave the "kingdom over Israel to David and his sons forever."

Ah, he dare not take away the entire kingdom from that royal line! Yes, we can say "dare not," and emphasize it, too. And we may also add, must not, cannot, or any and all such expressions as will voice our protest or express the impossibility of such a thing. Indeed, the Lord himself has uttered a stronger protest than ours could ever be. We say this because the Lord, in this Psalm which we have under consideration, after saying, "My covenant will I not break, nor alter the thing that is gone out of my lips," has, in the very next statement, made use of words which forever shut the door of retreat; for he not only took an oath, in which he pledged his own holy character, but he brought the physical universe into the contract, or at least that portion of it which involves the continued existence of the present arrangement of our solar system. His declarations are: "Once have I sworn, by my holiness, that I will not *lie unto David. His seed shall endure forever, and his throne as the sun before me. It shall be establshed forever as the moon, and as a faithful witness in the heaven.*" (Psa. 89:35-37.) Also, in the twenty-ninth verse of that same Psalm is the following: *"His seed also will I make to endure forever, and his throne as the days of heaven."*

If we are willing to give these words their full and natural meaning, then surely we must see clearly that it is the intention of the Lord that we shall understand that, so long as the sun, the "great light" which he created for a light by day, and the moon the "lesser light," which he created to rule the night, shall keep their appointed places in the heavens, traveling their orbits, continuing to make their proper changes, passing through their ecliptics, or completing their lunations,—*just so long* must they rise over, shine down upon, and set beyond, the limits of, a kingdom on this earth over which *some member* of the Judo-Davidic family is holding the sceptre. Just so long will they continue to say, by their very presence in the heavens,

"We are witnesses unto men throughout *all generations,* that the Lord God of Israel has not lied into his servant David."

Furthermore, it is certain that the expressions, "days of heaven," and "a faithful witness in heaven," as used in these Scriptures, are purely astronomic, and refer to the stellar and atmospheric heavens. Hence the throne, kingdom, sceptre and family of David must endure, "as the days of heaven," i. e., so long as the earth continues to revolve on its own axis, thus giving to itself that diurnal motion which causes day and night to succeed each other, and which enables the sun and moon to perform their functions of lighting the day and night.

"But," says one, "do not these sayings apply to the kingdom and throne in heaven, where Christ, the seed of David, is now sitting at the right hand of God? And is not the New Jerusalem, which is above, and is the mother of us all, the celestial capital of that kingdom?" To this we are compelled to give a negative answer; for that celestial city has "no need of the *sun,* neither of the *moon,* to *shine* in it; for the glory of God did *lighten* it, and the Lamb is the *light* thereof." (Rev. 21:23.)

"But," questions another persistent spiritualizer, "do not the seed and throne mentioned in these Scriptures refer to Christ, who is the 'Son of David,' in his *spiritual* kingdom, which is set up in the hearts of men?" Again we are compelled to reply in the negative, for the Holy Ghost is the divine illuminator of that kingdom; the sun and the moon having never been heavenly lights, only in an astronomic sense.

Furthermore, a mere glance at the context will reveal the fact that the Lord is dealing with a very earthly seed and kingdom; for, intermingled with the promises of an everlasting seed, throne and kingdom, the
declaration is made concerning the children of David
that, if they do not walk in his judgments and keep
his commandments, but forsake his law, and break
his statutes, then he will visit their transgressions with
the rod and their iniquity with stripes. But still, no
matter how wicked the ruler on the throne or the
subject in the realm, he will not suffer his faithfulness to fail,—his covenant with David must stand forevermore.

The only conditions to the covenant are such as are
entirely beyond the power of man either to control
or to break, viz., the faithfulness of God in keeping
and fulfilling his word, the holiness of his character—
for he cannot lie—and the omnipotence of his power to
keep the sun, moon and the earth rolling onward in
their present cycles and order until, by the good pleasure of his will, he shall change those ordinances and
bring into existence the new heavens and the new
earth.   Hence, the Holy Ghost has inspired Jeremiah
to write: "Thus saith the Lord: If ye can break my
covenant of the day, and my covenant of the night,
and that there should not be day and night in their
season; then may also my covenant be broken with
my servant, that he should not have a son to reign
upon his throne." (Jer. 33:20, 21.)

Previously, in this same chapter, and in the seventeenth verse, the Lord has said: "David shall never
want a man to sit upon the throne of the house of

Israel." Then he adds the following: "If my covenant be not with day and night, and if I have not appointed the ordinance of heaven and earth, then will
I cast away the seed of Jacob, and David my servant,
so that I will not take any of his seed to be rulers
over the seed of Abraham, Isaac, and Jacob." This,
too, after saying: As the host of heaven cannot be
numbered, neither the sand of the sea measured: so
will I multiply the seed of David my servant." (Jer.
33:22, 25, 26.)

In the statement, "David shall never want a man to
sit upon the throne," the word man is translated from
the Hebrew "ish" (*iysh*), which is defined as meaning "a man, a person, a certain one, any one."

In the declaration that David should always "have
a son to reign upon his throne," the Hebrew word from
which "son" is taken is *"Ben,"* which means "son,
man, or a builder of the family name."

In the other expression, "take any of his seed to be
rulers," etc., the word "seed" is taken from the Hebrew *"Zara"*—"a man, a person, a child, a nephew, a
grandchild, or relative."

This being the case—together with the fact that
when duration of time is being considered, there are
no stronger words in the Hebrew language than those
which are translated "forever," "evermore," and "everlasting," then these following propositions must
stand:

(1) The Lord God of Israel made a covenant with
David concerning the perpetuity of his seed, throne,
and kingdom, regardless of the good or evil conduct
of his descendants.

(2) The subjects of this Davidic kingdom must belong to the lineage of Abraham, Isaac and Jacob.

(3) Some person of the lineage of King David must be on that throne (seat of power) who holds the sceptre, and reigns over that kingdom.

(4) National afflictions will come upon them, as punishment for their unrighteousness; but they will not be utterly destroyed; for the kingdom must endure so long as there be day and night, and the subjects must continue to increase until they become innumerable.

(5) So long as the sun, moon and earth continue rolling onward in their appointed orbits, just so long must the seed, throne, and Israelitish kingdom of David be in existence, or we have no longer a holy God ruling in the heavens and watching over Israel.

(6) In order to prove that God has become unholy— i. e., lied—some man must yet find a fulcrum on which to rest his lever with which he can stop the rotation of the earth, and then find some way by which he can drive those witnessing lights from the sky; or in some way break up the appointed ordinances of heaven and earth, so that there cannot be day and night in their season. Otherwise, the holiness and omnipotence of God must not be questioned. This is the reason that David so triumphantly says to him: "Thou hast magnified thy word above all thy name." (Psa. 138:2.)

(7) The fact that God has thus magnified his word above his name would, in case of a failure on his part to perpetuate that which he swears shall be in existence forever, give us authority to impeach his testimony on every line, for it would undeify him.

CHAPTER II.

JEREMIAH'S CALL AND COMMISSION.

Having settled the question concerning the perpetuity of the covenant which God made with "David and his sons," together with the fact that he has given, as a pledge of their everlastingness, not only the astronomic order of producing day and night, months, years and seasons, but the very holiness of his character as well, we must now proceed to take up the thread of history which pertains to that sceptre, throne, kingdom and royal seed whose continued existence is balanced over against such weighty considerations as the power, integrity and immutability of the character and Word of God.

While dealing with the history of the Birthright and its inheritors, the house of Joseph, we had, of necessity, much to say concerning the history of the Sceptre and the royal family, its inheritors. Especially was this true when we contrasted that system of feudalism and continual overthrowing of dynasties which prevailed in the kingdom of Israel as compared with the one continuous dynasty and succession of the royal princes of the Judo-Davidic family, as they mounted the throne of their fathers and held the sceptre over the kingdom of Judah.

In order to have our historic thread complete we must resume our history of the Sceptre at the call of Jeremiah the prophet, which occurred at a period prior

to the time when the Jews were taken into the Babylonish captivity, but subsequent to the time when Israel, the Birthright kingdom, was taken into captivity
by Shalmanesar, king of Assyria, and deported into
the country of the head-waters of the Euphrates—the
country more generally known as Medo-Persia.

It is certain that we can never understand the
history of this covenanted throne, kingdom and family,
and the fact that they have been thus far built up
"unto all generations," unless we understand the history and accept with unfaltering faith the call and
commission of Jeremiah the prophet, in relation to
those things which God has given his pledge shall
endure forever. For if to be taught the distinction
between the two houses, and to understand the difference between the kingdoms of Israel and Judah, may
be likened unto the key which unlocks the outer sanctuary of our understanding of sacred history, then
surely a knowledge of the life and work of Jeremiah,
the son of Hilkiah, is the key which the Holy Spirit
can use to open that inner sanctuary, or Holy of Holies,
of our understanding in these matters upon which rest
the vindication of God.

According to the Divine record, there have lived in
this world only three men who were sanctified before
they were born. The first was this same Jeremiah,
who, in one of the darkest hours in all the history of
the Abrahamic nations which pertains to them as a
whole, was made the custodian of the sceptre, throne
and royal seed of David. The next was John the Bap-
tist, the forerunner and herald of the coming Prince of
the House of David. Then came the last and greatest

of all—our Lord and Saviour Jesus Christ, the Son of David, that Prince of whom the angel declared unto Mary at the time of the annunciation: "The Lord God shall give unto him the throne of his father David." (Luke, 1:32.) When this blessed Prince takes his seat he will be the last King to sit on that throne, or any other on this earth.

In the days of Josiah, the son of Amon, king of Judah, in the thirteenth year of his reign, while Jeremiah was still a minor, a mere youth, only seventeen years of age, he received his call as the "Prophet unto the nations," and was given his commission, the details of which he himself has given in the first chapter of his own prophecies, as follows:

"Then the word of God came unto me, saying: Before I formed thee in the belly I knew thee—before thou camest forth out of the womb I sanctified thee, and I ordained thee a prophet unto the nations.

"Then said I: Ah, Lord God! behold, I cannot speak, for I am a child.

"But the Lord said unto me: Say not, I am a child, for thou shalt go to all that I shall send thee, and whatsoever I shall command thee thou shalt speak. Be not afraid of their faces; for I am with thee to deliver thee, saith the Lord.

"Then the Lord put forth his hand and touched my mouth. And the Lord said unto me: Behold, I have put my words into thy mouth. See, I have this day set thee over the nations and over the kingdoms, to root out, and to pull down, and to destroy, and to build and to plant." (Jer. 1: 4-10.)

Called as the prophet of God; the words of the Lord put into his mouth with a touch from the Divine hand; and set by the Divine One "over the nations, and over the kingdoms." What! Surely he was not set over *all* the nations, neither *all* the kingdoms of the earth? No, there is nothing said about all nations; just simply and definitely—"the nations" and "the kingdoms." So far as the word which is translated "nations" in the text is concerned, it is the same word that is used when the Lord said to Abraham, "I have made the father of many *nations*"; and when he said to Rebekah, "Two *nations* are in thy womb." He now calls Jeremiah a "Prophet unto the nations," i. e., the "two nations," the "two kingdoms," the two houses—Israel and Judah; the "two families," the inheritors of the Birthright and of the Sceptre. It is to these nations, not to all the nations of the earth, that the Lord sends Jeremiah, his prophet, with a commission to root out, tear down, and destroy, on the one hand; but—hear it!—he was also Divinely commissioned to "BUILD AND PLANT"!

The fact that Jeremiah was commissioned to overthrow the commonwealth of Judah, destroy the Davidic kingdom, as it then existed among the Jewish people, throw down the throne of David which was in their midst, and root out that branch of the royal family which occupied the throne at that time—all this is so clear, so well known, that most, if not all, of the accepted authorities of Christendom proclaim it. But those same authorities do not seem to know, neither do they proclaim that which follows as a natural sequence, i. e.. that if it was the kingdom, sceptre, throne and seed of David which were to be overthrown, then it follows that it is those very same things which must again be planted and builded.

Hence we affirm that, as God is still holy, and did not lie to David, and if he did not sanctify, call, and commission Jeremiah in vain, then that throne of David was again set up, the seed planted, and the kingdom builded before Jeremiah died.

Mind you, we do not say that these were planted and builded among the Jews. That was not at all necessary in order to fulfillment. Indeed, we will show that it was *not* planted nor builded in Judah. For God "gave the kingdom *over Israel* to David forever, even to him and his sons by a covenant of salt." Nine-twelfths of the seed of Israel *never were members* of the *Jewish* kingdom.

The great wrong of which the standard authorities of Christendom have been guilty is that, with a wide-open Bible before them, they should be in such ignorance of the declared purpose of God, and have such a hesitating, apologetic faithlessness in his covenant promises,—wherein he has sworn by himself,—that they are blinded even to the necessity of accounting for the building and planting which God gave Jeremiah to do.

The great fault with their whole teaching, so far as the outcome of Jeremiah's work is concerned, is that they have either suffered, implied, or actually taught that the promises of God to David were allowed to go by default. And when an honest questioner would arise, as of necessity there must, he at once becomes an irresponsible, irregular, unarmored stripling, upon whom these regulars in the army of Israel insist on putting the armor of Saul. But the "heavy" armor of the should-be leader will not fit the bright young head and freer limbs of the little irregular; so he must go forth alone to slay the giant of infidelity, whose champions have been defying the armies of the living God. Meanwhile, these "regulars" stand on the hill of their self-importance and ask, "Who is this youthful stripling whom we see down in the valley picking up pebbles with which to meet the foe whose challenge has sent dismay among us for lo! these many days?"

CHAPTER III.

THE TEARING DOWN AND ROOTING OUT.

Pursuant to the object of Jeremiah's call and work, the first king on David's throne to be disposed of was Josiah, for it was in the thirteenth year of his reign that the call of God came to Jeremiah, as you may know by reading Jer. 1:1, 2. Jeremiah himself gives no account of the downfall of Josiah, but it is recorded in 2 Kings 23, and 2 Chr. thirty-fifth chapter. It took place in the days of Pharaoh-Necho, king of Egypt, and Charchemish, king of Assyria.

Josiah himself was a good man and a good king; he did all that could be done to restore the people to the worship of God. He had all the wizards, workers with familiar spirits, images, idols and abominations put out of the land; but the Lord would not stay his threatened punishment of the kingdom of Judea, which had become "worse" than Israel.

Concerning the goodness of Josiah, and also his inability to prevent the impending calamity, it is written: "And like unto him was no king before him, that turned to the Lord with all his heart, and all his soul, and with all his might, according to all the law of Moses; neither after him arose any like him. Notwithstanding, the Lord turned not from the fierceness of his great wrath, wherewith his anger was kindled against Judah, because of all the provocations that Manasseh (son of Hezekiah) had provoked him withal.

And the Lord said, I will remove Judah (the Jews) out of my sight, as I have removed Israel (the ten tribes). (2 Kings, 23:25-27.)

Not only was Josiah the best king they ever had, and not only did he put away those abominations, but he also kept the greatest passover that was ever held in Israel or Judah since the days of Samuel the prophet. To this passover that good king gave thirty-three thousand and three hundred cattle and oxen, and to this the princes and people gave willingly of their flocks and herds, until the number was swelled to many thousand more.

The sons of Aaron made themselves ready; the people made themselves ready; the sacrifices were killed; the blood sprinkled; the offerings were burned upon the altar of the Lord, and the people kept the feast of unleavened bread for seven days. But all this availed nothing, except a personal blessing to Josiah, that he should die in peace and not see the destruction of Jerusalem and the captivity of the people.

No, the eternal fiat of God had gone forth, and we think that no number of worshipers, no number of good kings, or good men, and surely no mighty army of bad men, could stay the downfall of that nation.

For the Lord says, "After all this," when Pharaoh-Necho, the king of Egypt, came up to fight against Charchemish, king of Assyria, Josiah rashly, without provocation, made it his business and went out to fight against the king of Egypt, who kindly tried to restrain him, and sent ambassadors to him saying: "What have I to do with thee, thou king of Judah? I come not against thee this day, but against the house (Assyria) wherewith I have war; for God commanded me to make haste: forbear thee from meddling with God, who is with me, *that he destroy thee not."* And the record continues: "Nevertheless, Josiah *would not* turn his face from him, but disguised himself, that he might fight with him and harkened not unto the word of Necho from the mouth of God, and came to fight in the valley of Megiddo. And the archers shot at King Josiah; and the king said to his servants, Have me away, for I am sore wounded. His servants there-fore took him out of that chariot, and put him in the second chariot that he had, and brought him to Jeru-salem, and he died, and was buried in one of the sepulchres of his fathers. And all Judah and Jerusa-lem mourned for Josiah. And Jeremiah lamented for Josiah." (2 Chr. 35:21-25.)

So Jeremiah saw that good king pulled down, and lamented him, together with the whole nation; and the singing men and women made an ordinance of lamen-tations for Josiah, and Shallum the son of Josiah ascended the throne. But the Lord had said, "I swear by myself" that this house of Judah shall come to deso-lation. So he says to this lamenting people: "Weep not for the dead, neither bemoan him: but weep sore for him that goeth away: for he shall return no more, nor see his native country. For thus saith the Lord touching Shallum, the son of Josiah, which reigned instead of Josiah, his father, which went out of this place, he shall not return any more: but he shall die in the place whither they have led him captive, and shall see this land no more." (Jer. 22:10-12.) Thus Jeremiah records the fact of another overthrow; and so the work goes on.

Jehoiakim, another son of Josiah, was next to take the throne of his fathers; but hear the judgment which was pronounced upon him: "Therefore thus saith the Lord concerning Johoiakim, the son of Josiah, king of Judah: They shall not lament for him saying (to each other), Ah, my brother! or, my Ah, my sister! They shall not lament for him, saying, Ah, Lord! or, Ah, his glory! He shall be buried with the burial of an ass, drawn and cast forth beyond the gates of Jerusalem." (Jer. 22:18, 19.) Another disposed of. Who next?

"As I live, saith the Lord, though Coniah, the son of Jehoiakim, king of Judah, were the signet upon my right hand, yet would I pluck thee thence; and I will give thee into the hand of them that seek thy life, and into the hand of them whose faces thou fearest, even into the hand of Nebuchadnezzar king of Babylon, and into the hands of the Chaldeans. And I will cast thee out, and thy mother that bare thee, into another country, where ye were not born, and there shall ye die. But unto the land whereunto they desire to return thither shall they not return."

"Is this man Coniah a despised broken idol? Is he a vessel wherein is no pleasure? Wherefore are they cast out, he and his seed, and are cast into a land which they know not? O earth, earth, earth, hear the word of the Lord. Thus saith the Lord: Write ye this man childless, a man that shall not prosper in his days; for no man of his seed shall prosper, sitting upon the throne of David, and ruling any more in Judah." (Jer. 22 : 24-30.)

Thus Coniah makes the fourth king who has been disposed of since the Lord called and commissioned Jeremiah; but there is still another, as recorded by that prophet: "And King Zedekiah, the son of Josiah, reigned instead of Coniah, the son of Jehoiakim." (Jer. 37: 1.)

Zedekiah, the successor to Coniah, ascended the throne about six hundred years before Christ. His reign lasted only eleven years, and he is the last king of the Judo-Davidic line who has reigned over the Jewish nation from that day to this. Yet God has said that he would build up David's throne unto all generations, and prior to that he declared: "The Sceptre shall not depart from Judah (his posterity), nor a law-giver from between his feet, until Shiloh come; and unto him (Shiloh) shall the gathering of the people be." (Gen. 49:10). With these facts before us it behooves us to look well into this history of Zedekiah, and learn his fate and also that of his family.

During the reign of Coniah, the predecessor of Zedekiah, the king of Babylon had come against the kingdom of Judah, subdued it and carried away the king, his mother, his wives, and others, into Babylon. Consequently at the time when Zedekiah ascended the throne, the country of Judah was a province of Babylon. But the then tolerant Nebuchadnezzar, king of Babylon, took Mattaniah, the third son of Josiah, who was of course brother to Jehoiakim, Coniah's father, and changed his name to Zedekiah, then made him king instead of Coniah.

We do not purpose, especially at this time, to go into endless genealogies, as it is generally confusing to the reader. In this Josiah family there were at least two Zedekiahs, and Zedekiahs along the family line for centuries back. There were also Shallums, and Shallums, and Shallums, and even Coniah's name is spelled three different ways. We will also say, for the benefit of the more critical student, that often a man is said to be the son of another when in fact he is grandson or even further removed. Christ is the "Son of David," and yet David is his great-grandfather twenty-eight generations back. "From David until the carrying away into Babylon are fourteen generations, and from the carrying away into Babylon unto Christ are fourteen generations." (Matt. 1:17.)

This Zedekiah of whom we write is the third son of Josiah, for we read, "And the king of Babylon made Mattaniah, his (Coniah's) father's brother, king in his stead, and changed his name to Zedekiah."

"Zedekiah was twenty-and-one years old when he began to reign, and he reigned eleven years in Jerusalem. And his mother's name was Hamutal, the daughter of Jeremiah of Libnah." (2 Kings 24:17-19.) Thus we find Jeremiah making the following record concerning Coniah's successor: "And King Zedekiah, the son of Josiah, reigned instead of Coniah, the son of Jehoiakim, whom Nebuchadnezzar, king of Babylon, made king in the land of Judah." (Jer. 37:1.) Hence

this young king, the fifth to occupy the throne of
David, since Jeremiah had received his commission,
was his own grandson.

The work of rooting out and tearing down has been
well done so far, and we may rest assured that, although the prophet's own flesh and blood are on the
throne and dwelling in the palace, the God-assigned
work will not stop. But if there should be any very
young or helpless members of that family survive the
wreck which must come during the tearing down and
rooting out period, who would have a greater claim
as their natural protector than one so closely allied by
the ties of blood as this very man whom God has
chosen for the work of building and planting, as well
as of tearing down and rooting out?

Jeremiah records the downfall of Zedekiah and his
sons, the royal princes, as follows: "In the ninth year
of Zedekiah, king of Judah, in the tenth month, came
Nebuchadnezzar, king of Babylon, and all his army
against Jerusalem, and they besieged it. And in the
eleventh year of Zedekiah, in the fourth month, and
the ninth day of the month, the city was broken up.
And all the princes of the king of Babylon came in, and
sat in the middle gate, even Nergal-sharezar, Samgar-
Nebo, Sarsechim, Rabsaris, Rabmag, with all the residue of the princes of the king of Babylon.

"And it came to pass, that when Zedekiah, the king of
Judah, saw them, and all the men of war, then they fled,
and went forth out of the city by night, by the way of
the king's garden, by the gate betwixt the two walls;
and he went out the way of the plain. But the Chaldeans' army pursued after them, and overtook Zede-

kiah in the plains of Jericho; and when they had taken him, they brought him up to Nebuchadnezzar, king of Babylon, to Riblah, in the land of Hamath, where he gave judgment upon him. Then the king of Babylon slew the sons of Zedekiah in Riblah before his eyes; also the king of Babylon slew all the nobles of Judah. Moreover he put out Zedekiah's eyes, and bound him in chains, to carry him to Babylon. And the Chaldeans burned the king's house, and the houses of the people, with fire, and brake down the walls of Jerusalem. (Jer. 39:1-8.)

In the fifty-second chapter of Jeremiah there is a statement of these events, to which, after recording the fact concerning the king's being carried to Babylon in chains, there is added the following: "And the king of Babylon * * * put him in prison till the day of his death." (Jer. 52:11.)

Thus ends the history of the last prince of the house of David who has ever reigned over the Jewish people from that time until the present; and we know that they are not now, as a nation, being ruled over by any prince of their royal family; for they are scattered among all the nations of the earth, and are now fulfilling, not the prophecies concerning their ultimate and most glorious destiny, but a class of prophecies which pertain to this period, or time, of being scattered, which are those of becoming "a hiss and a byword," "crying for sorrow of heart and vexation of spirit," and leaving "their name for a curse." When those events occurred which resulted in the overthrow of the Zedekiah branch of the royal house, a climax was reached, not only in the history of all those things which were involved in the Davidic covenant, but also in that predestined work, for the accomplishment of which God sanctified and sent Jeremiah into this world.

By this climax, the first part of his mission, in all its phases, was now most thoroughly accomplished—namely, the plucking up, throwing down, afflicting. Indeed, it was so well done, that the heretofore accepted authorities in theologic, historic and ethnologic matters have taught that the sceptre, throne and kingdom of David were wiped out of existence, together with the house of David, excepting only another branch of the family of Josiah, who were carried away into the Babylonish captivity, of whom came Christ, the son of David, who, according to the Scripture, must yet sit upon the throne of his father David. We will give but one example of that class of sophistical reasoning which has led the mind of the Christian world into this gross error.

Take, for instance, the well-known and much-used Polyglot Bible, published by Samuel Bagster & Sons, of London. The compilers of this work (whoever they are we know not) give what is called "A summary view of the principal events of the period from the close of the sacred canon of the Old Testament until the times of the New Testament." According to the system of chronology which this work adopts, the overthrow of Zedekiah occurred in the year 589 B. C. This proposed summary begins after the return of the Jewish people from the Babylonish captivity, but while they were yet under the dominion of the Kingdom of Persia; and when Artaxerxes Longimanus was the reigning king, who in his twentieth year commissioned Nehemiah to rebuild the walls of Jerusalem, an event which happened, according to the chronology used, in 446 B. C.

Then follows a brief record of the death and successions of kings, the rise and fall of dynasties, and the overthrow of kingdoms, powers, dominions and empires. But it is always shown conclusively that these ruling powers, whatever might be their nationality, were dominating the Jewish people.

The summary shows that Alexander the Great marched into Judea to punish the people for certain grievances which, in his mind, they had practiced against him as commander of the Grecian forces, and that God thwarted him in that purpose. It shows that when Alexander died the Grecian empire was divided among his four generals; that Palestine was given to Loamedon, one of those generals, and that it was soon taken away from him by Ptolemy, the king of Egypt, that they "rejoiced to submit to this new master," and what the consequences were. It shows what they suffered under Antiochus Epiphanes, especially after a false rumor had been spread concerning his death, which they believed and rejoiced in, and that in consequence of this rejoicing "he slew 40,000 persons, sold as many more for slaves, plundered the temple of gold and furniture to the amount of 80 talents of gold, entered the Holy of Holies, and sacrificed a sow upon the altar of burnt offerings, and caused the broth of it to be sprinkled all over the temple." No greater indignity than this could have been put upon that people. The summary continues, a truthful record of suffering after suffering, trouble after trouble, and indignity after indignity, heaped upon that conquered people, who during all those centuries were reigned over by their enemies, the Gentile nations; but not once does the record show—no not for even one generation—that they were ruled by a prince of their own royal house.

Finally, the summary ends as follows: "At length Antipater, a noble but crafty Idumæan, by favor of Julius Caesar, was made procurator of Judea, and Hyrcanus continued in the priesthood. After Antipater's death, his son, Herod the Great, by the assistance of Antony, the Roman triumvir, and through much barbarity and bloodshed assumed the regal dignity; which authority was at length confirmed by Augustus Caesar. He maintained his dignity with great ability, but with the utmost cruelty, in his own family as well as among others, till the birth of Christ. In the interval he built many cities, and, to ingratiate himself with the Jews, almost rebuilt the temple.

His cruel attempt to murder the infant Saviour is recorded by the evangelist; and soon afterward he died most miserably. After some years, during which the dominions of Herod were governed by his sons, Judea became a Roman province, and *the sceptre departed from Judah, for Shiloh was come* (the italics are their own); and after having been under the government of Roman procurators for some years, the whole Jewish state was at length subverted by Titus, the son of Vespasian."

The sophistry in the use of those italicised words, as employed by the compilers of that summary, is that they destroy the evident meaning of that prophecy to which they refer, by the substitution of various sceptres—held by various kings, of various Gentile nations, that have consecutively held dominion over the Jewish people—for one particular Sceptre, which the Lord promised should be held, *only* by some member of Judah's family line, and which should not cease to be held by those of his posterity *until* Shiloh should come.

If the view, as put forth in the closing sentence of that summary, is the true one, then the entire prophecy must, for several reasons, go by default.

(1) A sceptre did not depart from over the Jews when Christ came. Forty years after Christ had come and gone finds them still under the power of Rome. Shortly afterward they were dispersed and have since been scattered among all nations, where they remain unto this day, and are still being *ruled over.*

(2) If the first coming of Christ was his Shiloh-coming, then Shiloh failed; for the people did not gather unto him.

(3) The Lord declares: "Judah is my law giver." According to this summary and other accepted evidence, Judah as Lawgiver departed from the Jews 588 years before Shiloh came. Hence that unbridged chasm of nearly six hundred years stands like a gaping wound in the side of the Church of Jesus Christ, whenever she is compelled to show herself in naked honesty. The entire trend of this summary with its subtle reference to the prophecy in question seems to be that so long as the Jewish nation was ruled over, no matter by whom, and held together as a province or state, this prophecy was vindicated: whereas such vindication, conception,

or use of those words, is only an attempt to hold together, by daubing with untempered mortar, an edifice which is tottering and tumbling.

The most charitable construction which can be put upon such accommodating, mollifying, weak and abortive efforts to vindicate the truth of God, is that the persons are ignorant of just some such vital point as the fact that Jeremiah was called and commissioned of God to *build* and *plant* anew the plucked-up kingdom of David.

All who claim that Christ has come as Shiloh are compelled to resort to just such distortions of the Divine Word as the one under consideration, in order to fill up that gaping hiatus of 588 years, from the overthrow of Zedekiah until Christ.

Furthermore, after they have plastered over that gap to their own (questionable) satisfaction, they are still confronted with the fact that the Lord God did not give unto Christ the throne of his father David, nor cause him to reign over the house of Jacob—no, not even spiritually—for the Jews are a part of the house of Jacob: as these men themselves are compelled to admit. Also the Jews are enemies to the gospel of *grace* which Jesus Christ came to bring, "but as touching the election (of race), they are beloved for the fathers' sake."

Meanwhile, the great question which confronts us is this: Has God suffered his faithfulness to fail, or allowed any of his promises to go by default, or permitted his covenant either with Judah, David or Christ to suffer lapse? The very thought that such could possibly be the case causes us to feel the first chilling blight of skepticism to fall heavily upon our hitherto believing and happy hearts.

The next link in the chain of this divine history is of such deep import that it is impossible for us to over-estimate its value, as it is the connecting link between sacred history and prophecy; for you will notice in the first clause of the following text we find a record of events which have become history, but before the sentence is finished we are carried out into the field of prophecy. *"It shall come to pass that like as I have watched over them, to pluck up, and to break down, and to throw down, and to destroy, and to afflict," so will I watch over them,* TO BUILD *and* TO PLANT, *saith the Lord.*   (Jer. 31:28.)

The Lord here uses the already accomplished facts of history as a basis upon which to rest his promise concerning the accomplishment of those which are yet future. Hence, upon events which once were prophetic, but which have now become history, he predicts the fulfillment of others which are still in the future. But these events must follow as a sequence to those which have gone before, since both these which are past and those which are yet to come were originally couched in the same prophecy, in the same commission, and were to be accomplished by the same prophet, Jeremiah of Libnah.

The Lord has said that David should never lack a man of his seed to sit upon that throne.

Query—Where was the seed with which Jeremiah must "build and plant"?

CHAPTER IV.

Before we can gather up even the first link in the chain of history as regards the "building and planting" which Jeremiah must accomplish, we must take a glance at some of the facts concerning the prophet's own history.

We have already noticed that when the Lord was instructing Jeremiah in the work which he was to do, he said to him, regarding those that should oppose or fight against him, "Be not afraid of their faces, for I am with thee to deliver thee."

But Jeremiah seems not to have met with any special opposition until during the reign of Jehoiakim. This was at a time when the Lord commanded him to go into the court of the temple and speak to the people as they gathered from all the cities of Judah to worship; at the same time he told him to speak all the words which he, the Lord, had commanded him, and to "diminish not a word."

He was true to God, and faithfully delivered the Divine message. The message itself was full of mercy, and accompanied with a proviso that if every man would turn from his evil way then the Lord would avert the impending calamities which hung over the nation as judgments in consequence of their numerous and manifold sins. But it only resulted in the prophets, the priests, and the people

183

gathering themselves into an excited, surging and howling mob, which made a prisoner of Jeremiah, saying unto him, "Thou shalt surely die."

Later, when the princes of Judah heard these things, they came up to the temple, and in order that they might hear and judge for themselves, Jeremiah was permitted to speak again. This he did, still faithfully giving the unwelcome message of the Lord. In conclusion, he said: "The Lord sent me to prophesy against this house (the temple) and against this city all the words that ye have heard. Therefore now amend your ways and doings and obey the voice of the Lord your God; and the Lord will repent him of all the evil that he hath pronounced against you.

"As for me, behold, I am in your hand; do with me as seemeth good unto you. But know ye for a certain, that if ye put me to death, ye shall surely bring innocent blood upon yourselves, and upon this city, and upon the inhabitants thereof; for of a truth, the Lord hath sent me unto you to speak all these words in your ears." The princes were evidently touched somewhat by this appeal, and the people with them; for after this, both princes and people stood against the prophets and the priests, and said, "This man is not worthy to die." So a division arose among them, which resulted in Jeremiah's being spared for the time and set at liberty. But he continued his earnest expostulations with the people because of their sins, and continued just as before his startling annunciations concerning the impending ruin of temple, city and nation.

These truths were so unwelcome and painful for the people to hear, that other prophets soon began to appear who uttered contrary predictions, no doubt for the sake of the popularity which they should acquire among the people by prophesying the return of peace and prosperity. Hananiah was the name of one of these false prophets. On one occasion he broke a small wooden yoke which Jeremiah wore upon his neck, which had been put there as an object lesson by Divine direction. When this false prophet broke that yoke, he told the people that the Lord said that the yoke of Nebuchadnezzar, which was not only upon the neck of Judah, but upon all nations, should be broken within two years. But the Lord spoke to Hananiah, through his true prophet, Jeremiah, and told him that, because he had made the people trust in a lie, he should die that same year. And the record reads, "So Hananiah, the prophet, died the same year in the seventh month."

Shemeniah was another of those lying prophets who was dealt with in a manner which condemned him and exonerated Jeremiah. But still Jeremiah's enemies, the priests, false prophets, and certain elders, were not at rest, but continued their persecutions until the result was that Jeremiah was thrown into prison. With his liberty thus restricted he could not publicly deliver his messages, so he called Baruch, the scribe, to his assistance, and he wrote as Jeremiah dictated. This matter was inscribed upon a roll of parchment, with the view of having it read to the people in some public and frequented part of the city.

The favorable opportunity occurred on the occasion of a great festival, which was a feasting day, and which brought the inhabitants of the land from all parts of Judea together at Jerusalem. On the day of the festival Baruch took the roll and stationed himself at the entry of the new gate of the temple, and, calling upon the people to hear him, began to read. A great concourse of people soon gathered around him who listened, apparently with honest attention.

But one of the by-standers, Michaiah, went down into the city to the king's palace, and reported to the king's scribes and princes, who were assembled in the council chamber, that Baruch had gathered the people together in one of the courts of the temple, and that he was reading to them a discourse on prophecy which had been written by Jeremiah. He also told them all he himself had heard, as Baruch read the book in the hearing of the people.

This aroused such an interest and anxiety among them that they immediately sent Jehudi, an attendant at the palace, to tell Baruch to come to them and bring the roll with him. As soon as he arrived, they asked him to read what he had written. He did so, and they were evidently much impressed, for the Scripture statement is, "When they had heard all the words they were afraid, both one and the other."

Their fear must have been great, because they felt a conviction that these words were from the Lord, and that these predictions would surely come to pass. This very fear created in them a tender regard for both Baruch and Jeremiah, for they told him that they would be obliged to report the matter to the king; but they advised Baruch, saying: "Go hide thee; thou and Jeremiah, and let no man know where ye be."

When the matter was reported to the king, the subject matter of the book so angered him that when he had read only three or four leaves, he took out his pen-knife and cut the entire roll to pieces and threw it in the fire, and then ordered his officers to "take Baruch, the scribe, and Jeremiah, the prophet; but the Lord hid them." (Jer. 36:26.)

Strange, isn't it, that they should have Jeremiah in prison, and yet, when they come to look for him he cannot be found? But then, we believe that when the Lord does a thing it is well done. One thing we do know about this, that the Lord took him out of prison to hide him, and that when he again appeared among men, they did not imprison him on the old charge, for the Scripture saith: "Now Jeremiah came in and went out among the people; for they had not put him in prison."

Meanwhile, King Jehoiakim had received his promised burial, that of "an ass, drawn and cast outside the gates of Jerusalem," "and his dead body," as Jeremiah says, was "cast out in the day to the heat, and in the night to the frost."

The next time in which we find Jeremiah a prisoner is during the reign of Zedekiah, who, as we have before mentioned, was the prophet's own grandson. At this time Jeremiah's enemies represented to the King that the predictions which were uttered by the prophet were so gloomy and terrible that they depressed and discouraged the hearts of the people to such an extent that they were weakened in their power to resist, and that accordingly he must be regarded as a public enemy. So persistently were these claims urged that finally the King gave Jeremiah into the hands of his enemies and told them that they might do with him as they pleased.

There was a dungeon in the prison, to which there was no access except from above. The bottom was wet and miry and covered with filth and slime. It was the custom to let prisoners down into its gloomy depths and leave them there to starve. Into this filthy dungeon Jeremiah was cast and was left to die of misery and hunger. But God brought Jeremiah into this world to accomplish a work, for the accomplishment of which he himself had pledged his reputation as God; consequently he could not afford to let that man die then and there.

So the Lord began to trouble Zedekiah. His heart smote him, his fears confronted him, and he trembled with misgivings lest he had delivered a true prophet of God into the hands of those who, he knew, would surely put him to death. So he inquired what had been done with the prisoner, and learned that he had been practically buried alive. Then, with fear-tortured haste, he commanded an officer to take thirty men and get Jeremiah out of that horrible pit "before he die."

When they went to the dungeon and opened the mouth of it they found that he had sunk deep into the mire. They threw down some old clothes, which he was to fold and place under his arms and about those parts of his body where the ropes were to pass, and where the greatest weight would come in pulling him out of the mire and up out of that dismal pit.

After that Jeremiah had the freedom of the court of the prison, and the King secretly sought him and begged him to reveal the truth concerning his own fate and that of the kingdom of Judah. Jeremiah did this faithfully, and the King found out all that he sought to know; which proved to be much more than he cared to learn, especially concerning his own fate.

While Jeremiah was shut up in the court of that prison the word of the Lord came to him for the last time concerning the destruction of the city. At the same time the promise concerning the preservation of his own life was given, and was as follows: "But I will deliver thee in that day, saith the Lord, and thou shalt not be given into the hand of the men of whom thou art afraid. For I will surely deliver thee, and thou shalt not fall by the sword, but thy life shall be for a prey (booty or prize) upon thee." (Jer. 39: 17, 18.)

Jeremiah remained shut up in that prison until the Babylonish forces captured the city, broke down the walls, burned the Royal palaces and the houses of the people, thus making the inside of those prison walls the only place of safety in all that city.

Now, it is a remarkable fact, one well worthy of God and certainly one most worthy of note, that the Lord had promised not only that the prophet should be delivered from his enemies among his own people, but also that the enemies of his people should treat him well, and that amidst it all his life should be spared. It is also a remarkable fact that, in view of all this, we read: "Now Nebuchadnezzar, King of Babylon, gave charge concerning Jeremiah to Nebuzar-adan, the captain of the guard, saying, "Take him and look well to him, but do him no harm, but do unto him even as he shall say unto thee." (Jer. 39:11, 12.)

The effect of this command from the conquering king was so wonderful in its results, and the result was so absolutely essential in order that Jeremiah might be free to finish his Divinely-appointed task, that we are moved to give this result just as it is recorded in the Word of God:—

"And the captain of the guard took Jeremiah and said unto him, * * Behold I loose thee this day from the chains that were upon thy hand. If it seem good unto thee to come with me into Babylon, come and I will look well unto thee; but if it seem ill unto thee to come with me into Babylon, forbear; behold all the land is before thee; whither it seemeth good and convenient for thee to go, thither go. * * So the captain of the guard gave him victuals and a reward (money) and let him go."

Query: Where did he go and why?

CHAPTER V.

When Nebuzar-adan, the captain of the Chaldean guard, gave Jeremiah privilege to go where he pleased, and provided him with all that was needful for the journey, the record further declares: "Then went Jeremiah unto Gedeliah, the son of Ahikam, to Mizpah, and dwelt with him among the people that were left in the land." (Jer. 40:6.) The next verse of the same chapter states that the people who were still in the land were "the poor of the land, of them that were not carried away captive to Babylon."

This Gedeliah, the son of Ahikam, was the man whom the King of Babylon had made governor of what little there was left in Judea; for he had taken the masses of the people into captivity to Babylon and made servants of them.

It seems that, since the capital city of Judea was now destroyed, Gedeliah had been compelled to set up a provincial government in some other city and had chosen Mizpah. Also, when the refugees from among the Jews who had fled into Moab, Ammon and Edom heard that the King of Babylon had left a remnant in Judea and had set a governor over them, then they returned and put themselves under him. So also did the several captains of small outlying forces until, all told, there was quite a goodly number in this remnant, as it was called.

But the little province did not prosper long, for the King of Ammon entered into a plot with Ishmael, the son of Nethaniah, to assassinate its new governor. Johanan, the son of Kareah, discovered this plot and told Gedeliah.   At the same time he offered to slay secretly this Ishmael, the would-be assassin; but Gedeliah would not permit it, would not believe Johanan's story, and accused him of speaking falsely concerning Ishmael.

However, it was only a short time until the plot was successfully carried out; for Ishmael and nine of his confederates slew not only the governor, but all the Chaldeans, all the men of war, and all the Jews that were with him.   His object in all this was that he might easily make captives of the rest of the people, who were unarmed, and carry them away into Ammon to increase and strengthen the kingdom of the Ammonites.

To show that this was the object, we quote the full text of the tenth verse of the forty-first chapter of Jeremiah.   Still it is not of any very special interest to us to know that such was his object, but there is something in that text which is of the greatest possible interest to us.   The reason for Jeremiah's going to Mizpah is there.   The key to the possible fulfillment of Jehovah's promise to David is there.   The possibilities of the success of Jeremiah's commission are there.   The Divine support to our faith and an opening door for the complete vindication of God are there.

"Then Ishmael carried away captive all the residue of the people that were in Mizpah, even the *King's Daughters*, and all the people that remained in Mizpah, whom Nebuzar-adan, the captain of the guard, had committed to Gedeliah, the son of Ahikam; and Ish-mael, the son of Nethaniah, carried them away captive and departed to go over to the Ammonites."

What! "The *King's daughters?*" we hear you ex-claim.

Yes; but wait until we shall gather into one focus a few other points, and then we can see the way perfectly clear for Jeremiah to finish completely his God-given task.

When Johanan and the other captains of the fighting forces heard what Ishmael had done they gathered themselves together, started in pursuit and overtook him at Gibeon. At this juncture the Scripture says: "Now it came to pass that when all the people which were with Ishmael saw Johanan, the son of Kareah, and all the captains of the forces that were with him, then they were glad. So all the people that Ishmael had carried away captive from Mizpah cast about and returned, and went unto Johanan, the son of Kareah. But Ishmael, the son of Nethaniah, escaped from Johanan with eight men and went unto the Ammon-ites." (Jer. 41:13, 15.)

After Johanan had retaken this captive company, and Ishmael, the traitor, had escaped, then he became afraid of the Chaldeans, and feared that the King of the Chal-dean Empire, Nebuchadnezzar, who had placed Gede-liah over them, would, upon hearing what Ishmael had done, send his army and destroy them. So, under the distress and despair of the hour, Johanan, who was now their recognized leader, with all the captains and the people, from the least unto the greatest, made an ap-peal unto the prophet of God, "and said unto Jeremiah the prophet, Let, we beseech thee, our supplication be accepted before thee, and now pray for us unto the Lord thy God, even for all this remnant (for we are left but a few of many, as thine eyes do behold us); that the Lord thy God may show us the way wherein we may walk, and the thing that we may do."

In reply to this appeal Jeremiah told them that he would pray for them and inquire of the Lord for them, but that they must obey the Lord; for he would tell them just what the Lord said, whether it was good or bad, and that he would keep nothing back. To which they replied: "Whether it be good, or whether it be evil, we will obey the voice of the Lord our God, to whom we send thee; that it may be well with us when we obey the voice of the Lord our God." Then Jeremiah besought the Lord, and the Lord heard and gave instructions. Among other things the Lord told him to say to them, "Be not afraid of the King of Babylon, of whom ye are afraid; be not afraid of him, saith the Lord; for I am with you to save you, and to deliver you from his hand." He also told them not to go down to Egypt, as was their intention, thinking they would be safe if they placed themselves under the protection of the King of Egypt.

Furthermore, he told them that if they did go to Egypt the very thing which they feared would come upon them, and they should be destroyed, saying: "If ye wholly set your faces to enter into Egypt, and go to sojourn there, then it shall come to pass that the sword which ye feared shall overtake you there in the land of Egypt, and the famine whereof ye were afraid shall follow close after you there in Egypt, and there shall ye die."

The Lord also told Jeremiah that these people were dissembling in their hearts, when they sent him to pray for them and to make their request. So we are not surprised that it is recorded that Johanan said unto Jeremiah: "Thou speakest falsely: the Lord our God hath not sent thee to say, Go not into Egypt to sojourn there: But Baruch, the son of Neriah, setteth thee against us, for to deliver us into the hands of the Chaldeans, that they might put us to death, and carry us away captive into Babylon."

Neither are we surprised to read the result, which is recorded as follows: "But Johanan, the son of Kareah, and all the captains of the forces took all the remnant of Judah that were returned from all the nations whither they had been driven, to dwell in the land of Judah; even men, women and children, and the KING'S DAUGHTERS, and every person that Nebuzar-adan, the captain, had left with Gedeliah, the son of Ahikam, the son of Shaphan, and JEREMIAH, the prophet, and Baruch, the son of Neriah. So they came into the land of Egypt; for they obeyed not the voice of the Lord. Thus came they even to Tahpanhes." (Jer. 43: 5-8.)

Baruch, the scribe, was the companion of Jeremiah in prison, when the Lord took them out and hid them. He was also his companion in persecution and affliction and accusation. Now, since we find his name mentioned as one of this company which Johanan compelled to go to Egypt against the direct command of God, there is just one prophecy concerning him which we need to mention before we proceed further. It is as follows: "Thus saith the Lord, the God of Israel, unto thee, O Baruch: Behold, that which I have built will I break down, and that which I have planted I will pluck up, even this whole land, * * * but thy life will I give unto thee for a prey (booty or reward) in all places whither thou goest." (Jer. 45:2, 4, 5.)

Furthermore, when that company had reached Egypt and were at Tahpanhes, the Lord again used Jeremiah to prophesy concerning their destruction, and also concerning the King of Babylon and his coming against Pharaoh-Hophra, the King of Egypt, and many other matters; but we will only give a small portion—that which pertains to the destiny of the people whose history we are following.

The prophecy opens with these words: "The word that came to Jeremiah concerning all the Jews which dwell in the land of Egypt." Note carefully the following: "I will take the remnant of Judah, that have set their faces to go into the land of Egypt *to sojourn there*, and they shall all be consumed, and fall in the land of Egypt; they shall even be consumed by the sword and by the famine; they shall die, from the least even unto the greatest, by the sword and by the famine; and they shall be an execration, and an astonishment, and a curse, and a reproach." (Jer. 44:12.)

The complete destruction of that company is foretold in those words; yet the Lord has in that company a few persons whose lives he has promised shall be spared. So, before the prophecy continues much further the following proviso is given: *"None shall return but such as shall escape."* (Verse 14.)

And before the prophecy is ended abundant provision is made for the very few whom God has promised shall live. Hence we find in the prophecy as it continues the following: "Behold I shall watch over them for evil, and not for good; and all the men of Judah that are in the land of Egypt shall be consumed by the sword and by the famine, until there be an end of them. Yet a *small number* that escape the sword shall return out of the land of Egypt."

Remember that the masses of the house of Judah, of the Jewish people, were in captivity in Babylon, where they were to stay for seventy years. Also remember that this remnant which came into Egypt were only the ragged end of the nation, i. e., the poor of the land, and a few captains of small military forces. Now, the Lord proposes to destroy this rag-tag remnant, out of which "a small number shall escape." Now, let us take our bearings.

1. We have in this company, which has come down into Egypt from Judea, "the King's daughters." Since the plural form of speech is used there are at least two of them—history says there were three. These are the royal seed of the house of David, who are fleeing from the slayers of their father, Zedekiah, the last King of the house of Judah, and the slayers of their brothers, the sons of Zedekiah and princes of Judah.

2. In company with these princesses is Jeremiah, their grandfather, whom also the Lord has chosen to do the work of building and planting. In the princesses the prophet has royal material with which to build and plant.

3. In company with Jeremiah and his royal charge we have Baruch, his faithful scribe, whom expert genealogists prove to have been uncle to the royal seed.

4. God has promised that the lives of this *"small number,"* only five or six at most, shall be to them a prey (reward) in all lands whither they shall go.

5. Prior to this, at a time when Jeremiah was greatly troubled, when in his great distress and anguish of heart he cried unto the Lord, saying: "Remember me, visit me, and revenge me of my persecutors"; then the Lord said, "Verily it shall be well with *thy remnant;* verily I will cause the enemy to entreat thee well in the time of evil and in the time of affliction.   * * * And I will make thee to pass with thine enemies into a land which thou knowest not."   (Jer. 15: 11-14.)

Note the expression "thy remnant," i. e., Jeremiah's, for it is he who must build and plant that royal seed. Understand also that Jeremiah and his little remnant were well acquainted with Egypt, and since it was well known to them it could not have been their final destination. Hence, this escaping royal remnant must journey back to Judea, and then—whither?

"Into an unknown land!" Why? "For out of Jerusalem shall go forth a remnant, and they that escape out of Mount Zion (on which were the royal dwellings). The zeal of the Lord of hosts will do this.   And the remnant that is escaped of the house of Judah (royal line) shall again take root downward and bear fruit upward."   (Isa. 37: 32-31.)

Hear it! O hear it! Ye men of earth, HEAR IT! "Shall again take root downward"—be planted! "and bear fruit upward"—be builded! Where? God should tell us where in His Word, and he does.

CHAPTER VI.

THE PRINCE OF THE SCARLET THREAD.

While we leave our little royal "remnant" to make their escape, let us look about and out into the fields of revelation and history, to see if we can find some royal prince to whom shall be wedded one of these princesses who are fleeing into that "unknown land," where the Lord has promised that those who compose this remnant shall again take root and grow.

While we are making this search it will be well to remember that "God gave the kingdom over Israel to David forever," and that "Israel" is not the name of the Jewish nation, but that it is the name of the ten-tribed kingdom, which had been driven into "an unknown land" about one hundred and thirty-nine years prior to the flight of this remnant.

Let us also remember that the Sceptre, with all that belongs to it, was promised distinctively to the Judo-Davidic family, and not to the kingdom which bore the name of Judah, a name which, together with its corrupted form, Jews, is the Biblical historic name of the Jewish nation.

Judah, as we will remember, was the representative name of that nation which was composed of the smaller portion of Israel's seed, because it was to Judah's blessing and standard that the people gathered who afterward became separated from the rest of

Israel, and were known as the Jews. They are the descendants of these people who are still known as Jews.

On the other hand, according to a prophecy which shall be cited in due time, the descendants of the ten-tribed kingdom, which had been cast out into an unknown land, were to be called by another name.

The fact that they were not to be known by the name of Israel cannot annul the prophecy which was uttered by Abijah, as he stood upon a certain mount in Ephraim and said: "Hear me, thou Jeroboam, and all Israel; ought ye not to know that the Lord God of Israel gave the kingdom over Israel to David forever, even to him and to his sons, by a covenant of salt?"

Do you ask, "Is it possible that this little royal remnant shall have gone to that same unknown land to which they of the ten tribes had previously gone? Was it among that people that this remnant was planted, and over whom the preserved sceptre held its sway?" Let us examine the Scriptural evidence.

Ezekiel is believed to have lived contemporaneously with Jeremiah. By taking the testimony of chronology, together with the concurrence of many historic events, all may know that this is true.

Jeremiah states historic events and utters prophecies which relate chiefly to Judah, but gives only a little of that which pertains to Israel; while Ezekiel does the reverse of this, saying much that concerns Israel and but little that pertains to Judah.

Still, what he does say concerning the destroyed commonwealth of Judah, the plucked-up Sceptre and the overturned throne of that royal family whose history we are studying, does most undoubtedly furnish evidence which connects the remnant seed and their monarchical belongings with the exiled house of Israel, which has taken root, and whose people are gathering strength in a country the location and geographical character of which are described by the prophets, and which, at a time prior to the prophecies, was an unknown and an uninhabited wilderness.

Jeremiah tells us that "Zedekiah was one and twenty years old when he began to reign, and he reigned eleven years in Jerusalem."

At a period which synchronizes with the time when Zedekiah had reigned for six years, Ezekiel declares that the word of the Lord came to him saying that he should prophesy against Judah and Jerusalem, concerning the King of Babylon, who would come up against them with the sword, and that at that time he should set battering rams against the gates of the city, cast up a mount and build a fort. The result of this would be that the city would be taken.

At the same time the message from the Lord, which was delivered by the prophet Ezekiel to Zedekiah, was : "And thou, profane, wicked Prince of Israel, whose day is come, when (your) iniquity shall have an end, thus saith the Lord God : Remove the diadem, and take off the crown; this shall not be (upon) the same; exalt him that is low, and abase him that is high. I will overturn, overturn, overturn it; and it shall be no more (overturned) until he come whose right it is; and I will give it to him."—Ezek. 21 : 22-27.

We have no disposition to make an attempt to give words a meaning which they will not bear, nor to attach any signification to them which the context does not clearly indicate; but these words do most certainly give us to understand that there is a person, a male heir of the royal line, who is to be the immediate successor of Zedekiah to the Davidic throne. Also, these words teach that the crown is to be taken from off the head of Zedekiah, upon whom it rested at the time when this prophecy was given, and placed upon the head of this person whom the Scriptures designate as "him that is low."

These words further teach that when the royal diadem, the emblem of kingly power and exaltation, is taken from the one and placed upon the head of that other person, that then the one who was previously high is abased and brought low, but that the one who hitherto was low is then exalted and made high. This is essentially so, because the two men shall have then exchanged places.

Furthermore, the expression, "This shall not be the same," taken together with the prophecy concerning the overturns, leads us to expect a change of dynasty, at least on the side of the male line, and also a change in the territorial or geographical situation. This is still more apparent when we note that there are to be three overturns, and that after the third overturn shall have been accomplished, there are to be no more until another certain person comes. Also, after the diadem has been removed from the head of the prince who wore it at the time of the first overturn and placed upon the head of "him that is low," it is to be noted that then either this man, who is the person understood as the antecedent of the personal pronoun, "Him," or his lineage, is to be dethroned by the Lord in favor of that other person, who is designated as "he whose right it is," to whom it shall then be given.

The next question for us to settle is, Who is this legally possible person, that is to be the successor of Zedekiah, who is spoken of as "him that is low"? for he is spoken of as "low" only in the sense of non-ruling.

By consulting the thirty-eighth chapter of Genesis we will find a record of the conception and birth of twin boys, whose conception and birth were both accompanied by such extraordinary circumstances that the question of their parentage is forever settled; for Tamar, the mother, did willingly stoop in order that she might conquer Judah, the father, and compel him to do justice by her.

The never-to-be-forgotten manner in which Judah was forced to acknowledge that those children were his offspring and that their mother was more righteous than he, does most certainly place the fact of their royal lineage beyond the possibility of cavil.

When the mother was in travail and after the midwife had been summoned, there was the presentation of a hand. Then, for some reason either human or Divine, the midwife knew that twins were in the womb. So, in order that she might know and be able to testify which was born first, she fastened a scarlet thread on the outstretched hand. Since Judah's was the royal family in Israel, and the law of primogeniture prevailed among them, it was essential that this distinction should be made so that at the proper time the first born or eldest son might ascend the throne.

After the scarlet thread had been made secure **on** the little hand it was drawn back and the brother was born first. Upon seeing this the midwife exclaimed: "How hast thou broken forth?" Then, seemingly, she was filled with the spirit of prophecy and said: "This breach be upon thee," and because of this prophetic utterance he was given the name of Pharez, i. e., "A Breach." Afterward his brother, who had the scarlet thread upon his hand, was born, and his name was called Zarah, i. e., "The seed."

The very fact that Pharez was really born first would exalt him, and it eventually did exalt his heirs, to the throne of Israel, for King David was a son of Judah through the line of Pharez. But just so surely as this son of Judah and father of David, who was the first one of the line to sit upon that throne, was given the name of Pharez, just so surely must we expect—with that little hand of the scarlet thread waving prophetically before them—that a breach should occur somewhere along that family line.

That breach did occur. We are now considering its history and are well into its transition period, which began when the Lord God sanctified Jeremiah, sent him into the world, and gave him his commission to pull down and pluck up the exalted Pharez line, and afterward to build and plant anew the sceptre, throne and kingdom; while at about the same time the word of the Lord came to Ezekiel and moved him to predict the removal of the crown from the head of the one who is high, a proceeding which not only involves the transfer of the royal diadem to another head, but also an overturning; and when both the transfer and the overturning shall have been accomplished, then the one who was low will have been exalted and the exalted one will have been brought low.

The immediate posterity of this "Prince of the Scarlet Thread" is given as follows: "And the sons of Zarah; Zimri and Ethan and Heman and Calcol and Dara, five of them in all." (1 Chron. 2:6.) Thus the direct posterity of Zarah was five, while that of Pharez was only two.

For the reason that our Lord sprang out of Judah, through the line of Pharez, the unbroken genealogy of that family is given in the sacred records; but the genealogy of the Zarah family is given only intermittently. One thing is made quite clear in the Bible concerning the sons of Zarah, and that is, that they were famous for their intelligence and wisdom, for it was only the great God-given wisdom of Solomon which is declared to have risen above theirs, as is seen by the following: And God gave Solomon wisdom and understanding * * * and Solomon's wisdom excelled the wisdom of all the children of the East, for he was wiser than all men—than Ethan the Ezrahite, and Heman, and Calcol, and Dara. (1 Kings 4:29, 31.)

Furthermore, we find that two of them, Ethan and Heman, were also noted singers, as we find by consulting the fifteenth chapter of First Kings and the nineteenth verse. By noting the titles of the eighty-eighth and eighty-ninth Psalms we also see that one of them was composed by "Heman the Ezrahite," and that the other was the song of "Ethan the Ezrahite."

It is not at all unlikely and would be but natural that

the Zimri who overthrew Baasha, the third King of Israel (not Judah), belonged to the posterity of Zimri, the first-born son of Zarah, son of Judah and twin brother of Pharez. For, as we have shown, the seed of Jacob were at that time divided into two kingdoms, with the posterity of Pharez on the throne ruling over the kingdom of Judah. How natural it would be for the then living members of that family to think, and to say: "This is the long foretold breach for which we have been taught to look. This is the time to assert our royal prerogatives, take the throne, and rule over this the house of Israel."

It would be but natural for another reason, namely, there has always been an attempt to fulfill, in the natural, every promise that the Lord God has made to his chosen people. He promised Abraham and Sarah that they should have a son. In order that they might accomplish this end Sarah gave and Abraham took, Hagar her handmaid, and the result was Ishmael.

Before Jacob and Esau were born the Birthright was promised to the younger. Jacob, the younger, undertook to accomplish this in the natural by taking unjust advantage of his brother and deceiving his father.

So with Joseph: after God had promised the Birthright to him he undertook in the natural to take advantage of the blindness of Jacob.

Nevertheless, God in his own good time gave Sarah strength to conceive; settled with repentant, wrestling Jacob, and outwitted manœuvering Joseph.

So now, in his own good time, he has also made the predicted breach, which shall result in the bringing down of the line of Pharez, *"the high,"* and which shall exalt the prosperity of Zarah, *"the low."*

CHAPTER VII.

THE "PRINCE OF THE SCARLET THREAD" AND "THE ROYAL REMNANT" UNITED.

In connection with the record of the fact that the *"high,"* or ruling, Prince of Judah has been uncrowned and dethroned, and that the *"low"* has been crowned and placed on the throne, we find that a royal prince, a royal princess and the ten-tribed kingdom of Israel are all together in the same country, also that this royal pair are united and placed on a throne, and are ruling over the kingdom of Israel.

These facts are recorded in the seventeenth chapter of Ezekiel in the form of a riddle and a parable, which, together with their explanation, make up the subject matter of the entire chapter, which opens as follows: "And the word of the Lord came unto me saying, Son of man put forth a riddle, and speak a parable unto the house of Israel; and say, Thus saith the Lord God, etc." The Hebrew word which is here translated riddle is defined as "A puzzle; hence a trick, conundrum, dark saying, hard question," etc. These definitions correspond to our English thought of an enigma, or something proposed which is to be solved by conjecture; a puzzling question; or an ambiguous proposition. A parable, on the other hand, is more like a fable or an allegorical representation of something which is real in its relation to human life and thought, and is represented by something real in nature.

Thus the prophet in his introduction prepares us to expect that the words which follow shall be enigmatical; and, since the Lord commanded him to use this veiled language, we must adjust ourselves accordingly, remembering that "it is the glory of God to conceal a thing; but the honor of kings to search out a matter." So, then, let us, in a spirit that shall be worthy of kings, search out the matter of this riddle, which we will notice is put forth unto the house of Israel, and not to the Jewish people.

The first part of the riddle is given, as follows: "Thus saith the Lord God: A great eagle with great wings, long-winged, full of feathers, which had divers colors, came unto Lebanon, and took the highest branch of the cedar; he cropped off the top of his young twigs, and carried it to a land of traffick; he set it in a city of merchants."

A few moments' reflection will convince us that, whatever else it may mean, the great eagle is intended to represent a means of transportation; for the declaration is that *"it came"* to a certain place, *"and took"* something which was in that place to which it came, and *"carried it into"* some other *"land."*

We are also told that this means of transportation came to Lebanon. Since Lebanon is a mountain range in Palestine, then the place to which it came, and from which it departed is, most certainly, Palestine.

That which was taken away is declared to be *"young twigs,"* which were taken from *"the highest branch of the cedar"* of Lebanon. Since the personal pronoun *"his"* is used, having *"the cedar"* for its antecedent, it must represent a person. This person is of the masculine gender, and father of the *"young twigs"*; hence, these young scions are also persons.

Furthermore, it is a well authenticated fact that the cedar of Lebanon is a symbol of royalty. Since the riddle contains within itself such abundant evidence of this fact, which will be made clear as we proceed, we will not need to go elsewhere for proof.

Again, inasmuch as it is true of twigs that they must be set, grafted, or planted, in order that they may grow and bear fruit, or increase, so also it is declared of these young royal scions that they were *"set."* The place also where they were set was certainly well adapted for increase of population, or subjects; that is, *"a city of merchants, in a land of traffick."*

The second part of this riddle reads as follows: "He took also of the seed of the land, and planted it in a fruitful field; he placed it by great waters, and set it as a willow tree. And it grew, and became a spreading vine of low stature, whose branches turned toward him, and the roots thereof were under him; so it became a vine, and shot forth sprigs."

"The seed of the land" is most certainly the people of the land. The land from which *"he took"* this seed, or people, is Palestine; and the people of Palestine are distinctly Israelites. And numerically, hence preeminently, they are always the ten-tribed kingdom of Israel.

So these people who had been taken out of their own land were *"planted"* in another, and that other has become to them *"a fruitful field,"* which is located *"by great waters."* Not by the Mediterranean Sea, or the Great Sea, as it is called in Scripture. But the new home of this removed people is *"by great waters."* In their new home Israel *"grew and became a spreading vine."* And since this riddle is dealing with the breach—as we shall see—in which the *"high"* and the *"low"* princes of the royal house are to exchange places, we are not surprised that this spreading or out-reaching vine is said to be of "LOW" stature, nor that its branches and sprigs turned toward him, or that its roots, or growing power, was under him. If under him, then he was over them, i. e., their ruler.

This riddle further says: "There was also another great eagle with great wings and many feathers; and behold this vine did bend her roots toward him, and shot forth her branches toward him, that he might water it by the furrows of her plantation. It was planted in a good soil by great waters, that it might bring forth branches, and that it might bear fruit, that it might be a goodly vine." Here we have the record of the arrival of another passenger, who also came to that land of *"good soil,"* which is by *"great waters,"* and who was brought there by the same means of transportation, i. e., a *"great eagle with great wings,"* as that which brought the royal sons. This was not the same eagle, but "another" eagle, or ship, for we believe this means of transportation to have been the ships of Dan; since it is declared that "Dan abode in ships," and that "they have taken cedars from Lebanon to make masts" for their ships. We also know that the seaport of Tyre, in Palestine, was the port into which they must come for the cedars of Lebanon.

Yes, for the cedars of Lebanon!!! be they used as masts for their ships, or as types of their royal princes.

The tribe of Dan also used the eagle as their standard, and they are said to have used great carved eagles with outstretched wings as the figureheads on the bows of their vessels. Also it is a common thing to symbolize ships which are under full sail as flying birds; and in this riddle the *"long wings"* represent the long sails, which, like wings carry the *"great"* ship— the large bird, or eagle ship—and her passengers to the land of traffic.

We are forced to the conclusion that the object which the writer has in view in mentioning the coming of this second ship is, that we may guess that another important personage had arrived; for, after mentioning the ship's arrival, his next expression is: "Behold, this vine did bend *her* roots toward him."

Thus we learn that the person who came in the second ship was a woman, and that her inclination and desire was toward the prince who had preceded her into the same land.

Then, still under the similitude of a vine, and that which is essential to its life and growth, viz., land and water, there follows that which clearly indicates a unity of life, claims and purpose. In fact, there was a marriage between the *"her"* and the *"him"* of this riddle, the result of which was that she, too, was *"set"* or *"planted"* in that land of a *"goodly vine,"* albeit that goodly vine is of "Low Stature"; and bore *"fruit."* That is, offspring.

Since it is true that a prince can wed only with a princess, it will be well for us, at this juncture, to remember that we left Jeremiah and his little royal remnant of king's daughters on their way to a land which was strange, or unknown, to them; yet to a place where this preserved seed of David's line was to be "planted," again "take root," and "bear fruit."

Now, it is a fact that the man and the woman of this riddle were united. Also it is a fact that the woman was "planted" in that land of good soil, into which she did "take root," and these things were accomplished in order that she "might bear fruit." In other words, that which hitherto has been the subject of prophecy concerning Jeremiah's commission, and concerning his royal charge, is now recorded as a matter of history. The analogy is complete.

Still the explanation of this riddle makes all these things so plain that we are not left to conjecture. For at the eleventh verse the prophet says: "Moreover, the word of the Lord came unto me, saying, Say now to the rebellious house, Know ye not what these things mean? Tell them, Behold the king of Babylon is come to Jerusalem, and hath taken the king thereof and the princes thereof, and led them to Babylon."

The king of Babylon was Nebuchadnezzar, as we know. The king of Jerusalem, and the princes thereof, were, as we also know, Zedekiah and his sons.

Then follows a brief account of Zedekiah's treachery with the king of Babylon, how he rebelled against him, and sent to the king of Egypt for help.

Then comes a prophecy concerning the fact that King Zedekiah shall die in Babylon.

After this comes the prophetic account of that band

of fugitives going to Egypt, and the declaration that they should fall by the sword, etc., all of which we have given in detail.

But the outcome of it all, and that which pertains to our immediate subject, begins again with the twenty-second verse. The prophet, still using the symbols of the riddle, explains as follows:

"Thus saith the Lord God, I will take of the highest branch of the high cedar, and will set it." This is the royal prince who came in Ship Number 1. He then proceeds to say: "I will crop off from the top of his young twigs a tender one, and will PLANT it upon a high mountain and eminent." This is the second importation of royal branches, but this time it is the "top" or one whose right it is to rule, a "tender one." That is, it is a tender young girl, the topmost one of the young twigs that came in Ship Number 2.

Where was she planted? "In the mountain of the height of Israel," is the Divine reply. "What, ISRAEL?" Yes, Israel, national Israel. Israel as a nation; but not Jewish-Israel, for that kingdom is overthrown; the people are gone into the Babylonish captivity; the king, with his eyes put out, is doomed to die in chains in a Babylonish prison; the princes are dead; the king's daughters have escaped out of Jerusalem; and the topmost one of these tender twigs is planted here in the *height* of the mountains of Israel, i. e., the THRONE.

"And it (that which was planted) shall bring forth boughs, and bear fruit, and be a goodly cedar: and under it shall dwell all fowl of every wing; in the shadow of the branches thereof shall they dwell." The

purport of this is so glaringly plain that the most
obtuse mind can see that it refers to the mixed population which Israel, of necessity, must have gathered
while being sifted through other countries.

The prophet further declares: "And all the trees
of the field, i. e., all the people of that kingdom of
Israel, "shall know that I, the Lord, have brought
down the HIGH tree, have exalted the LOW tree, have
dried up the green tree, and have made the dry tree
to flourish. I the Lord have spoken and DONE it."
(Ezek. 17:24.)

"Done what?" Brought down the HIGH from the
throne, and exalted the LOW to the throne.

"What else?" Made the long-foretold breach, remembered his covenant with David, and kept faith
with Jeremiah.

For, since these trees are the royal cedars, and the
male heirs of the former reigning line have been dethroned in favor of him that was low, who also is the
"spreading vine of LOW stature" of the riddle, and
who is now exalted by being enthroned, and since a
royal princess found her way to the land of the *"vine
of low stature"* and united her interests with his, "that
he might water the furrows of *her* plantation," we are
safe in saying that God has taken the crown from off
the head of Zedekiah, the high, who was of the Pharez
line, and has placed it on the head of a prince of Zarah,
the low, to whom Zedekiah's daughter, the heir to
crown and sceptre, made her way, in company with
Jeremiah, who had charge of the royal paraphernalia,

and who was divinely commissioned to plant and build anew the plucked-up and overthrown kingdom of David.

Christ came through the family line of Judah, David, Josiah and Jeconiah, not through the breach; the breach ran through Judah, David, Josiah and Zedekiah. So, the two branches of the Judo-Pharez-David line diverge at Josiah. One of these lines eventually gave birth to the Messiah; and, as we shall prove, the other line, after having been united to the brother line of the Scarlet Thread, are still holding that preserved throne and sceptre, and raising up seed unto their fathers, Judah and David; so that there shall never be a lack of some one of David's children to sit upon that throne as rulers over the seed of Abraham, Isaac and Jacob, and that the sceptre may not depart from Judah till SHILOH COME.

Thus it is that one of these lines holds that sceptre, and wears that crown as a fact, but the Judo-David house has a greater son to whom they belong by "RIGHT." When he comes, as Shiloh, God will give it to him, for unto him shall the gathering of the people be. At that time the breaches will be healed, and he shall be called "The Restorer of the BREACH."

The question now is to find where that sceptre and throne are today, for we are not only confronted with the question of "Lost Israel," or the *"Lost Birthright,"* which involves the whole house of Joseph and the many nations into which they were to develop; but we are also confronted with the question of THE LOST SCEPTRE which involves the Zedekiah branch of the house of David and all its Heraldic Blazonry.

PART THIRD.

THE VEIL LIFTED FROM THE ABRAHAMIC NATIONS.

"**If** I have told you of *earthly things*, and ye believe not, **how** shall ye believe if I tell you of *heavenly things?*"—Jesus.

CHAPTER I.

The fact that a great nation, composed of ten tribes of the posterity of Abraham, Isaac and Jacob, is lost, or unidentified, among the nations of the world is well known to enlightened students of the Old Testament. This truth has been a source of such great mystery that it has both puzzled the minds and engaged the interest of men to such an extent that many of them who are the intellectual peers of the world have bent their best energies to the work of hunting for this lost nation.

Thus, for many years, devout minds have been investigating secular and sacred history, as well as sacred prophecy, which must have become, or which must yet become, history. These men have carefully traced, not only the perfectly connected outlines, but also the details of history. Hence they confidently assert there are no missing links in the chain of racial and national events.

A large per cent. of the men who have been thus engaged are eminent in religious, historic and scientific research. Men who have called to their aid chronology, astronomy, archæology, ethnology, pyramidology and philology. Indeed, they have used any and every science that could throw any possible light upon this subject; for they have been irrepressible in their search after facts, and are men who purpose, for the truth's sake, that the Word of God shall be forced to stand every test, be it ever so crucial, that its own internal matter demands.

It is the consensus of opinion among this class of men, the number of whom is increasing daily, that the once-lost ten tribes of Israel are found. Be they right or wrong, we are sure of this one thing—namely, that there is a race of people here amidst other races, who do not know their ancestral origin, and who possess all the distinguishing marks whereby the Scriptures declare the lost house of Joseph shall be found and recognized, not only by themselves, but by the rest of the nations of the earth.

Still, be this as it may, there is nothing for us to do now but to take up the thread of our story, which is a *"scarlet"* one and pertains to those members of the royal family whom we left on the throne of Israel, and who were holding the sceptre of David *de facto*, instead of the one to whom it belongs *de jure*, and to whom the Lord will give "it," and not the Sceptre which belongs to some other royal family, race or kingdom.

While dealing with the breach which occurred in the royal family—which had been prophesied of, not only in the words which were uttered by the midwife, but by the peculiar manner of the birth of the Judo-Tamar twins, which also had been used as a prophetic type or symbol—we said nothing about the three over-turns which are a part of Ezekiel's prophecy concerning some of the chief details of this same breach.

One reason for this omission was that we could not give the proof concerning the location of that *"goodly land"* to which the royal branches, i. e., Judah's prince and David's princess, were carried, and in which they were "set," without making many points in proof of the present whereabouts of the still preserved seed, and the perpetuated Crown, Throne and Sceptre of David. For it was not our desire to give any such proof until we should first prove that the building and planting which Jeremiah's commission involved, had been accomplished, and that the transfer of the crown had been made, that the high branch had been dethroned, and that another branch—one equally high by birth, but "low," only in the sense of non-ruling, and because of the law of primogeniture—had been exalted by being enthroned.

Now, since we have shown that the Word of God emphatically declares these things to have been accomplished, we are prepared to show that the three prophetic overturns took place, and that they took place in connection with these same royal ones, together with their succession, whom we have followed to a new country.

It is not possible to follow the history of these overturns, nor to follow further the history of that branch of the royal family which came into power when the breach was made, and to do so independent of lost Israel; for it was to Israel that Jeremiah fled with the "king's daughters"—the same people with whom the royal line of Zarah had been for more than a century prior to the time when Jeremiah joined them, and since that time, nationally speaking, the fortunes and history of the Sceptre and Birthright have become one.

We must remember that the place where this prince

and princess were planted was in the "Height of Israel"; that it was all the trees in the field of Israel that were to know the low tree had been exalted; that it was Israel, the dry tree, which is made to flourish, and that has been dry hitherto for lack of royal honors and royal blood, but now that a prince and princess of the blood are on the throne, the once dry tree doth flourish, but the former green tree, the Jewish kingdom—not the nation—is dried up.

We must remember that Israel is the ten-tribed nation, the Birthright people, whose ancient capital was Samaria, whose representative name is Ephraim, the second son of Joseph, to whom pertains the birthright; and that his two sons, Ephraim and Manasseh, were to "grow into a multitude in the midst of the earth," that they were finally to separate, Manasseh to become a "great nation," and Ephraim to develop into many nations, a multitude of nations, or a company of nations, as it is variously given.

The first of these overturns is the one whose history we have essentially given while dealing with the preservation of King Zedekiah's daughters, and is the overturn of the kingdom from Palestine to that goodly land, by the side of great waters, where it took root, grew, flourished and became a spreading vine.

A ripple of holy joy went pulsing through our heart when we found that the prophet had, in his riddle, used the expression, *"spreading vine"* in connection with Israel. The Hebrew word, *sawrakh*—spreading, as here used, is defined in Strong's Exhaustive Concordance, "to extend, to spread, to stretch exceedingly, to extend even to excess." Thus this new country, this strange and unknown land, in which the royal remnant found the cast-out people of Israel, is the place from which it is declared that they shall spread out, that they shall exceedingly extend their borders and so fulfill their national destiny.

How perfectly this harmonizes with the promises concerning the "place" which the Lord made to David in connection with the promises concerning the perpetuity of his seed, throne and sceptre, and which was given at the same time, as follows: "Moreover, I will appoint a place for my people Israel, and will plant them, that they may dwell in a place of their own, and move no more; neither shall the children of wickedness afflict them any more, as beforetime."

At this juncture we feel impelled, for fear you will not think it out for yourselves, to point out the fact that the Lord had cast Israel out of her land, and cast her afar off; and while going to that far-off land she was to be "sifted through the nations as corn is sifted in a sieve"; but after they have reached their far-off destination, their God-appointed place, then they are to move no more. For it is in reference to this same casting out of the Ephraimic nation that Hosea declares: "The children of Israel shall abide many days without a king, and without a prince." But now, with this prophetic riddle fulfilled, their king is with them, and the monarchy of Israel is flourishing as a green, or living, tree.

Our next effort will be to find this far-off land, whose history has been one of spreading out—yea, spreading out exceedingly, even excessively.

The very fact that the Jews have a record of the birth, call and commission of Jeremiah, and the history of the execution of the first part of his commission, i. e., the tearing down, rooting out and plucking up of the house and throne of David—this, considered in the light of the fact that they can give no account of him after his sudden disappearance from among them, is evidence that he neither died nor completed his God-ordained task among them. And all the civilized races of the world know that he did not *build* that seat of power, nor *plant* those royal scions among the Jews.

But since we find it on record that Jeremiah's work has been accomplished, we know that it must have been he who did it; even if his name is not mentioned in the Scriptural account of the doing of it. For God would not permit some other man to do that work, after having sanctified Jeremiah before he was born, and brought him into the world for that purpose. We must bear in mind the fact that the sacred account of the building and planting is in the form of a riddle or parable, and that metaphors instead of names are used for those concerned; the *high* and the *low,* the *enthroned* and the *dethroned,* the *young twigs* and the *tender twigs,* the *planted* and the *planter.* But we must remember also that the name of "Israel," the special national name of the ten-tribed kingdom, is mentioned as the receiver of the planted and enthroned pair. And since the historic testimony declares Jeremiah's work to have been accomplished in Israel, it is only in Israel that we may hope to find evidences of that fact.

This necessitates the finding of Joseph-Israel, and they shall be found, for God says they shall; and when they are found, manifestly, there must be found with them a branch of the Judo-Davidic family, who are their sovereigns.

Since the East is left in such utter darkness, not only as to the fate of Jeremiah and his little Royal Remnant, but also as to the destination of "the dispersed" ten tribes, who had been lost, even to the Jews, so long before Christ came, that some of them thought that no person except the Messiah could go to them, or might even know where to find them, we must look elsewhere. Also, because of their lack of historic data concerning the completion of Jeremiah's work, and because his disappearance was almost as marvelous as was the translation of Elijah, they were ready to say that the Christ was Jeremiah. (Matt. 16:14.) Their thought was, no doubt, that Jeremiah, like Elijah, was still alive, and that God would yet use him in connection with the building and planting anew, or the restoration of the kingdom among them, to which they looked forward with great anticipation and hope.

But, as we were saying, since there is no light in the East concerning these matters, let us scan the pages of prophecy to see if there are any straws which point West. And since it is said of straws that they show which way the wind blows, it will be well for us to know that Hosea gives a prophecy concerning Ephraim, in which he declares: "Ephraim, followeth after an East wind." As an East wind is one which blows from the East and travels to the West, this makes it certain that Ephraim did not travel Eastward. For had he gone in an Easterly direction, he must needs have gone facing an East wind; then he surely went WEST. And since he was "cast afar off," he must be in the far-off West.

When Jehovah confirmed his promise to David concerning the perpetuity of his kingdom, throne, sceptre and house, and took oath by his holiness that he would not lie to him, he said: "I will set his hand (sceptre) in the sea." The clues which the prophet Ezekiel gives in his riddle, as to the location of Israel and the royal pair, are, that it is "a land of traffic," that it has "good soil" and that it "brings forth branches"; that is, that it is fruitful and populous. We are told it has a "city of merchants," that "fowl of every wing dwell under the shadow of its branches," i. e., mixed, or various people dwell under the protection of its rulers; and that its location is by "great waters," which, for reasons that will become more and more apparent as we proceed, we affirm to be the Atlantic Ocean. For the Lord gives a message to Ephraim through Jeremiah, saying: "I am a father to Israel, and Ephraim is my first born. Hear the word of the Lord, O ye nations, and declare it in the isles afar off, and say, He that scattered Israel will gather him." In this declaration we find that the far-off home of Ephraim-Israel is in, not an island, but "the isles," i. e., a group of islands. Thus Ephraim, also, is located in the sea, in the isles afar off.

The prophet Isaiah, in the forty-ninth chapter, addresses these same people, saying: "Listen, O isles, unto me; and hearken, ye people from afar. * * * Thou art my servant, O Israel, in whom I will (still in the future) be glorified." And when speaking, in the twelfth verse of this same chapter concerning the future return of this same people to Palestine, their former home, at which time he will be more fully glorified in them, the Lord causes the prophet to make proclamation: Behold, these shall come from far off, and lo, these from the north and from the west."

In the Hebrew there is no compound word for north-west as we use it; hence the expression north and west. There is a group of isles out in these *"great waters,"* which are just as directly north-west from Palestine as the lines of latitude and longitude can lay them, namely, the British Isles. And we may just as well jump into the midst of our proofs at once, since that is the place where Ephraim-Israel shall chiefly be found. If not there, it is because they have "spread out," from these VERY ISLES, for it is a well-authenticated fact that Jeremiah went to Ireland, where he died, and that his grave is one of the well-known and proudly-named spots of that country, whose history is one of the mysteries of the world.

It is a well-known fact that the history of no country on the face of the earth has so puzzled historians as that of Ireland. There is both a sacred and secular reason for this. The secular reason is that Ireland steps into the arena of history with a monarchical kingdom running in full blast, and men do not know how it got there. The sacred reason is because God has issued a mandate, saying: "KEEP SILENCE before me, O islands, and let the people renew their strength." (Isa. 41:1.)

In the next verse the Lord asks the question: "Who raised up the righteous man from the EAST?" Then in the fourth verse he answers his own question, saying, "I the Lord, the first, and the last; I am he," and in the eighth verse of the same chapter, still addressing the dwellers in the isles, he says: "Thou art Israel, my servant Jacob, whom I have chosen, the seed of Abraham my friend. Thou whom I have taken from the ends of the earth." i. e., literally, from the rising of the sun, from the beginning, or from the East.

This statement, coming from such high authority, forever settles the question as to the origin of the peoples who dwell in those far-off northwest isles.

We have read many authors on the subject of the Hebrews in Ireland, who claim to have searched carefully and critically through all available chronicles, records and histories and they all agree that a perusal of these various authorities is not only heavy reading, but that they are very obtuse, and that they are actually confusing, bewildering and tormenting to all who do not take the word of God as an ally in the work of unraveling their mysteries; for, all of these authorities do agree in stating the following facts:

1. About 585 B. C. a "notable man," an "important personage," a patriarch, a saint, an essentially important someone, according to their various ways of putting it, came to Ulster, the most northern province of Ireland, accompanied by a princess, the daughter of an eastern king, and that in company with them was one Simon Brach, Breck, Brack, Barech, Berach, as it is differently spelled; and that this royal party brought with them many remarkable things. Among these was

the harp, an ark and the wonderful stone called Liafail, or stone of destiny, of which we shall have much
to say hereafter.

2. This eastern princess was married to King Herremon on condition, made by this notable patriarch, that
he should abandon his former religion, and build a
college for the prophets. This Herremon did, and the
name of the school was Mur-Ollam, which is the name,
both in Hebrew and Irish, for school of the prophets.
He also changed the name of his capital city, Lothair
—sometimes spelled Cothair Croffin—to that of Tara.

3. The name of this Eastern princess is given as
Tea-Tephi, and it is a well-known fact that the royal
arms of Ireland is the harp of David, and has been for
two thousand and five hundred years.

Ezekiel in his riddle, when speaking of the coming
of the female passenger who came to that land in the
second vessel, whom he afterwards proves to be a
princess, speaks of "the furrows of her plantation." It
is a truth, and, to us, a marvelous one, that the province of Ulster used to be called the "Plantation of
Ulster," as any one may know if they will take the
trouble to consult Chamber's Encyclopedia on the word
Ulster.

Further, the crown which was worn by the sovereigns of that hitherto unaccounted-for kingdom in Ireland *had twelve points.* Who shall say that "the king's
daughter" was not planted there; and that the first
of the three of Ezekiel's prophetic overturns was not
from Palestine to Erin?

CHAPTER II.

JACOB'S PILLOW-PILLAR STONE.

When the Abrahamic covenant promises were given to Jacob, he was making a journey from Beersheba to Padan-aram. He had but recently received from his father Isaac the *"Blessing,"* which carried with it those much desired covenants and the special blessings and promises which pertained to them. When Isaac gave this blessing to Jacob, he told him not to take a wife of the daughters of Canaan, the land in which they were then living, but to go to Laban, his mother's brother, and to take a wife from among his daughters.

It is hardly to be supposed that Jacob was traveling entirely alone, for that was not the Oriental custom. We learn, from incidental remarks that are dropped elsewhere in reference to this journey, that he had with him a tent which was pitched at night, and that the journey was made on foot, for he walked with a staff. The sacred record deals chiefly with that which took place between Jacob and the Lord, with but the slightest incidental mention of details, as concerning a certain sundown, and stones for pillows. The first mention of stones for pillows, with reference to this occasion, is plural; but suddenly one of those pillow stones is brought into great distinction.

The facts which brought that special stone into such prominence may be quickly read, for the Bible account of them is very short; but we doubt whether many who have read the record of those facts realize their true symbolic import. We doubt also whether we shall be able to explain, even approximately, not only the great distinction which has been bestowed upon that stone as a symbol, but also the exalted place it has occupied ever since it came into historic notice, or the supreme greatness of that position to which prophecy declares it shall yet be raised. If we read the prophets aright, no such glorious prominence, highly-honored use, or divinely-declared purpose, has ever been given to any other inanimate thing on the earth, as that which is yet in reserve for that special pillow stone upon which Jacob rested his head on that certain night, when he camped before Luz, while on his way to Padan-aram.

It seems to have been the custom among Oriental travelers, when they pitched their tents for the night, to take stones for headpieces, or bolsters, in order to raise that part of their bedding on which their heads rested to a comfortable position for rest and sleep. At least, this is what Jacob did, and as he slept, he dreamed. In his dream he saw what is called a ladder, but which may be called a staircase, or an open way that reached from earth to heaven, for "the top of it reached to heaven." The angels of God were ascending and descending by this existing way, which for the time was made visible to the inheritor of the covenant promises; and, at the top, above all that throng of radiant comers and goers, the Lord stood, and gave Jacob the full text of the covenants, as formerly given to Abraham and Isaac.

Upon hearing and receiving these promises from the Lord, Jacob awoke, startled, convicted and afraid; startled because, as he thought, he had accidentally got into God's house, and stumbled through the gate which led away from this world to that pure one of which he had just caught a glimpse; afraid, just as any man would be who had defrauded his brother, and taken advantage of the love and confidence of a blind and aged father; convicted! It could not have been otherwise, for he had caught a glimpse of the holiness of God and the purity of a sinless world. Hence, in the agony of that psychical fear, which must ever be experienced by the wicked when brought in contact with absolute holiness, he cried out, *"How dreadful is this place! This is none other but the house of God, and this is the gate of heaven."*

That which would have been a great joy to a holy man was only a means of torture to this sinful one, who was fleeing from the anger of an outraged brother. But he soon began to yield himself to God, and as he yielded there came to him that ever accompanying desire, i. e., the desire to worship. With these things there came also spiritual intuitions of coming events, and of their importance to him in his relations to the divine covenants. Then Jacob, awed by the sublime majesty of the Holy One, deeply impressed by the greatness of the promises made to him, stirred in the depths of his inner nature by the heavenly vision, pressed by the weight of responsibility, yet encouraged by the dawning gladness in his heart, and moved by the spirit of prophecy, took the stone upon which his head had rested, and set it up for a pillar of witness.

At the same time he anointed it with oil, called it Bethel, used it for an altar at which to worship, and upon which to make a vow unto the Lord God of his fathers, saying: "If God will be with me, and keep me in this way that I go, and will give me bread to eat, and raiment to put on, so that I come again to my father's house in peace; then shall the Lord be my God: and this stone, which I have set for a pillar, shall be God's house: and of all that thou shalt give me, I will surely give the tenth unto thee."

It is a most significant fact that the name Bethel, or God's house, should have been given to this stone by the one who was the father of the twelve patriarchs, who were the progenitors of that great multitude which is also called "The House of God," "The Host of God" and "The Families of God." Also in the eighty-third psalm, The House of Israel, the Hidden Ones, which, while hidden, are to develop into many nations, are called "The Houses of God."

We must bear in mind the fact that Jacob gave the name of Bethel not only to the place, or locality, where the stone was set up, but also to the stone pillar, for he emphatically declared: "*This stone*, which I have set for a pillar, *shall be God's house.*" We understand, however, that God inspired both the choice of this stone and its name, for when he next spoke to Jacob he said: "I am the God of Bethel." That means, I am the God of *God's house;* or, in other words, the God of the Bethel stone which is in the place called Bethel. Thus the Lord associates himself not only with the place where he appeared to Jacob, but also with the Bethel rock.

Twenty years later Jacob returned to the land of Canaan with great riches, and with the knowledge that his prosperity was the result of divine favor and intervention; for the Lord had shown him how one who is called "The Angel of God" was given power to control the breeding of the cattle. Thus Jacob was made to know that God had accepted and met all the conditions which he had made to him by vow on the Bethel pillow-pillar stone.

Before Jacob reached Canaan he had confessed his wrongdoings, and made peace with his brother; and God had taken away from him not only the name of supplanter, but also the inborn supplanter nature, and given him the victorious name of Israel.

It is a well-known fact that the place called Bethel and the city of Luz were so near each other that the two names are used interchangeably in the Scriptures, or rather that the name Bethel often included the little city, which was previously called Luz. But before we can understand the true relation of both Bethel and the Bethel rock to our general subject, we must know to whom, or to which one of the tribes, Bethel was given as a possession.

The sacred historian, when describing the boundaries of the *"lot"* in Canaan which fell to Joseph, describes one of those border lines as follows: "And (it) goeth out from Bethel to Luz, and passeth along unto the borders of Archi to Astaroth." (Josh. 16:2.) Also, in the description of that portion which fell to the children of Benjamin—their portion lay between Judah and Joseph, Judah being to the south, and Joseph to the north of Benjamin—we have the following: "And the border went over from thence (Beth-aven) toward Luz, to the side of Luz, which is Bethel, southward." (Josh. 18:13.) From this we perceive, not only that Benjamin's border was south of Bethel, but also that Bethel, the place where Jacob set up the Bethel pillar-stone, was on the south side of the city proper.

Further, it is recorded that the children of Dan could not conquer the Amorites, but that the Amorites drove them into the mountains, and occupied those portions of Dan's inheritance which best suited them. But it is also recorded that the house of Joseph did conquer those Amorites, that they compelled them to become their dependents, and that they fixed their boundary lines. In the description of these boundaries we have the following: "And the coast of the Amorites was from the going up to Akrabbim, *from the rock,* and upward." (Judges 1:36.) Some may think that this reference to the rock refers to the rock Etam, or Etam-rock. This is not possible, because both Etam, the city, and the rock Etam are southwest of Jerusalem in the hill country of Judea, and had nothing whatever to do with the borders of Joseph, Dan or the Amorites. Hence the phrases, "from the rock and upward," can mean only Bethel, the place of the rock, or, from the BETHEL ROCK, and up into the mountains of Eph-raim-Samaria-Israel.

Again, concerning the house of Joseph, Bethel and Luz, we have the following: And the house of Joseph, they also went up against Bethel and the Lord was with them. And the house of Joseph sent to descry Bethel. (Now the name of the city was Luz.) And the spies saw a man come forth out of the city, and they said unto him: Shew us, we pray thee, the entrance into the city, and we will shew thee mercy. And when he shewed them the entrance into the city, they smote the city with the edge of the sword; but they let go the man and all his family. And the man went into the land of the Hittites, and built a city, and called the name thereof of Luz." (Judges 1:22-26.) Thus, with the building of that other Luz, the name of Luz not only departed forever from Bethel, but it is never again mentioned in sacred history.

Finally, when Jeroboam, of the house of Joseph, was made king of the ten tribes, and became fearful that the people would, if allowed to go up to Jerusalem to worship, kill him, and go again to Rehoboam, king of Judah, he, to prevent this, made two golden calves, of which it is said: "He set the one in Bethel, and the other put he in Dan." His right to place one in Bethel was undisputed, because it was not only "the king's sanctuary," but it was also in his own tribal territory. He had a sovereign's right to place one in Dan, for all who went there to worship were confederate with him. The Dan referred to was the city of Dan, which was situated in the northern part of his realm.

Now, one point is settled beyond the possibility of doubt, and that is, that Bethel was a part of the inheritance which fell to the house of Joseph when the land of Canaan was divided among the children of Jacob. This brings us to a vital point concerning the subject in hand, namely:

That not only Bethel, the city, or place, but also that Bethel the pillar-rock was given to the birthright family; and that Israel carried that rock with them into

Egypt and in their subsequent journeyings in the wilderness.

Proof: Jacob died in Egypt, and his posterity were in Egypt at the time. When dying, "Jacob called unto him his sons and said, Gather yourselves together, that I may tell you that which shall befall you in the last days." When his sons, in response to this call, came together, he gave a prophecy concerning that which the posterity of each of them would be in the last days. But while he was making the prophecy concerning Joseph and his house, to whom he had just given the birthright, he stopped in the midst of his prophetic utterances, and used the following parenthetical expression: "(from thence is the shepherd, the stone of Israel:)"

"Thence," as herein used, is an adverb used as a noun, and is equivalent in value to *that place,* or the place to which it refers. The phrase, *from thence,* means "out of there, out from thither, (or) out of that place. Since the place from whence* the stone came was the inheritance of Joseph, and since Bethel, the place of the stone, was the inheritance of Joseph, we must know that it came *from thence,* i. e., Bethel. Thus, the very fact that Jacob, when dying in Egypt, made use of those words in reference to that Bethel stone, carries proof on its very face that the stone was not, at that time, in the place where it had formerly been, but that it was with them there in Egypt, and had previously been committed to the care of the house of Joseph.

---

*Whence, present form of the old word *thence.*

It has been estimated that the number of the Israelites which came out of Egypt in the exodus were two millions and a half. All who will take time to think will soon comprehend how impossible it would be, even for a fertile country, much less a desert, to supply such a multitude, as well as their cattle, of which not a hoof was left behind, with food and water unless special arrangements were made for an extra supply. But in this case, as a matter of course, that was not done; hence it became necessary for God to furnish the supply of food and water for that vast concourse of people, and also for their herds and flocks.

It is a well-known fact that the Lord continually provided food for Israel during these forty years of wanderings in the desert-wilderness. But, because there are only two instances recorded in which the Lord supernaturally provided them with water, most people think these were the only instances in which water was thus provided. Yet, all who will give the subject just a little investigation will soon know that such is not the case.

The first mention of no water for the people to drink was while the Israelites were encamped at Rephidim. Without previously selecting one special rock, the Lord said unto Moses: "I will stand before thee there upon *the rock* in Horeb, and thou shalt smite *the rock,* and there shall come water out of it." The phrase, "There in Horeb," points out the place where the rock was at the time, and if the Lord, when he spoke of the rock, had used the demonstrative form, and said "That rock," then we should know that he was designating which one, or a certain one not yet selected, but the

fact that he said *"The rock"* is proof to us that he was speaking of a rock with which they were already familiar. May it not have been the Bethel pillar rock, *"the* shepherd, *the* stone of Israel," which had been committed to the keeping of the house of Joseph?

This possibility is more clearly manifest in the account of the other circumstances when there was no water, which occurred at Kadish, a city in the border of Edom, the country which belonged to the descendants of Esau. At this place the people of Israel were very bitter against Moses and Aaron, and said unto them, "Why have ye brought up the congregation of the Lord into this wilderness, that we and our cattle should die there? And wherefore have ye made us to come up out of Egypt, to bring us into this evil place? It is no place of seed, or of figs, or of vines, or of pomegranites; neither is there any water to drink. And Moses and Aaron went from the presence of the assembly unto the door of the tabernacle of the congregation, and they fell upon their faces, and the glory of the Lord appeared unto them.

"And the Lord spake unto Moses, saying: Take the rod, and gather the assembly together, and speak ye unto *the rock* before their eyes; and it shall give forth his water, and thou shalt bring forth to them water out of the *rock;* so thou shalt give the congregation and their beasts drink. And Moses took the rod from before the Lord, as he commanded him. And Moses and Aaron gathered the congregation together before *the rock,* and he said unto them: Hear now, ye rebels; must we fetch water out of *this rock?* And Moses lifted up his hand, and with his rod he smote *the rock* twice: and the water came out abundantly, and the congregation drank, and their beasts also." (Num. 20:5-11.)

We have quoted this account in full, from the beginning of the complaint by the people until the water was given, that our readers may see that, although the phrase "the rock" is used four times, there is not the slightest indication that there was any selection, or indication of preference for any certain rock in the vicinity of Kadish, or that one was not already chosen, and in their midst. It was to show also that at the very first mention of water for the people from "this rock," all that was necessary, as a preparatory measure, was for the Lord to say to Moses, "Speak to the rock"; and also that when the people were commanded to "gather before *the rock*," they understood so well which rock it was that, in all that vast company of two and a half millions, no explanations were necessary. Hence, it must have been among them before this, and well known. Let us also bear in mind that this name, *"The Rock,"* was used in the same relation at Rephidim, and yet the children of Israel had removed, journeyed and pitched their tents twenty-one* times after leaving Rephidim, and here at Kadish there is with them that which is still familiarly known as "THE ROCK."

We all know that stones are rocks, and that rocks are stones, so that a rock or stone is only one rock or stone, and the appellation "The Rock," and "The Stone," must refer to some special or particular stone or rock. As we have seen, Israel must have been in

---

*See Numbers, 33d chapter.

possession of just such a special rock, i. e., the Bethel stone, and that Jacob set it up and called it a "Pillar." Later, in the days of Athaliah, after she tried to destroy all the males of "the seed royal," but did not succeed, for the reason that an infant son of Ahaziah, whom Athaliah succeeded to the throne, was stolen from those whom she had ordered slain and hidden. The stealing and hiding of this infant was so cleverly done that it was not missed by the court slayer. This infant, whose name was Joash was kept hidden from the wicked queen for six years. During this time she reigned, not knowing that there was a male heir to the throne who could dethrone her. But in the seventh year the secret was revealed to the "rulers over hundreds," and to "the captains of the guards," and quiet arrangements made to proclaim the seven-year-old prince as their king. The plans were successful, and Athaliah knew nothing of it until she heard the people in the temple shouting "God save the king!"

Thus it is recorded: "And when Athaliah heard the noise of the guard and of the people, she came to the people into the temple of the Lord. And when she looked, behold! the king stood by a pillar, as the manner was." (2 Kings 11: 13-14.) Concerning this pillar, Dr. Adam Clark's translation reads, "Stood on a pillar," which he explains is "The place or throne on which they were accustomed to put their kings when they proclaimed them." But in the revised version it is rendered, "Standing by the pillar, as was their custom," the article denoting that particular pillar by, or upon, which it was the custom of Israel to crown their kings.

Again, when the good king Josiah made a covenant before the Lord, in the presence of all the people, that he would destroy idolatry out of the land, it is written, "And the king stood by a (or the) pillar and made a covenant before the Lord." (2 Kings 23: 3.) There is, in the Second Chronicles, a recapitulation of this circumstance concerning Josiah, which gives the following, "And the king stood in his place." His place, we are told, was by the pillar, which might properly be translated *pillar-stone,* upon which all the kings of Israel were crowned, made covenants, took oaths, or made vows, as did Jacob when he first set it up for a pillar and made it God's house.

This stone is not only called "The Pillar," "The Rock," "Bethel," and "The Stone of Israel," but, wonderful to tell, it is also called "The Shepherd." And since it is really *the stone of Israel* we should expect it to be with them to whom it belonged, but since it is also *the Shepherd of Israel,* its very name and character,—for with God names are always characteristic—demand that it should be with Israel in all their wanderings. Hence, *this* SHEPHERD—though it is only a stone—as any other shepherd would do, must go with His flock.

We have said that this stone of Israel, was a type, or symbol. For proof, let us go back to the place called Bethel. There we shall find that Jacob, after setting up "The Rock" for a pillar, also anointed it with oil, which in sacred symbols is typical of the Holy Ghost. And, according to sacred history, this Bethel stone is the only single, individual stone that has ever been anointed; hence, among stones it is pre-eminently

"the Anointed One." When Christ, the great prototype, came, and was anointed with the Holy Ghost,
he was pre-eminently, among men, *"the Anointed
One."*

Also, concerning "The rock" which accompanied
Israel, the Lord could say to Israel's leader, *"Speak
to* THE ROCK." But, on the other hand, Israel also
could say, concerning that divine presence which went
with them, *"Let us sing unto* THE ROCK of our salvation."

Again, this stone is called *"The Shepherd of Israel."*
But there is also a divine one unto whom Israel
prayed, saying, "Give ear, *O Shepherd of Israel."*
Later, when this same Shepherd was manifest in the
flesh, he said, "I am the *Good Shepherd,"* and his
apostles spoke of him as "The Great Shepherd" and
"The Chief Shepherd." Hence, the oft-repeated metaphor of "sheep" and "flock," in both the Old and the
New Testaments.

Further, Israel had a pillar-rock, which went with
them as their shepherd in all their journeyings in the
wilderness; but it is also written that "The Lord went
before them by day in A PILLAR of a cloud, to lead them
in the way; and by night in A PILLAR of fire, to give
them light!"

Still further, that the Scriptures might be fulfilled,
Israel's divine Shepherd-rock was smitten, for it is
written, "Smite the Shepherd." So, too, Israel's literal Shepherd-rock was smitten. The Lord knew that
he must be smitten for the sins of the people, and, that
the type and prototype might agree, he gave command,
"Smite the rock." Oh, the pain of it all!—especially

to him; but he shall yet see the desire of his heart, i. e., his emotional nature, his soul, and be satisfied.

It is also said of Israel that they "Did all drink the same spiritual drink, for they drank of that *Spiritual Rock* that followed them, and that *Rock* was Christ." It is also true that they did all drink from the same refreshing stream which flowed from that *literal* Rock which also went with them, for it was their Shepherd-rock. No doubt Israel was supplied with water from this rock in the wilderness, as well as at Rephidim and Kadish, for the country between these two places is much more desert than these cities. At Kadish Moses sent messengers to the king of Edom, asking permission for the Lord's host to pass through his country, and told them to say, "Thus saith thy brother Israel, Let us pass, I pray thee, through thy country: we will not pass through the fields, or through the vineyards, *neither will we drink of the water of the wells;* we will go by the king's highway; we will not turn to the right hand nor to the left, until we have passed thy borders. * * * If I and my cattle drink of thy water, then I will pay for it: I will only, without doing anything else, go through on my feet."

Just imagine a company of two and one-half million traveling on foot through a country which is several hundred miles in length, giving assurance to its ruler that they would keep to the highway, and not turn to the right and left, for any reason, nor drink water out of the wells (i. e., pits, fountains, springs, or wells; literally their water supply) of that country. Israel could afford to make this proposition, for both their Shepherd-rocks were with them, i. e., the literal and the spiritual rock, and they knew that he, who had hitherto furnished them with food and water, would still continue to supply them until the end of the journey. Otherwise Moses would never have made such a promise.

True, there was a conditional promise made, in which there is a promise to pay for any of the water of Edom which might be used. But this, as you see, was made chiefly, if not altogether, on account of the cattle, which they might not be able to control and keep to the dusty highways, while passing by the cool and tempting pools and springs of water. This might prove to be a difficult task for the drovers, especially in the heat of the day; hence this proviso. They were not supposed to get water from the rock until they had completed their day's journey and pitched their tents.

Thus we have seen that among the Israelites there were two rocks, two houses, two kingdoms, two nations, or a Sceptre and a Birthright company. Of these two great divisions, Judah and Joseph are the representatives. By divine appointment one of these rocks was given to the Birthright family, and the other to the Sceptre family. The Bethel-Pillar-Shepherd-Stone of Israel was given to Joseph, but to Judah was given the Spiritual Rock, for it is written that "Our LORD sprang out of Judah." BOTH OF THESE ROCKS, each in a different way, HAVE BEEN REJECTED, but EACH OF THEM SHALL YET BECOME THE HEAD OF THE CORNER.

CHAPTER III.

THE OTHER OVERTURNS.

In connection with the prophecies concerning the removal of the crown of David from the head of Zedekiah to the head of a prince who belonged to the hitherto non-ruling branch of the royal family of Israel's race, the Lord said, "I will overturn, overturn, overturn it; and it shall be no more (moved or overturned) until he comes whose right it is; and I will give it to him." These words teach that, after the removal of David's crown from the head of the then ruling prince, there were to be three overturns—no more, no less—and that after the third overturn the crown must rest, or stay in the place where it is left by the third overturn, until that person comes to whom it belongs by right. Then at least one more overturn will be necessary, for that seat of power must yet go back to the city of David.

The first of these overturns we have already traced from Palestine to the islands of the north-west, which are in the "great waters." We now propose to show that the other two of these predicted overturns took place in those self-same islands, or, in other words, that these three overturns landed the sceptre and throne alternately in Ireland, Scotland and England; and that, even after the third overturn, the kingdom is still, as the word of God declares, "in the isles afar off," and "in the sea."

It will be impossible to follow the history of the overturns of this kingdom, unless we again take up the thread of history as it concerns the pillar stone, upon which the kings of Israel were crowned; for, strange as it may seem to some people, both ancient and modern history come honestly to the rescue of prophecy, and follow that stone through each of these overturns.

We have already seen, according to Josephus, that, prior to the return of the Jews from Babylon, Ezra (Esdras) received a letter from Xerxes, which was so full of offered favors, love, and fraternal greetings, that he sent a copy of it to the ten tribes in Media-Persia, and asked them to return with the Jews to Jerusalem. But the ten tribes refused this offer, and Josephus tells us that the entire body of Israel remained in that country. On the other hand, Ezra (Esdras), who was in a position to know more about them, says that they decided not to return, and also that they took counsel among themselves, and resolved that they would go further away into an unknown country. In accomplishing this, Esdras says, "They entered into Euphrates by the narrow passages of the river. For the Most High then shewed signs for them, and held still the waters till they were passed over. For through that country there was a great way to go, namely, of a year and a half." This is in harmony with the following: "The breaker is come up before them; they have broken up, and have passed through the gate and are gone out of it, and their king shall pass before them; and the Lord on the head of them." (Micah 2:13.)

The clause, "They have passed through the gate," and the one by Ezra, "They have entered into the narrow passages," are parallel, and refer to the same circumstance and place. This *gate*, or *narrow passage*, which is up among the headwaters of the Euphrates, is now called the Caucasian Pass, or the Pass of Dariel. As Israel goes out through this pass, Micah says that the Lord is on the head of them, but it is left for Ezra to say that the Lord gave Israel evidence of his presence, because he gave them signs and held still the floods, as he did at Jordan, until they passed over.

But while the Lord is with Israel, it is said of their king that he shall pass before, or precede them to that unknown country to which they are going. It is for this reason that Hosea says, "The children of Israel shall abide many days without a king, and without a sacrifice, and *without an image*," or, as the marginal reading gives it, "*without a standing pillar*." Young, in his Exhaustive Concordance, gives among other definitions of the original Hebrew word, both that of *memorial stone* and *pillar*. Other scholarly men who have investigated this text, in connection with its context, even give us *pillar-rock* and *pillar-stone* as the correct rendering.

All this, supplemented by the fact that the word of God associates the absent king with the absent pillar-stone, justifies our conclusion, that the pillar in question is the Bethel pillar stone which was used as a coronation stone, consequently it was left with the royal family which ruled over the Jews until the overthrow of Zedekiah.

We must also remember that Jeremiah and his little remnant were taken, against their will, and against the direct command of God, to Egypt, and that while there they dwelt in Taphanhes. Morton W. Spencer says, "It is an undeniable historical fact that about 580 B. C. (i. e., the very time of the captivity of the Jews in Babylon), that a princess from the East did arrive in the north of Ireland. Her name was Tephi, a pet name like "Violet," denoting beauty, fragrance. Tea Tephi was her full name, found in Hebrew. The Tea, a *little* one, and Tephi answering to a surname. *Taph,* the root word, is used in many scriptures (Gen. 34:29, and Deut. 1:39) (*Vide* Concordance). Her names were interchangeably used as Tea, Taffe, Taffes, Tephi, the Eastern Princess, the Daughter of Pharaoh, and Tea Tephi; either of these serve to identify her as "The King's Daughter." In Egypt she was offered protection, and from her the city of Taphanhes or Dahpnæ was named, doubtless, and to this day we are shown the site of "The Palace of the Jew's Daughter," by the Arabs. The fact that she fled the country is still preserved in her name, Tarah, meaning one banished or flight.

The name of Pharaoh is neither a given nor a surname, but it is the Egyptian name for king or monarch. The very fact that Irish historians called Tea Tephi "The Daughter of Pharaoh" is proof that they knew her as "The King's Daughter." Also this name, "The King's Daughter," is the only one used in the Bible account of the first overturn to designate that daughter of Zedekiah who succeeded him to the inheritance of David's throne, excepting, of course, that metaphorical name, "Tender twig," of Ezekiel's riddle. Since the name Tea means *"little one,"* and since a *tender twig* is also a *little one,* it certainly takes no great stretch of faith to believe that these two names belong to one and the same person. Especially is this the case when we consider that in the Tea Tephi of Irish history we have a king's daughter, with a Hebrew name, who not only came from the East, but also from Egypt, and who is the daughter of a Jew.

But there are still other facts connected with the arrival of this princess in Ireland, which, as we consider them, will strengthen our faith more and more. Tea Tephi was accompanied by an aged guardian, who was called *Ollam Folla,* more Hebrew words which mean revealer, or prophet. The prophet was accompanied by a man who was his scribe, whom the chronicles of Ireland called Brug, or Bruch. Baruch was Jeremiah's scribe while they were in Judea; he went with the little remnant to Egypt, and escaped when the rest did; for his life, like the lives of the rest of his party, was to be preserved in all places whither he should go. This little company disappeared from Egypt, but surely they reappeared in Ireland, for, marvel of marvels! they brought with them a pillar-stone, which has ever since been used as the *coronation stone of the kingdom.*

Later, Tea (sometimes spelled Teah) Tephi herself was crowned upon this pillar-stone, and the name of Erin's capital was changed from Cathair Crofin to Tara, which is also another Hebrew word. But at this juncture history comes to our help, and with unquestioned authority declares that, from that time until the present, every king and queen who has reigned in Ireland, Scotland or England has been crowned upon that self-same pillar or coronation stone. Queen Victoria herself was twice crowned upon that stone, the first time as Queen of England, and the second time as Empress of India.

On the occasion of Queen Victoria's coronation, June 28th, 1837, an article appeared in the London *Sun*, which gives a description of the coronation chair and the coronation stone, as follows: "This chair, commonly called St. Edward's chair, is an ancient seat of solid hardwood, with back and sides of the same, variously painted, in which the kings of Scotland were in former periods constantly crowned, but, having been brought out of the kingdom by Edward I, in the year 1296, after he had totally overcome John Baliol, king of Scots, it has ever since remained in the Abbey of Westminster, and has been the chair in which the succeeding kings and queens of this realm have been inaugurated. It is in height six feet and seven inches, in breadth at the bottom thirty-eight inches, and in depth twenty-four inches; from the seat to the bottom is twenty-five inches; the breadth of the seat within the sides is twenty-eight inches, and the depth eighteen inches. At nine inches from the ground is a board, supported at the four corners by as many lions. Between the seat and this board is enclosed a stone, commonly called Jacob's, or the fatal Marble, Stone, which is an oblong of about twenty-two inches in length, thirteen inches broad and eleven inches deep; of a steel color, mixed with some veins of red. History relates that it is the stone whereon the patriarch Jacob laid his head in the plains of Luz." This, as you see, was published more than sixty years ago, before it was thought possible that the Anglo-Saxons were the descendants of Joseph, the inheritor of the birthright blessing which God gave to his fathers, Abraham, Isaac and Jacob.

This article further says that "this stone was conveyed into Ireland by way of Spain about 700 years before Christ. From there it was taken into Scotland by King Fergus, about 370 years later; and in the year 350 B. C., it was placed in the abbey of Scone, by King Kenneth, who caused a prophetical verse to be engraved upon it, of which the following is a translation:

" 'Should fate not fail, where'er this stone is found,
The Scots shall monarch of that realm be crowned.'

"This antique regal chair, having (together with the golden sceptre and crown of Scotland) been solemnly offered by King Edward I. to St. Edward the Confessor, in the year 1297 (from whence it derives the appellation of St. Edward's chair), has ever since been kept in the chapel called by his name; with a tablet affixed to it, whereon several Latin verses are written, in old English characters. * * * The stone maintains its usual place under the seat of the chair."

Prior to the time that King Kenneth had his verse engraved on that Coronation Stone, there was a

prophetic verse which had attached itself to it, which
Sir Walter Scott has rendered, one word excepted, as
follows:

"Unless the fates are faithless grown,
 And prophet's voice be vain,
Where'er is found this sacred stone
 The Wanderers' Race shall reign."

Think of it! For more than seven hundred years this
stone has been in Westminster Abbey. Dean Stanley,
in his "Memorials of Westminster Abbey," says: "The
chief object of attraction, to this day, to the innumerable visitors to the Abbey, is probably that ancient
Irish monument of the empire known as the *Coronation
Stone.*" He calls it a "Precious Relic," and says that
King Edward I. said that "It is the one primeval monument which binds together the whole empire." The
Dean further adds: "The iron rings, the battered surface, the crack, which has all but rent its solid mass
asunder, bear witness to its long migrations. It is
thus embedded in the heart of the English monarchy,
an element of poetic, patriarchal, heathen times,
which like Araunah's threshing floor in the midst of
the temple of Solomon carries back our thoughts to
races and customs now almost extinct, a link which
unites the throne of England with the traditions of
Tara and Iona, and connects the charm of our complex
civilization with the favors of Mother Earth, the stocks
and stones of savage nature. Faithful or foolish, the
sentiment of the nation has, through three hundred generations of living men, made it *felt* that Jacob's Pillar
Stone was a thing worth dying for in battle. By the

treaty of Northampton in 1328, the emeralds, pearls, and rubies were carried off without a murmur. But the Ragged Old Stone—Oh no!—the Londoners would have died for that! The stone of Scone, on which it was the custom for the kings of Scotland to be set at their coronation, the Londoners would *on no account suffer* to be sent away."

Dr. Poole says: "This stone is a dull, reddish or purplish sandstone, with a few small embedded pebbles; one of these is quartz and two others of a dark material. The rock is calcareous and is of that kind which masons call freestone. Chisel marks are visible on one or more of its sides." There is no rock of this kind in England, Ireland or Scotland. But the Rev. Canon Tristram says that there is a stratum of sandstone near the Dead Sea just like this stone, which by the English people is called Jacob's Pillow Stone.

This stone is called by the Irish and by the Scotch "Lia Fail" and "The Stone of Destiny." In Irish *Lia* is stone and *Fail* is fate, hence, the stone of fate, or the stone of destiny. But it is that only because it is Jacob's Pillow-Pillar Stone. This is the reason that Tea Tephi was called "The Daughter of God's House." (*Log,* or Lug, Celtic for God, and *Aidh*, a house; hence the word Lughaidh.) Amergin, chief bard to King Dermod, monarch of Ireland in the sixth century, in the "Notes of the Annals of the Four Masters," refers to Tea Tephi as follows:

"A rampart was raised around her house,
For Teah, the daughter of Lughaidh,
She was buried outside in her mound,
And from her it was named Tea-mur."

The parentage here assigned to Tea Tephi could have been for no other reason than that she was the daughter of "God's house," to the people to whom she brought "God's house," the Stone, which was their Shepherd-stone, i. e., Bethel. Morton W. Spencer says that *Lia* (sometimes spelled Leag) is an Irish word and means "a stone," but that Phail is Hebrew, and is itself a Scripture word, and is of the deepest import, for it means *wonderful,* and is so translated in Isa. 9:6. This we have verified, and it clinches our thought that the Bethel stone, or Lia Fail, the Stone Wonderful, is indeed a symbol of that Divine Rock, that *Wonderful One,* THE ROCK OF OUR SALVATION.

The fact that there are iron rings in the stone which is in the Coronation Chair, and that they are worn, is remarkable. The question arises, How and when were they worn? It could not have been in the royal halls of Tara, nor in the abbey of Scone, nor since it came to Westminster, nor in the temple of Jerusalem; but surely it could have been when, for forty years, Israel journeyed through the wilderness, and had both literal and spiritual drink from their Shepherd rocks that followed them.

The modern classic Hebrew uses little dots like periods to represent the vowel sounds. These dots are placed in various positions about the alphabetical characters which represent the consonant sounds. But it is a well known fact that in ancient Hebrew writings, both secular and sacred, there are no characters, not even the little dots, to represent the vowel sounds. Hence, the vowels are absolutely unwritten, and the consonants of a word are so arranged that the speaker is compelled to give the vowel sound while pronouncing the consonants. Take, for instance, the word Bethel. There, in the original, we have only that which is equivalent to the English B-th-l. At Bethel, as we have already shown, when Jacob set up the Bethel stone, he used it for an altar, at which he worshipped, and upon which he made his vow. Prof. Totten, of New Haven, says: "The altars of ancient Ireland were called Botal or Bothal, meaning the house of God." That is, it is the Hebrew word B-th-l, and has the same meaning.

Thus the Bethel stone again proves itself to be a perfect type of Christ, for although Christ is many other things, he is also the Christian's altar. Proof: Jesus said to the Pharisees: "Whether is greater, the gift or the altar that sanctifieth the gift?" In this we see that the altar is that which sanctifies. Elsewhere we are told that "Jesus Christ, of God, is made unto us sanctification." Since it is the altar which does the sanctifying, then he who sanctifies is the altar. Thus, it is written, "We have an altar, whereof they have no right to eat which serve the tabernacle. * * * Wherefore Jesus also, that he might sanctify the people (i.e., do that which the altar does) with his own blood, suffered without the gate."

Yes, the Altar-Shepherd was smitten, and concerning that other rock, Dean Stanley speaks of the crack, which, he says, "has all but rent its solid mass asunder." Could it be possible that rent was made when and because Moses smote the rock when he was told to speak to it? But, be this as it may, history has made it impossible to escape the fact that, like a true Shepherd, this stone has followed the fortunes and misfortunes of its people for two thousand five hundred years.

Joshua, at one time, took a stone, set it up, and said unto all Israel. "Behold, this stone shall be a witness unto us; for it hath heard all the words of the Lord which he spake unto us: it shall be therefore a witness unto you lest ye deny your God." Thus we see that a stone may be a witness; and the historians of Great Britain, either wittingly or unwittingly, have made Lia Fail (sometimes spelled Leag Phail) a witness to an unbroken line of sovereigns, for it has been the *throne* upon which their rulers have been consecutively crowned, ever since it was landed in Ireland.

Further, there have been just three overturns of this kingdom. The first, as we have shown, was from Palestine to Tara, in the plantation of Ulster, through Tea Tephi, Jeremiah's ward, the "King's Daughter." The second overturn was from Ireland to Scotland, through Fergus, who sent for Lia Fail, the Stone of Destiny, and had it brought from Tara to Iona, where he was crowned. The third OVERTURN was from Scotland to England. At this time the throne was brought from Scotland and placed in Westminster Abbey, where it *rests* under the protection of the greatest monarchy on earth.

Hence, if this Coronation Stone which is in Westminster, which the English call Jacob's Pillow, and which their Scotch and Irish ancestors called "God's house," "B-th-l," "The Stone of Destiny," and "Leag Phail," "The Stone Wonderful,"—we say, if this stone is indeed what these names and what its history declare it to be, then it is indeed the veritable *throne* of Israel,

upon which the sons of David were formally crowned
in the Temple of God at Jerusalem. Consequently, in
this also, God has kept faith with David, and preserveu
his *throne* through all generations that are past.

This makes us feel like singing the Doxology, because it is just as it should be. When the Bethel stone
was in Bethel place, it was "God's house," in God's
house; when it was in the Temple, it was still God's
house, in God's house; when, as one of the jewels of
empire, it was taken by Teah, the *"tender* twig," and
placed in the *heights of Israel in the islands of the sea,*
it was still God's house, in God's house. The descendants of Teah and Herremon are the custodians
of that rock today, and their subjects possess all the
distinguishing marks whereby prophecy declares the
lost *house of God* shall finally be recognized and found.
And in the midst of this great national or racial house
there is a house of God, a *"spiritual house,"* which is
by some called "Spiritual Israel," and which is, *like literal Israel was,* FOUNDED ON A ROCK.

CHAPTER IV.

DAN—THE SERPENT'S TRAIL.

The question naturally arises, "How did the prince, the highest branch of the cedar of Lebanon, get to the isles of the sea?" To get to the bottom of that which is involved in the reply to this question we will need to understand some of the characteristics, and acquaint ourselves with some of the prophecies, which pertain to the tribe of Dan.

The prophecies which dying Jacob gave concerning what the posterity of each of his sons was to become in the last days, is recorded in the forty-ninth chapter of Genesis. In the seventeenth verse is a part of the prophecy concerning the tribe of Dan, the first clause of which, according to the King James' translation, reads as follows: "Dan shall be a serpent by the way." But a better translation is as follows: "Dan shall be a serpent's trail." A few points in the history of the children of Dan will show us how they became a serpent's trail.

In the division of the land by lot, a narrow strip of seacoast country, west of Ephraim and Benjamin, fell to Dan. But this country soon became too small for the tribe, as we are told in the following: "The coast of the children of Dan went out too little for them; therefore the children of Dan went up to fight against Leshem, and took it, and smote it with the edge of the sword, and possessed it, and dwelt therein, and called Leshem, *Dan, after the name of Dan, their father."* (Joshua 19:47.)

Concerning the Danites, we have also the following: "And there went from thence of the family of the Danites, out of Zorah and out of Eshtaol, six hundred men appointed with weapons of war. And they went up, and pitched in Kirjath-jearim, in Judah; wherefore they called that place Mahaneh-*dan* unto this day." (Judges 18:11-12.)

Again we are told concerning this same company of six hundred that they came to Laish, "A people that were at quiet and secure; and they smote them with the edge of the sword, and burnt the city with fire.... And they built a city and dwelt therein. And they called the name of the city DAN, *after the name of Dan, their father,* who was born unto Israel; howbeit the name of the city was Laish at the first." (Judges 18:29.)

A company of Danites went to Leshem, and it became *Dan.* A company of *Dan*-ites went to Kirjath-jearim, and it became Mahaneh-*Dan.* They went on to Laish, and it ceased to exist, but they left their trail, i. e., DAN, *the name of their father,* and thus their trail can be traced, not only from *Dan* to Beer-Sheba, but to the islands of the sea both by land and by water, for Dan had an inland country and a coast country. The inland company of Danites went west with the Overland Column, and the coast company went by water, for "Dan abode in his ships."

Thus we have the prophecy concerning the ships of Tarshish, i. e., the ends of the world: "Be still (margin: silent) ye inhabitants of the isles; thou whom the merchants of Zidon, that pass over the sea, have replenished." (Isa. 23:2.) Also, in the sixth verse, is the following: "Pass ye over to Tarshish; howl, ye inhabitants of the isle. Is this your joyous city (Tyre) whose antiquity is of ancient days? Her own feet (means of travel) shall carry her afar off to sojourn."

In these scriptures we are informed that the isles of the sea were replenished by the ships whose seaports were Tyre and Zidon, which were ports of Palestine. Also the people by whom the islands were replenished, or peopled, are commanded to keep silent; just as this same prophet, in another place, commands Israel in the island to keep silent until they should renew their strength.

When Shalmanesar descended upon Israel, he did not disturb those portions of the tribes of Dan and Simeon, which were dwelling on the southwest coast of Palestine, for the kingdom of Judah was then at peace with Assyria and lay between them and Samaria. However, both Dan and Simeon had large colonies in the interior, Dan in the north (Judges 18) and Simeon in the east, at Mount Sier, the region formerly occupied by the Amelekites (1 Chron. 4:42-43). These portions of Dan and Simeon went with the rest of Samaria-Israel into Assyria, and with them passed out through the Caucasian Pass. The territory into and through which the ten tribes made their escape was just north of the Caucasus, which in ancient geography, as may be seen by consulting ancient maps, was known as the territory of the Sarmatians, while the pass, or gate, was sometimes called "The Sarmatian Gate." Not a few have shown, and upon good grounds, that the name of Sarmatia was derived from Samaria, the earlier home of these wandering people, whose general name among themselves was Scoloti, but whom the Greeks called Scythians, or Nomades. From that word *Scoloti* we have the more modern name *Scoti,* and the still more modern *Scots,* which, of course, mean the same as the Greek, Scythia and Nomades, i. e., wanderers.

But this is only one of the many names by which these wanderers, or Scots, may be traced, for in their western march across the European continent, which was necessarily slow, Ephraim did obey the prophetic injunction, *"Set thee up waymarks."* (Jer. 31:21.) And just here we must keep in mind the fact that in the ancient Hebrew there are no written vowels, and that in the word *Dan* there are only two letters used which are equivalent to the English D and N. Hence it makes no difference if the word is Dan, Don, Dun, Din or Den, it is equal to the Hebrew D-n, in which the speaker sounds the vowel according to characteristics of his own dialect.

On the west side of the Black Sea, there is, according to ancient geography, a region which was called "Moesia," signifying the land of the Moses-ites, and the people of which were called Moesi, or Mosesites. These people had such great reverence for a person whom they called Zal-moxis, whom Herodotus, the father of history, supposed to be their God, and concerning whom he concludes his account as follows: "Zalmoxis must have lived many years before

Pythagoras; whether therefore he was a man or a deity of the Getae, enough has been said of him." T. R. Howlett says, "Zalmoxis, whom Herodotus supposed them to worship as a god, is without doubt Moses; Zal signifying "chief," or "leader," while *Moxis* and *Moses* are but the Greek for the Hebrew *Mosie,* which is also rendered *Moses* in our tongue."

Moesia was bounded on the south by Mace-*Don*-ia and the Dar-DAN-ells, and on the north by the river DAN-ube. In the territory of Sarmatia, which in some maps is Scythia, in others Gomer, there are the rivers D-n-iper, *D-n*-ister, and the DON. The fact that the Dnieper and the Dniester are written without a vowel between the D and the N is quite as significant as the fact that the Don has one.

Professor Totten says: "There is no grander theme upon the scrolls of history than the story of this struggle of the Anglo-Saxons westward. The very streams of Europe mark their resting-places, and in the root of nearly all their ancient names (Dan, or Don) recall the sacred stream, Jor-*dan*—river of rest—from whose banks, so far away, as exiles, they set out. It was either the little colony of Dan, obeying its tribal proclivity for naming everything it captured (Jud. 18:1-12-29) after their father, or else the mere survival of a word and custom; but, none the less, it serves to trace these wanderers like a trail. Hence the *Dan*-ube, the *Dan*-ieper, the *Dan*-iester, the *Dan*-au, the *Dan*-inn, the *Dan*-aster, the *Dan*-dari, the *Dan*-ez, the Daci and Davi, the *Dan,* the *Don,* the U-*Don,* the Eri-don, and the thousand other dans and dons of ancient and early geography, down to the Danes in Dan-emerke, or

"Dan's last resting place." To this we would add, that, during all these years of blindness concerning the birthright tribes, the people of Den-mark have been called DAN-es, and that the people in contiguous countries, while having different local names, have been called by the same generic name, i. e.,

*Scan-*DIN-*navians.*

Also that Denmark, the modern form of Danemerke, means "Dan's mark": that too, to the people of the lost birthright. The very people who have hunted most for the way-marks which God told them to set up.

All that Scandinavian country, and much more, once belonged to Denmark, which is now reduced to a comparatively small region. Yet we believe that little kingdom will stand until the end of this age. When dying Jacob called his sons together about him that he might tell them what their posterity should become in the last days, he began his prophecy concerning Dan as follows: "Dan shall judge his people as one of the tribes of Israel." Then, immediately following, is the expression, "Dan shall be a serpent by the way." (Isaac Leeser's translation.)

In this prophecy Jacob does not say, as many seem to think, that Dan in the last days shall become the ruler of the other tribes of Israel; for the Eternal One has said, "Judah is my law giver." But what Jacob does say is, that Dan *as one of the tribes of Israel* shall render a verdict, or judge his people Israel. How? Because he shall, like a serpent, leave his mark or trail, that Israel may find it in the last days, and that they may say, "There is one of the lost tribes of Israel." When this verdict has been rendered, then Dan will have judged his people Israel. It may be that the word Israel, as used in the prophecy above, is used in its broadest sense, and includes both the house of Israel and the house of Judah. We are inclined to this opinion, for reasons which follow:

When Dan was born, Rachel said: "God hath judged me, and hath also heard my voice, and hath given me a son; therefore she called his name Dan." The word in Hebrew means *"Judge,"* and Daniel means *"The judge of God."* Thus Dan "judge," and El "God," hence Daniel, the judge of God. Thus Jacob in his last day's prophecy concerning the tribe of Dan plays on their tribal name, and says the judge shall judge, or, in other words, that *Dan* shall *Dan.* What? Dan shall Dan! Yes; and he certainly has *Dan*-ed, and *Dan*-ed, and *Dan*-ed, and kept on *Dan*-ing until he has given abundant evidence to his people that he is one of the tribes of Israel, for they now see the mark of his trail, i. e., Dan.

It is now more than two hundred and fifty years since a Danish peasant, who, with his daughter, was following their plow in their native country, when the daughter's plow turned up a bright and glittering something, which upon examination proved to be a golden trumpet. It was taken to the authorities, and, beyond all doubt, identified as one of the Seven *Golden Trumpets used in the altar service of the temple at Jerusalem.* This trumpet, which is now in the National Museum at Copenhagen, is ornamented with a lily and pomegranate —the lily being the national flower of Egypt, and the pomegranate that of Palestine—thus showing the half

Egyptian and half Israelitish origin of the birthright nation of which the tribe of Dan was a part.

Just before Moses died, he, like Jacob, gave prophecies concerning each tribe in Israel, and of Dan he said: "Dan is a lion's whelp; he shall leap from Bashan." Bashan was on Palestinean territory, hence Dan is to leap from that country, but it is left for history to tell where that leap landed him. And it is a well-authenticated fact that, after the coast colonies of Dan and Simeon knew that their king and their brethren were defeated, then they embarked in their ships and fled to the islands of the sea which are to the northwest of Europe. For the people who are known by all historians to have been the first settlers of Ireland are called "Tuatha de Danaans," which literally means "The tribe of Dan." These *Danaans* of Ireland correspond to the *Danaoi* of the Greeks, and Latin *Danaus*, and the Hebrew *Dan*.

The Lord, by the mouth of the Psalmist, declares that "He breaketh (or driveth) the ships of Tarshish with an east wind." As these Si-*don*-ians from the port of Si-*don* are driven, like Ephraim, WEST by an east wind, they not only leave their trail along the shores of the Mediterranean in Dens, Dins and Dons, but on the Peninsula of Spain. Just before passing out through the strait into the great waters they left a mark that remains unto this day, i. e., Me-*din*-a Si-*don*-ia.

That Dan's leap landed him in Ireland is evident, for in that island we find to this day *Dans*-Lough, *Dan*-Sower, *Dan*-Monism, *Dun*-dalke, *Dun*-drum, *Don*-e-gal Bay and *Don*-egal City, with *Dun*-glow and

Lon-*don*-derry just north of them. But there is also *Din*-gle, *Dun*-garven and *Duns*-more, which means "More Dan's." And, really, there are so many more that we have no space for them, except to mention *Dan*-gan Castle, where the Duke of Wellington was born, and to say that *Dunn* in the Irish language means just what *Dan* means in the Hebrew, i. e., *a judge*.

It is remarkable that there is not only a river *Don* in Scotland, but also a river *Doon*, and that there is also a river *Don* in England. Also that these countries are as full of *Dans, Dons* and *Duns* as Ireland, for in them are not only such names as *Dun*dee, *Dun*kirk, *Dun*bar, *Dun*raven, and many others, but the name of DAN, the son of Jacob, son of Isaac, son of Abraham, lies buried in the name of their capital cities, i. e., E-*din*-burgh and Lon-*don*. Surely Dan hath Dan-ed, or *judged among his people*, and thus fulfilled the sure word of prophecy.

We are told that, in the days of Solomon, "Every three years came the ships of Tarshish." Eight hundred and sixty years before Christ we are told that Jonah went to Joppa, a seaport within the borders of Dan, and found a ship going to Tarshish, and that he took passage in it to go to Tarshish from the presence of the Lord. Just how long the ships of Palestinean seaports had been replenishing, or colonizing, the isles, even before the Assyrian captivity of the ten tribes, is not known, but historians place the time as early as 900 B. C. This gives abundant time for some prince of the Zarah branch of Judah's family to have preceded Israel to the isles, and to have had a large colony even before the Birthright went to Assyria, an event which did not occur until 721 B. C. That one of those princes did precede Israel to the isles of the sea is evident; first, because God says he did, and, second, because it is recorded in the *Milesian* records of Ireland that the

Translated from Latin

Rongens Segl (1241).

The Kings Seal (1241).

prince Herremon, to whom Tea Tephi was married, *was a prince of the "Tuatha de Daanans."*

Mark this! If that prince was a prince of the tribe of Dan—and authentic history declares he was—then he was a prince of the family of Judah, for there can be no *Prince of Dan* other than a prince of the *royal family of* HIS RACE, and that family has but one fountain head, i. e., Judah, the fourth son of Jacob and Leah, to whom pertains the sceptre blessing.

But this rule seems to have worked both ways, for the family ensign of Judah is a lion, and since one of his whelps (young lion) went to the northwest isles with Dan, as a matter of course the ensign of his family, the royal family, went with him. Thus it became associated with the "Tuatha de Daanans," the tribe of Dan, and in time found its way into their national seal. See the accompanying cut.

The figure on this seal is described as *"A Lion's Whelp with a Serpent's Tail."* The largest of these represent Denmark, and the other two Norway and Sweden, which were at that time *under* the dominion of Denmark.

CHAPTER V.

ISRAEL IN THE ISLES.

We must keep in mind the fact that the Lord cast Israel *afar off to the isles of the sea,* and then, through the prophet Isaiah, commanded silence for a certain period, or until the people should have renewed their strength. This same prophet, in the first verse of the forty-ninth chapter, again addresses the people who dwell in the isles as follows: "LISTEN, O isles, unto me: and hearken, ye people from *afar";* and then makes the declaration: "Thou art my servant, O Israel, in whom I will be glorified."

Israel, as we know, was cast out of her land for idolatry, and Baal-ism was one of her chief idolatries. Before she was cast out she seems to have acquired the habit of attaching the name of the god Baal to places and cities, for on the ancient maps of Palestine we find *Baal*-meon, *Baal*-gad, *Baal*-ath, *Baal*-shalisha, *Baal*-tamar, *Baal*-peor, *Baal*-hazor, *Baal*-zephon, Mt. *Baal*-ah, and others.

But surely these people carried that same proclivity with them to the islands, for in Ireland this name of the god Baal is found just as frequently, if not more frequently, a circumstance which shows that this idol was honored and worshipped by her eastern colonists. The Rev. T. R. Howlett furnishes us with the following list of Baal-it-ish names found in Ireland: *Baal*-y-Bai, *Baal*-y-gowan, *Baal*-y-Nahinsh, *Baal*-y-Castell,

Baal-y-Moni, *Baal*-y-ner, *Baal*-y-Garai, *Baal*-y-nah, *Baal*-y-Con-El, *Baal*-y-Hy, *Baal*-y-Hull-Ish, *Baal*-Nah-Brach, *Baal*-Athi, *Baal*-Dagon.

Regarding the evidence given by these names, Howlett says: "These certainly are memorials of the Baal worship once prevailing in Ireland. In them we have not only the name of Baal, but its conjunction also with other Hebrew names. How can this be accounted for, except as they were so called by emigrants from Phoenicia and Palestine?

One thing that particularly marks the Hebrew origin of these names is their attachment to *places* but not to *persons*. The Canaanites and Phœnicians, attached the names of their gods, *Baal, Bal, Bel* to *persons*, as Eth-*Baal*, Itho-*bal*, Asdru-*bal* and Han-i-*bal*. These were family names among the heathen nations surrounding Israel. In like manner, we find among the chosen people the names of their God associated with and forming a part of family and personal names; as "El" and "Jah," in Isra-*el*, Ishma-*el*, Lemu-*el*, Samu-*el*, Ezeki-*el*, *El*-isha *El*-ijah. Baal never found favor among the Hebrews as a personal name, though used freely for localities. They gave it to their towns, but not to their children. Its use in Ireland is proof of the Israelitish origin of the earliest settlers—philological evidence of racial unity."

But this custom of thus using the name of Baal has long since passed away from the descendents of those who settled in "INNIS PHAIL"—an Island Wonderful—and her sister isles. These islands need no longer keep silent, for their people have renewed their strength and thus the isles are yielding up their secrets. Hence, we should not be surprised that the name of Baal is no longer in the mouth of their people. By the mouth of the prophet Hosea, whom the Lord used to declare that he would hedge up the way of Ephraim Israel, so that she could not find her paths, he also says: "I will take away the names of Baal-im (plural of Baal) out of her mouth, and they shall no more be remembered by their name." (Hosea 2:17.)

But just prior to this saying the Lord has given a prophecy, of which this is but a part, the sequence of that which precedes it, and which reads as follows: "Behold, I will allure her, and bring her into the wilderness (the hitherto uninhabited country), and speak comfortably *to her heart* (Margin). And I will give her vineyards from thence (there), and the valley of Achor (sorrow) for a door of hope; and she shall sing as in the days of her youth, and as in the day when she came out of the land of Egypt. And it shall be at that day, saith the Lord, that thou shalt call me Ishi (my husband); and shalt call me no more Baali. For I will take away the names of Baalim out of her mouth."

All idolatrous names were taken from the mouth of Israel, not so much because they had reached that God-appointed place where they were to be moved no more, and where the children of wickedness were not to waste them *as at the first,* but because they had passed out from their former sorrow through the door of hope, which was caused by the fact that their Lord had spoken comforting words to their hearts, and because she could look up in love to him and say, "Ishi—my husband." The reason for this heart-experienced hope will become clearer as we proceed with the prophetic history of this people, whose centralization of racial life and power is in those islands which are northwest of Palestine.

But in this same forty-ninth chapter of Isaiah, after letting us know that Israel is located in the isles, the prophet foretells some events in the future history of that island nation. Among these predicted events we find the following: "Thus saith the Lord, the Holy One: In the time of favour (grace) have I heard thee, and in the day of salvation (the Christian era) have I helped thee: and I will preserve thee, and I will appoint thee, *as a people of the covenant*, to establish the earth, to cause (thee) to inherit the desolate heritages."

In this quotation we have, for the sake of clearness, followed in part both the King James and the Isaac Leeser translations. The italicized phrase is from Leeser, and is remarkable for its clearness, especially in its use of the article *a* before people, because Ephraim-Israel, although not *all* the people, is distinctly *a people*, of the covenant; and *as a people of the covenant* she is appointed to establish, people, or cause to be inhabited, the desolate, uninhabited places of the earth. These desolate localities are given to Israel as an inheritance, and she has needed them in fulfilling the destiny of the Birthright Kingdom of Israel—that of becoming many nations, or a company of nations.

But we must now notice the word covenant, since it is used in the phrase *as a people of the covenant*. The Hebrew word for covenant is Beriyth, which in Judges 8:33 and 9:4 is used as a proper name, and, for that reason, it is simply transferred into the English text without being translated. It is given there as the name of one of the idols of Israel, namely: Baal-beriyth, and means *Baal of* (the) *covenant.* Also the Hebrew words *Ben-iysh Yemiyniy* are translated "Son of a man of Jemini. Thus *Ben* means "a son"; *Iysh*, "*a man*," and *Yemiyniy*, Jemini. The anglicized form of these words are Ben, ish and jamin, and, taken together, they mean "A man of Benjamin, or a Benjaminite."

We have brought you through this group of words to show that *ish* in Hebrew means *a man*. Now take the Hebrew word which is translated covenant, which in its original form has no vowel, but which in its Anglicized form retains the vowel *i* to preserve the *y* sound, and we have *Brith,* which joined with *ish* is *Brith-ish,* and means "A covenant man." Today the BRITISH people, or men of the covenant, are called Britons, and are dwelling in the British Isles!!!

We are told that the people of W*aels* call themselves, in ancient Welsh, "*Bryth y Brithan,*" or Briths of Briton," which means "The Covenanters" of "the land of the Covenant." The first form of this phrase is almost vernacular Hebrew.

It is also unmistakably recorded in British history that the earliest settlers in Wales and southern England were called *Simonii.* They came by the way of the sea in the year 720 B. C. At this time there was the greatest influx of the *Tuatha de Daanan* to Ireland, and this synchronizes with the deportation of the Israelites of the commonwealth of Ephraim to Assyria, and the flight of Dan and Simeon from the seaports and coast country of Palestine. That *Simonii* is the plural of *Simeon* we need scarcely mention.

But all evidences of the fulfillment of this prophecy are not philological, for Isaiah, still addressing the Israelites who dwell in the islands, predicts the following: "For thy waste and desolate places, and the land of thy destruction (the destruction of their identity), shall even now be too narrow (pressed, straightened) by reason of the inhabitants, and they that swallowed thee up (the Assyrians) shall be far away.

The children which thou shalt have, after thou hast lost the other, shall say again in thine ears: The place is too straight (small, crowded, cramped) for me; give a place to me that I may dwell." (Isa. 49:19-20.)

Here are a people called Israel who are living in the isles of the sea. They have lost one company of people, and yet their children say that the place is still too small, cramped and crowded, because there are too many inhabitants for such a small country. Consequently they ask the *Mother Country* to give them a place also. Or, according to Leeser's translation, they say, "Make room for me to dwell," and the Mother Country must do it, because it is she to whom the Lord has given the desolate heritages of the earth.

Mark this! It is also said of the mother country, or Mother Israel, that she *"lost"* her first children before other of her children asked for territory in which to dwell.

England is the only country on the face of the earth where these conditions obtain. Her first child was called New England, but she LOST it, and now it— together with that which, for various reasons, has been annexed—is called *The United States of America.*

But, after losing her American colonies, her work of

colonizing non-populated portions of the world kept right on; until today through the power of these colonies she holds possession of Prince Edward's Island, New Brunswick, Nova Scotia, British Columbia, Vancouver's Island, New Foundland and Canada. All of these are unitedly called the Dominion of Canada, and to these are added the six States of Australia, New Zealand, Tasmania, British India, the Fiji Islands and parts of Africa, Egypt and China. So that now the sun never sets on the realm of the United Kingdom.

But we should expect this, and even more, for according to Jer. 31:910, the Israel which is located in the Isles is none other than Ephraim, the Abrahamic Birthright People, of whom the Lord says: "I am a father to Israel, and Ephraim is my first born."

Ephraim, as we have shown, was the second son of Joseph. But when the birthright blessing was given to Joseph in his sons, Ephraim, the younger, was set before Manasseh, the elder. They were to remain together, however, until they grew into a multitude in the midst of the earth. After that they were to separate; then Manasseh was to become a *"great" people*, or nation, and Ephraim was to become "a multitude, or company of nations."

The people in the British Isles did certainly grow together until they became a multitude of people in the earth, and then they separated. The separated people has become a great nation, and those who were left in the isles have become a multitude of nations. The government of the separated people is democratic, the people in the isles still live, as they ever must, under a monarchy, but the two peoples are, as Joseph's two sons were, brothers; and they even call each other *"Brother John"* and *"Brother Jonathan."* There are no other nations on earth who thus brother each other.

The facts recorded above are also in fulfillment of another prophecy given by dying Jacob concerning Joseph, which reads as follows: "Joseph is a fruitful bough, even a fruitful bough by a well (water), whose branches run over the wall." (Gen. 49:22.)

An objector has said: "But I believe the words 'a multitude of nations' means a multitude of different nationalities." If this be the true meaning of these words, then surely England, with her sixteen nations in British India, her Indians and Esquimaux of British America, her Fiji Islanders and New Zealanders, and her subjects of still other nationalities, which are absolutely too numerous to mention—surely England is a multiplicity of nationalities. Still we do not believe this to be the meaning of the words under discussion, but we do believe that this fact of England's thus ruling so many nationalities, and of America's holding dominion over the Sandwich Isles, Cuba, Haiti, Porto Rico and the Philippines is the fulfillment of a promise that Israel shall inherit the lands and labor of the heathen, which is given as follows:

"He brought forth his people with joy, and his chosen with gladness: and gave them the lands of the heathen; and they inherited the labour of the people; that they might observe his statutes, and keep his laws. Praise ye the Lord." (Psa. 105:43-45.) The Bible follows Anglo-Saxon conquests, and some of the people in all these nations both receive and keep the law of God.

We must remember that Ephraim and Manasseh, as the representatives of the house of Joseph, both together received the birthright blessing under the hands of the dying patriarch, and that since they thus jointly hold the birthright blessing, even though Ephraim was set before Manasseh, we may expect that they shall hold many of its blessings in common. Take, for instance, the blessing pronounced upon the land of Joseph, as given by Moses on the day of his death, which is only an enlarged edition of that which was given by Jacob on the day of his death, and which is as follows: "And of Joseph he said, Blessed of the Lord be his land, for the precious things of heaven (rain), for the dew, and for the deep (ocean) that croucheth beneath (his vessels), and for the precious fruits brought forth by the sun, and the precious things put forth from moon to moon, and through the chief (best) things of the ancient mountains, and for the precious things of the everlasting hills, and the precious things of the earth and the fullness thereof, and for the good will of him that dwelt in the bush: let this blessing come upon the head of Joseph, and upon the top of the head of him that was separated from his brethren. His glory is like the firstling (firstborn) of his bullock, and his horns are like the horns of an unicorn (the unicorn is in the national seal of England): with them he (Joseph) shall push the people together to the ends of the earth; and they are the ten thousands of Ephraim, and they are the thousands of Manasseh." (Deut. 33: 13-17.)

This promise of wealth on land and sea, of abundant harvests, of rare gems and precious stones, of the richest and the greatest mining interests in the world, is fulfilled in England and America. It is also true that these nations, not only *push* the aborgines of their possessions into the ends, or corners, of their countries, but they also *push the people* of other nations with whom they war into corners. Concerning America and her aborigines, we need only say, "Lo, the poor Indian," and ask, Where is he? And then ask the same question concerning the aborigines of the countries which fall into the hands of England. Just here the alien testimony of the Russian Vernadsky is pertinent. He says, "Britain is a spider whose web encompasses the whole world within her own dominions. She has all the resources of all the continents. Her empire is stronger and vaster than any coalition of other states. She is a standing menace to all other powers, and her increasing strength is destructive to the balance of power. Nevertheless, unsatisfied and insatiable, she is grasping for more territory. Yesterday she seized Fiji; the day before she took the Diamond fields; today she annexed Transvaal, and tomorrow she will clutch Egypt. It is only too clear that the power of Britain is too great to be compatible with the general safety, and that the aggressive empire, unless speedily checked, will establish a universal dominion over all the people of the earth."

Our reply to this expressed fear concerning Britain's "universal dominion," is that England alone will not gain this, but that England and America will yet form an alliance and that then they *shall push the people to the ends of the earth,* for it is foretold that they, Ephraim and Manasseh, *"together"* shall do this, and also that, *"Israel shall blossom and bud, and fill the face of the whole* WORLD *with fruit."* (Isa. 27:6.)

The fulfillment of these promised blessings, which were pronounced upon the land of Joseph, by the people in the isles and their *"separated"* brother, is the cause of the fulfillment of another prophecy given by Isaiah concerning this same people, which is as follows: "Be still, ye inhabitants of the isle; thou whom the merchants of Zidon (Palestinean seaport), that pass over the sea have replenished. And by great waters (same place as in Ezekiel's riddle) the seed of Sihor, the harvest of the river is her revenue; and *she is the mart of nations."*

The Sihor is a river in Egypt. Israel dwelt in Egypt for four hundred and thirty years, hence they were formerly from Egypt, latterly from Palestine, now in the isles of the *Great Waters!!!* Moreover, the birthright holders were born Egyptians. Thus the Lord says, "When Israel was a child, then I loved him and called my son out of Egypt." It is for these reasons that, in the Bible, the Ephraim Israelites are in two places called Egyptians.

This fact of calling Israel out of Egypt is doubly true in the case of Israel; first in the fact that when Israel was a child (a young nation), the Lord called her out of Egypt; second in the fact that the Lord's son, Ephraim his first born was called out of Egypt. This was also true again, after the flight of Joseph and Mary into Egypt with the babe under the protection of an angel, for it is again written, "Out of Egypt have I called my son."

But there is another prophecy in Isaiah which has been most wonderfully fulfilled in the history of Ephraim and his brother Manasseh, i. e., England and America, the long lost house of Joseph. It is the following: "The Lord sent a word into Jacob, and it hath lighted upon Israel. And all the people shall know, even Ephraim, and the inhabitants of Samaria." (Isa. 9:8-9.)

Here we have the names of Samaria-Ephraim-Israel, the birthright kingdom, used prophetically. In connection with these names is the fact that the Lord sent a word to Jacob, and that it lighted not upon Judah, but upon Israel, and that all the people of Ephraim "shall know" this.

Hear this!

"Ye chosen seed of Israel's race—
Ye ransomed from the fall!"

Again we say, hear this! "In the beginning was the WORD, and the WORD was with God, and the WORD was God. The same was in the beginning with God. All things were made by him; and without him was not anything made that was made. In him was *life;* and the *life* was the *light* of men. And the WORD was made *flesh,* and dwelt among us——full of *grace* and *truth.* He came to his own (Judah) and his own (the Jews) received him not." So he said to his disciples, "Go to the lost sheep of the house of Israel." Christ, the Divine WORD was "SENT" "into Jacob," bringing life, light, grace, and truth, *but Judah rejected the word sent from God,* so it lighted upon Israel. Thus, the Apostle Paul, who was brought up at the feet of Gamaliel, and who was raised a Pharisee of the strictest sort, understood himself perfectly, when he said, "Israel (as a whole) hath not obtained that which he seeketh for; but the election (Ephraim-Israel) hath obtained it, and the rest (Jewish-Israel) were blinded." Who, "as concerning the gospel are enemies; but as touching the election (racial) are beloved for the fathers' sakes." Hence, "blindness in part (or blindness to a part) is happened to Israel, until the fullness of the Gentiles be come in."

But of that part of the elect race which is appointed to be the recipients of the *Word* which God *sent*. Paul says, "There is a remnant according to the election of grace," and it is the people who belong to the election of grace, that follow the colonies of that elect race, and plant the standard of the gospel of the grace of the Son of God among the nations of the earth. Thus the Messianic promise, which the Lord made to Abraham, that in his seed all the nations of the earth should be blessed, has received a double fulfillment, in that those who carry the message of the *One Seed*, are also the seed of Abraham. This is true either nationally or spiritually, for all who have been baptized into Christ have put on Christ, are Abraham's seed and heirs according to the promise. And it is also true that the Anglo-Saxons are pre-eminently the evangelists of the world.

CHAPTER VI.

A FEW MORE IDENTITIES.

In Ezekiel's riddle concerning the kingdom of Israel which is in the northwest isles of the sea, that fruitful land by the great waters to which those two ships of Dan carried their royal passengers, we are told that the kingdom became a green tree after the royal pair were united and placed on the throne in the height of Israel, and that it became a goodly cedar. Of that tree it is said, "Under it shall dwell all fowl of every wing; in the shadow of the branches thereof shall they dwell."

All understand, of course, that the prophecies of this riddle are given in veiled language, mostly metaphor, but we know of no prophecies in all the word of God that have been any more perfectly fulfilled than those of this riddle, and we affirm that there can be found no race on the face of the earth in which the conditions, as given in the above, are so completely fulfilled as in the Anglo-Saxon race; first in England and her colonies, and then in America.

"Fowl of every wing," i. e., people of every nation, all dwelling under the royal cedar, whose scions came from Lebanon (Palestine territory), or under the extended shadow of its branches; that is, directly under the central power, or under the dominion of one of its protectorates, or else under the protection of the separated brother of the house of Joseph, i. e., Manasseh, the brother of Ephraim, or America, England's brother nation.

The fact that these two nations have with them in their home country so many people of other nationalities has been used as an argument to prove that it is not possible for the Anglo-Saxons to be the lost house of Israel; but the very fact that this is so, and that men of other nations can come among us, take out their naturalization papers, become citizens, and have equal rights with those who are home-born, has on its very face the proof that we are Israel. For the Lord gave commandment unto Israel saying, "When a stranger shall sojourn with thee *he shall be as one that is born in the land*. One law shall be to him that is home-born, and unto the stranger that sojourneth among you." (Ex. 12:48-49.)

The political conditions mentioned above do obtain in Anglo-Saxon countries, and in no other countries of the world.

The reason given for the establishment of the law that permitted stranger to become as home-born citizen in Israel, is, that they were strangers in the land of Egypt; as before them Abraham their father was a stranger in the land of promise. The fact that this law prevailed in Israel, and that it is the law in all Anglo-Saxon commonwealths, shows that they are one and the same people, and accounts for the following state of affairs in Ephraim, which we must remember is the representative name of the house of Joseph:

"Ephraim, he hath mixed himself among the people; *Strangers* (foreigners) *have devoured his strength, and he knoweth it not.*"   (Hosea 7:8-9.)

Foreign labor, anarchy,* and Romanism!

In both England and America many of these strangers are naturalized and become as home-born, only that they may secure official authority, power, and prestige in their affairs of state so as to help the non-citizen foreign hordes to devour the strength of their government, and yet, apparently, they know it not.

Surely, these identities, as given above, are some of the *"waymarks"* which the Lord commanded Ephraim-Israel to set up.   (Jer. 30:20-21.)   But there are yet others.

We have certainly made it clear, that the *Tuatha de Danaans* of northern Ireland were those of the tribe of Dan who belonged to the seacoast colony, or at least that part who abode in their ships and thus escaped.   But where Dan is there Israel must be also, for Dan was a part of Israel, and was to judge or Dan his people, as one of the tribes of Israel.   It is a well authenticated fact of history that the Milesians, or Scots, inhabited the north of Ireland as well as the tribe of Dan, that they were the same race of people, and that the word *Scots* means wanderers.   Prof. Totten says: "Scythopolis has been traced to Sikytopolis (city of Siccuth), a corruption of Succoth, or Scothotti, the city of the Scots, Scyths,

*Since these words were written the President of the United States, William McKinley, has fallen a victim to Anarchy.

Sacs, or *wanderers,* i. e., "dwellers in booths." When Ephraim was cast out, Hosea declared, "they shall be *wanderers* among the nations," and this is in harmony with Amos, who says that they should be sifted through the nations, as corn is sifted through a sieve, and yet not one grain, or *stone* (margin) was to fall to the ground. Hence, they were to wander through the nations until they reached the isles of the sea, that God-appointed place for his people, where their enemies should not *waste* them, and where they should renew their strength.

But where Israel and Dan are, there, too, must the Canaanite be, and it is a well-known fact that the settlers of *southern* Ireland are a vastly different people from those of *northern* Ireland, and that the difference is in their origin, for they sprang from a different race. Moses said to Israel: "But if ye will not drive out the inhabitants of the land before you; then it shall come to pass that those which ye let remain of them shall be pricks in your eyes and thorns in your sides, and shall vex you in the land wherein ye dwell." (Num. 33:55.) The Lord also said, "If ye do in anywise go back and cleave unto the remnant of these nations, even those that remain among you, and shall make marriages with them, and go in unto them, and they to you; know for a certainty that the Lord your God will no more drive out any of these nations from before you; but they shall be snares and traps unto you." (Josh. 23:12-13.)

The Philistines most *certainly* did become a snare to the tribe of Dan, for they were the first tribe of Israel to fraternize with them, and the first who joined with them in the worship of their god Baal. Simeon soon joined with them, and so eventually did both Israel and Judah.

The evolution of the name of this Canaanitish nation is from Philistine to Phœnician, then Phenesian, then Venetian, and then Fenian. The Fenians of Ireland boast of their Phœnician origin, had the sixteen letter alphabet, and many evidences to justify their claim. These people lived with Dan and Simeon in Palestine, and came with them to Ireland. They are still "hewers of wood and drawers of water," and certainly "thorns in the sides and pricks in the eyes" only of England and America. This is the vexing "Irish question." For, "These are the nations which the Lord left, *to prove Israel by them.*" (Judges 3:1.)

The physiognomy of Israel must be different from that of the Jews. We must remember that although Benjamin was with the kingdom of Judah, they were the children of Rachel, and that they differed much from the characteristic Jew, both in looks and in speech. The Galileans were Benjaminites; hence all the apostles of Christ, except Judas, were Benjaminites, for they were Galileans; and while Christ was in the Judgment Hall, some of those who stood by said to Peter, "Surely thou also art one of them, for thy speech betrayeth thee." Also Esther, that lovely daughter of the captive people, and Mordecai, that "Jew of the Jews," could pass in and out of the palace of Ahasuerus, and not betray the fact that they were of Abrahamic blood, *because they were Benjaminites.* (Esther 2:5-10-20.)

If these differences were noticeable in the case of those tribes, which differences lay in the fact that they were only half-brothers, how much more so would they be in the case of the house of Joseph, who were still further removed from Judah, in that they were half Egyptian! Hence, the Abrahamic origin of the Anglo-Saxon has not been disproved, when its opponents assert that we do not possess *"crooked noses."* But we assert that, if they had the same *"shew of countenance"* that is peculiar to the Jewish people, they could not be the house of Joseph. But we Saxons get our *straight noses* from our royal Egyptian ancestor. We say royal Egyptian ancestor, because Joseph married Asenath, the daughter of Poti-pherah, Prince of On, instead of a "Priest of On," as you may see by consulting the original reading of Genesis 41:45, whereas the Saxon has neither a decided aquiline nose, or its pronounced opposite, the Egyptian acute angle, but he has an exquisite Egyptio-Jacobic blend, which is much more handsome.

It has been made clear to our readers that Omri, the sixth king of Israel, built the city of Samaria, the third and permanent capital of Israel, and that eventually' the entire country, formerly called "All Israel," became known as Samaria, because that was the name of its capital; also that Samaria became one of the national names of Israel, and is so used in some prophecies concerning them. Hence Omri is regarded as the real founder of the kingdom of Samaria, and Samaria-Israel was often referred to by other nations as the House of Omri.

When Shalmanesar, the king of Assyria, who led Israel into captivity, made a record of that captivity on the tablets of Assyria, he called them the House of Omri (Beth Khumree); also when Israel was confederate with Resin, king of Syria, and went against the Jews, and the Jews besought Tiglath-Pilesar, who was at that time king of Assyria, to become their confederate, he also in his records referred to Israel as the *Beth-Khumree.* In the annals of Sargon, who was also a king of Assyria (Isa. 20:1), successor of Shalmanesar, and predecessor of Senacharib, Israel is called Beth Khumree (House of Omri), and their capital city Khumree. On the Nimroud obelisk, "Jehu, the son of Omri," is written "Yahua-abil-Khumree." Prof. Rawlinson, who does not believe this truth we are enforcing, says: "Jehu is usually called in the Bible the son of Nimshi—although Jehosaphat was his actual father (2 Kings 9:20), but the Assyrians, taking him for the legitimate successor to the throne, named as his father, or rather ancestor, "Omri," the founder of the Kingdom of Samaria—Omri's name being written on the obelisk, as it is in the inscriptions of Shalmanesar, where the Kingdom of Israel is always called the country of "Beth Omri." Dr. Hincks also says: "The title, 'Son of Omri,' is equivalent to that of *King of Samaria,* the city which Omri built, and which was known to the Assyrians as *Beth Omri,* or Khumri."

The tribes of both Dan and Simeon belonged, of course, to the *Beth Khumree,* when used as meaning the Kingdom of Omri, or Samaria. Simeon seems to have clung to this name far more tenaciously than did Dan, for they still call themselves and their country *Kimry.* Saville says: "This name Kymri, or Cymry, as it is more commonly written, is in reality the plural of *Kymro,* meaning a Welsh-man, and the country of the Kymry is called by themselves *Khymru,* which has been Latinized into the well-known name of *Cambria.* The letter *v* in the Welsh language has two powers, and both these powers are active in the word *Kymry.* This letter *v sounds as u, except when it stands in the last syllable of a word, and then it has the sound of the Italian i or the English ee!* Hence, the correct pronunciation of the country of Wales, or land of the Cymry, in its ancient tongue would be as near as possible to the names Kumree, Khumree, or Kumri."

Thomas Stephens, in the preface to his "Literature of the *Kymry,*" says: "On the map of Britain, facing St. George's Channel, is a group of counties called Wales, inhabited by a people distinct from, and but very imperfectly understood by, those who surround them. Their neighbors call them Welsh-men. Welsh or Walsch is not a proper name, but a *Teutonic* term signifying 'strangers,' and was applied to all persons who were not of that family: but the proper name of these people is *Kymry.* They are the last remnant of the *Kimmerioi* of Homer, and of the *Kimry* (Cimbri) of Germany. From the Cimbric Chersonesus (Jutland) a portion of these landed on the shores of Northumberland, gave their name to the county of Cumberland, and in process of time followed the seaside to their present resting-place, where they still call themselves *Kimry,* and give their country a similar name. Their history, clear, concise and authentic, ascends to a high antiquity. Their language was embodied in verse long before the languages now spoken rose into notice, and their literature, cultivated and abundant lays claim to being the most ancient in modern Europe." Thus we find that the Khumree, Kumri, Kimry, Cumbre, Cimbri, or Cambrians, as the name is variously called in different tongues, were strangers and wanderers among the nations until they settled in the isles of the sea with the rest of their brethren, the Brith-ish or covenant people.

"Herodotus, the 'Father of History,' tells us much about the *Khumbri,* a people who, in his day, dwelt in the Crimean peninsula and thereabout. He particularly notes that they had come into that territory from Media, which he remarks was not their original home or birth-place."—Our Race.

We have thus conclusively followed the word *Khum-ree,* for the reason that the people who are known as Angles, Saxons, Danes, Celts or Kelts, Jutes, Scots, Welsh, Scyths (or Scythians), or Normans can trace themselves back to Media-Persia, *but no further,* and find their ancestors in the *Khumree,* at the place, and at the very time, when Israel was losing her identity and was actually known in the history of that country as the Beth Khumree.

We cannot take time or space to deal with the origin of all the above names, but we feel that we must say something concerning the name Saxon, as it is the most general name of the race—really the present generic name of the house of Joseph.

It seems to be a well-known Hebraism, and for some reason it certainly was a very common custom among the Israelites, to drop the first letter of a proper name. Bible examples of this custom are: Oshea, otherwise Hoshea; Hagar, otherwise Agar; Jachan, otherwise Achan; Heber, otherwise Eber, etc. Scholars tell us, if we have caught their thought, that this Hebrew idiom is peculiar to the possessive case, and also to allow the introduction of an affix.

When Jacob transferred the birthright to the sons of Joseph he, with one hand resting on the head of each, prayed: "Let my name (Israel) be named on them, and the name of my fathers Abraham and Isaac." The birthright kingdom did, as we have seen, inherit the name of Israel, and also that of Isaac. For Amos says: "And the high places of Isaac shall be desolate, and the sanctuaries of Israel (Bethel and Dan) shall be laid waste, and I will rise against the house of Jeroboam with the sword." (Amos 7:9.) Here we have *Isaac, Israel* and *the house of Jeroboam* used as interchangeable names for the ten-tribed kingdom. Amaziah also says to Jeroboam, the king of Isaac-Israel: "The Lord said unto me, Go, prophesy unto my people Israel. Now, therefore, hear thou the word of the Lord, (but) thou sayest, Prophesy not against *Israel,* and drop not thy word against the house of *Isaac.*" (Amos 7:16.)

Thus the name of Isaac was named upon the house of Joseph, and it is true, both in race and name, that, "in Isaac shall thy seed be called." It seems that the Jews had a preference for the name of Jacob, but Israel clung to the name of Isaac, especially after they were taken into captivity; they dropped the name of Israel and called themselves "Saac"—Sacae, or Saxae, as per Latin derivation—which is nothing more or less than the Hebrew name of Isaac, from which the initial letter I has been dropped.

It is now a well-authenticated fact that the word Saxon is derived from the Hebrew name of I-saac, together with an affix which means sons of. Prof. Totten says: "In most of the Eastern languages 'sons of' is written 'sunnia.' It is equivalent to the Scottish 'Mac' and the English and Irish 'Fitz'—Mac Donald, son of Donald; Fitz Henry, son of Henry. So, in the distant home of our ancestors, Saac-Sunnia means sons of Isaac. Stambul is formed of Istambul by dropping the prefix I, and so the Saxon is a direct descendant of our father Isaac. Dr. W. Holt Yates accepts this derivation of the Saxon name as positive, and the Rev. W. H. Poole, D. D., speaks of it as follows: "It is a little curious to glean from the ancient nations and from the stone monuments of the early times the various forms in which this word is to be found. I will here insert a few from a list of my own gleaned from ancient history, thus: Sons of Isaac, Sons of Saac, Saac-Sunnia, Saac-Suna, Saac-Sena Saaca-pena, Esak-ska, Sacae-Amyrqui, Beth-Sakai (House of Isaac), Sunnia-Sakai, Sakai-Suna, Saca-Suna, Sacae-Sunnae, Sackisina, Sacka-Sunia, Saca-cine, Saka-Suna, Sacas-Sani, Sakas-Saeni, Saxi-Suna, Sach-Suni, Sachi, Sacha, Sakah, Saachus, Saacus, Sacho, Saxo, Saxoi, Saxonia, Saxones, Saxae, Sach-sen, Sack-sen, Saxe-sen, Saxone, Saxony, Saxon."—"Our Race."

Concerning the etymology of the word Saxon, Yatman says: "Its history is as follows: The Persians used the terms Sacae and Scythian as *convertible*, whether from a corrupt rendering of one from the other or because the Sacae, a great tribe of Scythians (wanderers) bordering upon them, were so called by a tribal name. Of the fact of the *identity* of the Sacae and the Scythians there is not the shadow of a doubt, and it is clear that these people called their country Sacasena. It is equally clear that the Saxons of England were the Scythians or Celte-Scythians. Their geographical position in Europe is accurately described by Plutarch, Tacitus, Ptolemy, and other authors."

To this testimony all the historians agree. Strabo asserts that the most ancient Greek historians knew the Sacaea as a people who lived beyond the Caspian Sea. Diodorus says: "The Sacaea sprung from a people in Media who obtained a vast and glorious empire."

Ptolemy finds the Saxons in a race of Scythians, called *Sakai,* who came from Media.

Pliny says: "The *Sakai* were among the most distinguished people of Scythia, who settled in Armenia, and were called Sacae-Sani."

Albinus says: "The Saxons were descended from the ancient *Sacae* of Asia."

Prideaux finds that the Cimbrians came from between the Black and Euxine (Caspian) seas, and that with them came the Angli.

Sharon Turner, the great Saxon historian, says: "The Saxons were a Scythian nation, and were called *Saca, Sachi, Sacki, Sach-sen.*"

Gawler, in "Our Scythian Ancestors" (Page 6), says: "The word 'Saacae,' is fairly and without straining or imagination, translatable as Isaacites."

But why has it been necessary for the historians of these various nations thus to trace this name, search

records, tablets and monuments, and hunt for the
origin of the Anglo-Saxons? Are they an obscure
people? Are they a feeble nation? Are they an ignorant folk? Are they an uncivilized race? No; they are
diametrically opposite to all this. They are in every
way the greatest race on earth, but they do not know
where they originated, nor who were their ancestors—
they are lost.

Some of these historians whom we have quoted do
not agree among themselves as to the origin of the
Saxons, but belong to different schools of contention,
and are wrangling over the question whether these
lost people belong to the Aryan, or to the Semitic
race. The only use which we have, just here, for
their contention is to show that they all trace the Saxons to the very place where the captive ten tribes of
Israel were deported by Shalmanesar, the King of
Assyria. These same historians also show that the
Sax-ons sprang into existence, in so far as their
modern and mediæval history is concerned, about three
years after the Israelites were taken to that country,
and that there they lose them and can trace them no
further.

Since both the Saxons and Samaritan-Israelites are
lost, and since those Israelites are the sons of Isaac,
and were so called in sacred history, and since both
people bear the name of their father I-saac, we have
no hesitancy in saying that they are one and the
same, and that the lost are found. And since these
people have been told that they were not the chosen
people of God, we, together with many others, now

declare unto them that they are the natural children of Abraham, the national sons of God.

It is a most significant fact, that *Lia-F-ail*, the name of the Bethel stone, is the same, whether read from right to left, as the Hebrews do, or whether it is read from left to right, as the Saxons do. Also, the word has just seven letters (the perfect number), and if we start with the fourth (the human number), or central letter, and read from that, either to the right or to the left, we have in both instances the same word, i. e., f-a-i-l, in which if we use *ph* for the f sound, we have that Hebrew word *wonderful*, which is one of the names of the Messiah. Or if we start either with the right or left, read to the central letter and then back again to the place from which we started (l-i-a-f-a-i-l), then we have the full name of Liafail.

In a former chapter, when quoting from Irish chronicles concerning Liafail, we showed that one form of the word, or one of its names, was written Leagael. This word has the same peculiarities as that of Liafail in that it also has seven letters, and that when it is read either from left to right or from right to left, it is the same word, or by beginning either to the right or left and reading to the central letter, and back again, we still have Leagael, and by beginning with the fourth, or central letter, and reading either from left to right as the Saxons do, or from right to left, as the Hebrews do, we have in each case the same word, i. e., *gael*.

This word *gael* is a Hebrew word, and yet it is absolutely one of the most important words in all the history of the Saxon people; for it is the name of that tongue, speech, or dialect, which is the very root of the "King's English," as that language is sometimes called, which is now known as the mother tongue of the Saxons, but which evidently is not the original language of that race, for it is only several hundred years old, and these historians from whom we have quoted trace them back along the line of history for two thousand five hundred and twenty years.

The fact of this change in the language of the Saxons, as the years have been rolling by, dovetails into the history of Ephraim-Israel as foretold by the prophet Isaiah, who in the first verse of the twenty-eighth chapter says: "Woe to the crown of pride, to the drunkards of Ephraim." Remember we are not dealing with a race of saints, but with a people who have largely gone away from their God, although to begin with, they were a people who were *"wholly a right seed."* Nationally speaking, while other nations are opium eaters, and have other vices which cling to them as a people, the Saxons are the drunkard nation of the earth. Great Britain, in drunkenness, is worse than America; but America is bad enough in this respect to be so recognized by the more temperate nations of the world. But our chief object in giving this quotation is to show that the prophet was addressing Ephraim, of whom he further says: "For, with stammering lips and another tongue, will he (the Lord) speak to this people." The Hebrew word, which in this text, is translated *stammering* is that word *Gael.*

It is a remarkable fact that Young in his "Analytical Concordance" gives us the word *Leag,* as the

original Hebrew word, while Strong in his "Exhaustive Concordance" gives us the equally correct word
Gael, from the same Hebrew word. But be it *Leag*
to the Hebrew or *Gael* to the Saxon, it is the same
word to the same people, which they have reversed
and given to their newer language, which is called
the Gael, or Gael-ic tongue, which is not only the foundation of the English language, but is yet spoken in
its primitive simplicity in many places in Wales, Scotland and the north of Ireland.

Wa-els is only another form of Gaels, and the people
whose language was called Gael were themselves often
called Gaels. At first when a person needed to speak
of but one of these people, the custom was to say:
"One Gael," but as the language changed, the form of
one changed to *an* before a vowel sound, and to *a*
before a consonant sound. Thus *one Gael* became
Angael. And since the Hebrew word *ish* means man,
we can understand how things would get a little mixed,
and how very easy would be the evolution from AN-
GA-EL-ISH-MAN to

AN ENGLISHMAN.

Also, since these same people were called Angli,
and Sax-es, the combination and evolution of these
names into *Anglo-Saxon* would be inevitable.

CHAPTER VII.

A STUDY IN "SCARLET."

In giving further proof concerning that prince of the scarlet thread, whom historians tell us was married to Tea Tephi, the Eastern princess, we know of nothing that will be so helpful, satisfactory and convincing as to give his genealogy; beginning with his fathers, Juda and Zarah, and come down from father to son until we reach him. We are able to do this, but only because Prof. Totten has faithfully scanned the pages of ancient and modern history, and as a result has compiled and given to the world the genealogy of the Zarah branch of the royal family, which was exalted to the throne when the breach was made in the line of Pharez in the days of Zedekiah.

Culling from a genealogical diagram found in No. 5 of "Our Race" we have the following: Judah, begat Zarah; Zarah, begat Ethan; Ethan, begat Mahol; Mahol, begat Calcol; Calcol, begat Gadhol; Gadhol, begat Easru; *Easru,* begat *Sru;* Sru, begat *Heber Scot;* Heber Scot, begat Boamhain; Boamhain, begat Ayhaimhain; Ayhaimhain, begat *Tait;* Tait, begat Aghenoin; Aghenoin, begat Feabla Glas; Feabla Glas, begat Neanuail; Neanuail, begat Nuaghadh; Nuaghadh, begat Alloid; Alloid, begat Earchada, Earchada, begat Deagfatha; Deagfatha, begat Bratha; Bratha, begat Broegan; Broegan, begat Bille; Bille, begat Gallam (or William, the conqueror of Ireland); Gallam, begat Herremon, (who married Tea Tephi, and *Heber* and Amhergin his two brothers.

Of course, it is impossible to give Prof. Totten's argument by which this genealogy can be verified, but we can call attention to a few *straws,* which, you know, *show which way the wind blows.*

First, you will notice that we have italicized some of these names, two of which are Heber, and one Tait. In giving this genealogy we have given the direct line from father through only one son, but some of these men were the fathers of more than one son. Sru, for instance, the father of Heber Scot, had two other sons. Tait, who begat Aghenoin, had a son by the name of Heber. The fact that there are three Hebers in this branch of the royal family is most significant, for that is the name from which comes one of the national names of their race, i. e., Hebrews.

Also, we have told our readers of the confusion which most students of history find in trying to straighten out the history of Ireland, but it is generally conceded that there are two distinct phases to the Hebrew story of Ireland. The one is that concerning Jeremiah and the king's daughters, and the other is that which is told in the Milesian records, in which we have the story of the prince who married one of Jeremiah's wards. The Milesian story takes its rise in Egypt and Palestine amid the scenes of Israel's infancy. Now we are ready to call your attention to two other names in the genealogy of Zarah's royal house, which we have italicized, i. e., Easru and Sru, for in the Milesian records the descendants of these men, and some of their predecssors, were called by a name which to this day means *the children of the Red (or scarlet) Branch.*

The prince in the Bible story, as given in Ezekiel's riddle, is called a young *twig*, and the highest *branch* of the high cedar, and, after Zedekiah's sons were slain, it was not possible to find a prince who was eligible to sit on that throne unless he belonged to the line of the scarlet thread, for the other line, from which Christ came, was with the Jews in Babylon. Hence these children of the *"Red Branch"* must have belonged to the *Scarlet-thread branch* of the royal family. The Milesian records also call them *"Curaithe na Cruabh ruadh,"* the "Knights of the Red Branch."

"The term Milesian is derived from the mediæval title of Gallam, the conqueror of Ireland, who was called Milesius, or the Milesian, i. e., *the soldier,* a term derived from the Latin *miles,* whence we derive our word militia."—Totten.

"Furthermore, these knights of the Red Branch, of whom Gallam, the conquering Milesian, was one, called themselves *Craunnogs,* or 'the crowned.' The true meaning of their name is 'Tree tops,' for it comes from words common to all dialects: *craun* 'a tree,' and *og* 'a tuft' or 'termination.' We use the same word for a 'crown,' as they did, and the very use of it in common language would be enough to verify this identity of race were there not other reasons in their history and legends to establish it conclusively."—Totten.

One hundred years ago Joseph Ben Jacob, a Celt, and a Catholic, in a work called "Precursory Proofs," said: "Among the five equestrian orders of ancient Ire-

land was one called *Craobh-ruadh* (the Red Branch).
The origin of this order was so very ancient that all
attempts at explanation have hitherto failed. Some
suppose that it originated from the Ulster arms, which
are 'luna, a hand sinister, couped at the wrist, Mars.'
But these admit it should in such case be called crobh-
ruadh, or of the bloody hand."

This man was really proving the Hebrew and Egyptian origin of the Irish Celts, but was applying all the
evidence that he found to Joseph, knowing nothing of
the story of the breach in the royal family of Judah,
and of the exaltation of the *Scarlet Branch*, who landed
in the plantation of Ulster. Else he would have known
where to place the meaning of that ensignum of the red,
or bloody, hand "couped at the wrist" with a scarlet
thread which found its way into the royal arms of
Ulster.

The prophet Nahum, while speaking of "the excellency of Israel," says: "The shield of his mighty
men is made red, the valiant men are in scarlet." Scarlet is the characteristic color of the English army, and
they certainly wore "red coats" during the Revolu-
tionary War. We were recently in an English city, and
we took particular note of the scarlet thread, or stripe
which ran up the front, around the neck, down the
arms and up the pantaloon legs of the uniform of the
post men of the province.

A British consul once told us that every official
order he received was tied with a *scarlet thread*, and
showed us one which he had just received. This same
thing is true also with all English officials, to whom

written orders are sent, and from this custom comes that well-known political and diplomatical metaphor, "Red-tape."

We have also learned, from sources which we deem authentic, that a scarlet thread is woven into the material from which all ropes are manufactured, which are to be used in the construction of vessels for the British government, or navy. This is done so that under and all circumstances these vessels may be identified as the property of Great Britain, even though they be sunk in many fathoms of water at the bottom of the sea.

When Jacob blessed the sons of Joseph, he was under the necessity of crossing his hands in order that he might get his right hand on the boy that the Holy Spirit was designating as the one whom God had chosen as the birthright inheritor; and in thus crossing his hands Jacob necessarily made this sign (✖), or the sign of the cross. This is the *pre*-Christian cross of which relics are found along the trail of Israel, as they were being sifted through the nations to the isles of the Northwest, and which Ignatius Donnelly finds not only in Egypt and Ireland, but almost everywhere else. Donnelly's object in discussing the pre-Christian cross is to prove that the cross has been a sacred emblem ever since the creation of man, and that it originated in the garden of Eden, because of the four rivers which parted in Eden and became four heads. Donnelly finds that in Egypt, Assyria and the British Isles, the pre-Christian cross was emblematical of creative power and eternity. He also finds carved on Egyptian monuments (see cut) a very ancient sacred emblem, which he says Sir Gardener Wilkinson says was called "The cross-cake," which is, as you see, a cake with a cross on it, and as soon as we read this in Donnelly's "Atlantis," instantly we associated the Egyptian Cross-cake with the following: "Ephraim is *a cake* not turned." We know that Ephraim was associated with the cross that Jacob made, that he came from Egypt, and if he was not in some way associated with that cake with which are associated both Egypt and a cross, why should God use the metaphor, *"cake,"* in a prophecy concerning Ephraim's people? Here is a question for all grades of skeptics, from the "Higher Critics" up to the honest infidel, to answer. Thank God, that, when it comes to this question of critics, there is a superlative degree; i. e., Highest Critics!

CROSS FROM EGYPTIAN MONUMENTS.

This sign (✖) has floated in what is known as the "Union Jack," from the flagstaffs of the United Kingdom, and from the mast heads of English vessels for as many centuries as the kingdom has any history. It is also in that which is now accepted the world over as the national flag of the British people, which is described as a *scarlet* field with the union on a field of blue, to which are now added certain Christian crosses, one of which is *scarlet,* and across the others there is a narrow strip or thread of *scarlet.*

Ephraim as a cake unturned must mean, whatever else it may mean, that he has a hidden or unseen side, and that he is not altogether the fresh young nation that he seems to be. This new side is the Saxon side, with this sign (SaXon) buried in the very heart of his name, and the other side is the Ephraim-Israel side, but it is the same old cake, with its name of *Saac's sons* burnt through until it shows on this side.

If it be true that the sign of the cross became sacred in the garden of Eden, then surely, after the giving of the birthright, it became doubly so to the house of Joseph; but now it is thrice sacred to them, for on the cross their Saviour made full atonement for sin.

We believe that when Jacob said to Joseph: "I know it, my son, I know it!" he not only knew he had his right hand on Ephraim's head, which Joseph thought should have been on Manasseh's, but that he also knew why he blessed the sons of Joseph with the sign of the cross above their heads. For while he prayed with his hands thus crossed he said, "God, ... the Angel, which *redeemed me from all evil*, bless the lads," and we know there is no other name given among men whereby we can be saved, except the name of Him who shed his blood upon the cross to redeem men.

To us it is indeed significant that the birthright blessing was given with the sign of the cross. That the cross was sacred Jacob certainly knew. That God sent his Divine Word unto Jacob, we Christian Saxons (sons of I-saac) certainly know; and that Judah rejected that WORD made flesh, we also know. That Ephraim-Israel would receive that Word, divine prophecy declares; and that the Saxons did receive that rejected One and the word of his grace, is simply undeniable. Then, surely, that triple cross, together with one which has a thread of scarlet blood streaming down its rugged side, must mean more—yea, much more—to the people of one certain race, than it ever can to some other races. For He who shed that blood said: *"I am not sent but unto the lost sheep of the house of Israel."*

Our readers now know that the name "House of Israel" was the Biblical-historic and the prophetic name of the birthright people, over and against the name "House of Judah," for the Jewish people. So, if the people, known as the Jews, and they only, be national Israel—i. e., *"all of it,"* as has been taught by Christendom for lo! these many centuries—then the coming of Christ *to the seed of Abraham* was a failure in every sense. And if this be so, why should the angel Gabriel tell Mary, the daughter of Joseph (Mary's father's name was Joseph, as well as her husband's), that her divine child should "reign over the house of Jacob forever"? Or why should Mary, after receiving the salutation of Elizabeth, say: "He (God) hath *holpen his servant Israel* in remembering his mercy, as he spake to our fathers, to Abraham, and to his seed forever?" Or why should Zacharias, being filled with the Holy Ghost, say:

"Blessed be the Lord God of Israel; for he hath visited and redeemed his people, and hath raised up an horn of salvation for us in the house of his servant David; as he spake by the mouth of his holy prophets, which have been since the world began; that we should be saved from our enemies, and from the hand of all that hate us, to perform the mercy promised to our fathers, and to remember his holy covenant; the oath which he sware to our father Abraham, that he would grant unto us, that we being delivered out of the hand of our enemies might serve him without fear, *in holiness and righteousness before him,* ALL THE DAYS OF OUR LIFE"? (Luke 1: 69-75.)

We may also further ask, Why should Isaiah say: "Unto us a child is born, unto us a son is given; and the government shall be upon his shoulder; and his name shall be called Wonderful, Counselor, The Mighty God, The Everlasting Father, The Prince of Peace. Of the increase of his government and peace there shall be no end, upon the throne of David, and upon his kingdom to order it, and establish it with judgment and with justice from henceforth even forever. The zeal of the Lord of hosts will perform this. The Lord sent a word unto Jacob, and it hath lighted upon Israel. *And all the people shall know, even Ephraim.*"—Isa. 9: 6-9.

'Mark that! *All the people of Israel*—Ephraim-Israel—*shall know.* Yea, they do now know. Whether they be in the "High Church," or in the "Low;" whether they are Catholic or Protestant; whether they attend service at a costly cathedral, in some great palatial church, or in "the little church around the corner;" whether they pray in the uptown, or in the downtown church; whether they listen to the preached word in the independent mission, or in that little mission, the child of some uptown church, which they are holding off at arm's length; whether they attend the revival services of the popular evangelist, or whether they stand on the streets of our Anglo-Israel cities, and hear all sort of evangelists from very good to very inferior; yes, surely, whether they listen to any, all, or none (for they hear it as they go), all the people of Ephraim do know this one thing, namely: "Unto *us* a child is born."

It is conceded by all Christendom that those who accept the benefits of the new covenant, of which the testator must die before the testament could be in force, have the law of that covenant written in their hearts. Indeed, Paul when speaking of the New Testament covenant, which he says was "established upon better promises" than the Mosaic covenant, the failure of which necessitated the making of the new, says: "Because they continued not in my covenant, and I regarded them not, saith the Lord. For this is the covenant that I will make with the house of Israel after those days, saith the Lord; I will put my laws into their mind, and write them in their hearts; and I will be to them a God, and they shall be to me a people."—Heb. 8:10.

Thus we see that the journey of Israel from Lo-ammi (not my people) to Ammi (my people), is by the way of the blood-stained cross. But it is literal, fleshly Israel, that must make this journey. This is why God, by the mouth of the prophet Isaiah, says: "Hearken unto me, ye that know righteousness, the people in whose heart is my law," "Hearken to me, ye that follow after righteousness, ye that seek the Lord: look unto the rock whence ye are hewn, and to the hole of the pit whence ye are digged. Look unto Abraham your father, *and unto Sarah that* BARE YOU."—Isa. 51: 7 and 1-2.

When the house of Judah rejected Jesus, he asked them if they had read in the Scriptures concerning a stone which was rejected, and which became the head of the corner; and then he told them that the kingdom of God should be taken from them and given to another nation. Israel had been rejected, cast out, forsaken, divorced; but in order to be consistent with the prophecies of the Old Testament, and many passages in the New Testament, we contend that the other nation to which Jesus referred could have been none other than the house of Israel, that other nation of the two nations into which the seed of Abraham were divided.

"But" says one, "Paul said, I turn to the Gentiles, I am the apostle of the Gentiles, I magnify mine office." True, and in this he was obeying the order, "To the Jew first," but the Lord certainly sent him also to the Gentiles. The trouble with this word *Gentiles* to the ordinary English reader is, that to his mind it always excludes God's chosen people; whereas it only excludes the Jewish portion of the chosen race. There are three Greek words in the New Testament which are translated Gentile, and Gentiles. One of them is *Hellen,* and its various forms, which means Greek, Greece, or Grecian, but is sometimes used in the sense of non-Jewish. The other two words are *Ethnee,* and *Ethnos,* from which comes our word *ethnology,* which is defined as: "The science which treats of the different races and families of men." These two words are simply the singular and plural forms of the same root word. Liddell & Scott's Greek Lexicon defines, *Ethnos,* the singular, as, "A number of people living together, a company, body of men, a host, a tribe, a people. But, *Ethnee,* the plural, is, of course, defined by this same authority as, "The *nations,* hosts, tribes, and peoples."

God said to Abraham: "Thou shalt be the father of many nations."

Also, "The father of a multitude of *nations* have I made thee."

"I will make *nations* of thee, and kings shall come out of thee."

"She (Sarah) shall be a mother of *nations;* kings of *people* shall be of her."

God also said to Jacob, "That thou mayest be a company of *peoples;*" and, also, *"A nation* and *a company of nations* shall be of thee."

Jacob, by the command of God, said to Joseph: "Behold, I will make thee fruitful, and multiply thee, and I will make of thee a multitude of *people.*"

God, in turn, said to Joseph, through Jacob, "He (Manasseh) also shall become *a people,* and he shall be great: Howbeit his younger brother shall be greater than he, and his seed shall become a *multitude of nations.*"

Indeed, we have neither time nor space to tell of all the host and hosts, the people and peoples, the nation and nations, that are involved in these covenant promises; but, surely, these will suffice to show that these covenant promises are ethnical in the fullest and broadest sense. Hence when Jesus sent Saul of Tarsus to the *Ethnee;* i. e., the nations, we dare to say that he included, if he did not wholly mean, *the nations* of the birthright kingdom of Israel; for he said to Ananias in a vision concerning this same circumstance of Paul's call and commission: "He is a chosen vessel unto me, to bear my name before the (Ethnee) Gentiles, and kings, and the *Children* of ISRAEL."—Acts 9:15.

It was that Paul might go to the children of Israel that the Holy Ghost hindered him from going into Asia, and sent him into Macedonia, which included the country once known as Mosei, and where many of the *Saacs* still lingered. Then Paul pushed on into Illyricum, a country which lies still further to the northwest. This also is Paul's reason for wanting to go into Spain, whither he finally went. Irænus, one of the early Church Fathers, writing concerning the work of Paul, says: "He established many Christian churches among the Keltoi (Celts)." Also Clement, of Rome, of whom Paul speaks as having his name in the book of life, says of Paul, that he was the "Herald (of the Gospel of Christ) in the West," and that "he had gone to the *extremity of the West.*" This could not have been said by a writer at Rome without implying a journey into some countries much further to the West. Chrysostom, another early Church writer, says: "Paul preached in Spain," and, according to the testimony of several others, Paul also preached the Gospel to the Britons. At all events, they received the Gospel, and Jesus Christ, the son of David, became a "Light to *the nations,* and became the glory of *his people Israel,*" who were ruled over by the descendants of the Prince of the *scarlet thread;* and who put a *blood-stained cross,* the cross of St. George, into the heraldry of their nation. Later they and their brother nation became the evangelistic nations of the world. Thus through the many nations of Abraham's seed has the *One* Seed, the testator of the new covenant, been *a blessing to all the nations of the earth.*

Well, indeed, may Jesus say: *"If ye believe not his (Moses') writings,* HOW SHALL YE BELIEVE MY WORDS?"

CHAPTER VIII.

"Now Israel loved Joseph more than all his children, because he was the son of his old age, and he made him a coat of many colors." A souvenir of this coat of many colors which Jacob made for Joseph is still found in the many-colored plaid, as worn by the Scotch Highlanders, not only at home, but by Highlander societies, which exist in nearly every large Anglo-Saxon city. The use of this vari-colored plaid, and the custom of wearing it, can be traced as far back as the Scottish people have any history, and yet its origin among them is unknown; that is, it was unknown until they began to know that they were the descendants of Joseph.

Also, once upon a time, the Gileadites were at war with Ephraim-Israel, "and the Gileadites took the passages of Jordan before the Ephraimites; and it was so, that when those Ephraimites which were escaped said, Let me go over; that the men of Gilead said unto them, Art thou an Ephraimite? If he said, Nay; then said they unto him, Say now Shibboleth, and he said, S-iboleth; *for he could not frame to pronounce it right.*" The Ephraimites seem to have had trouble to pronounce the letter *h,* and many of Ephraim's people still have trouble with their *h's,* especially the modern "Cockney."

The Gileadites seem to have worsted Israel in this war to which we have referred, but, according to prophecy, there was to come a time when Ephraim would nevermore be conquered by a Gentile nation. And it must have been to this end that the Lord told the islands to keep silent, "until my people renew their strength." For of this same people, this Israel that is dwelling in the isles, the Lord says: "Behold, all that were incensed against thee shall be ashamed and confounded; they that strive against thee shall perish; they shall be as nothing. Thou shalt seek them, even them that contended with thee; they that war against thee shall be as nothing, and as a thing of naught. For I, the Lord thy God, will hold thy right hand, saying unto thee, Fear not; I will help thee. Fear not, thou worm Jacob, and ye men of Israel; I will help thee, saith the Lord."—Isa. 41:11-14.

When Balak, the king of Moab, hired Balaam to curse Israel, and he could not, but was compelled by the Lord to bless Israel, he said: "God brought him forth out of Egypt; he (Israel) hath, as it were, the strength of an UNICORN; he shall eat up the nations his enemies, and shall break their bones, and pierce them through with his ARROWS. He crouched, he lay down as a lion, and as a GREAT LION. Who shall stir him up? Blessed is he that blesseth thee, and cursed is he that curseth thee."—Num. 24: 8-9.

Now, it is a most remarkable fact that two of these racial emblems, the LION and the UNICORN, which were given to Israel with that compulsory blessing, are in the coat-of-arms of Great Britain. This insignia, or national seal, is, in part, the "Harp of David," which was brought to the isles by Dan and Simeon, with the *Unicorn* reared on one side and the *Great Lion* on the other. The Lion is both Judah's and Israel's, so also is the Unicorn not only Israel's, but Joseph's, and yet in a special sense it belongs to Ephraim, because he had the precedence in birthright. Thus Moses, on the day of his death, while he was reiterating and enlarging upon the prophecies and promises made by Jacob to each of the tribal heads, said, concerning the blessings of Joseph: "His glory is like the firstling of his Bul-

lock, and his horns are like the horns of Unicorns; with them he shall push the people together to the ends of the earth; and they are the *ten* thousands of Ephraim (the thousands of each of the ten tribes) and the thousands (of the one tribe) of Manasseh."

The English have not only the lion and the unicorn, but they have also that which to them may mean only a circle divided into four quarters. Still it is really a reproduction of Ephraim's cake, for the four quarterings are made by a cross. (See cut.) In one of these quarterings is David's harp, and in each of the other three are young lions.

That Manasseh was a separate tribe is known from the following: "There was also a lot of the tribe of Manasseh, for he was the first-born of Joseph."— Joshua 17:1. Also the following: "For the children of Joseph were two tribes, Manasseh and Ephraim; therefore, they gave no part unto the Levites in the land, save cities to dwell in, with their suburbs."— Joshua 14:4. Thus was the land divided by lot as the Lord commanded, "But unto the tribe of Levi (the priests) Moses gave not any inheritance; the Lord God of Israel was their inheritance." Thus with Joseph's *two tribes*, which was his promised "double portion," there were *thirteen* tribes in Israel, and only twelve divisions of the land, so the Levites could have no land inheritance; but they had the Lord, which was far better, and they were allowed to eat the meat of sacrifice from off the holy altar.

But Manasseh was not only a separate tribe, but as a partaker of the birthright blessing, he and Ephraim were to grow together until they became a multitude in the midst of the earth; then he was to be separated from his brethren, and become a *great nation*. This is the reason of the prophecy, "Joseph is a fruitful bough, even a fruitful bough by a well (literally by the water), whose branches run over the wall." Thus God said: "Let the blessing come upon the top of the head of him that was separated from his brethren."

Since there are thirteen tribes in Israel, and since Ephraim and Manasseh were adopted after all the rest were born, and Ephraim is counted for Joseph, or rather that they are counted interchangeably, there is no other chance for Manasseh, numerically speaking, but that he is number thirteen.   Now, it is a significant

MANASSEH:

"He also shall become a People, and he also shall be Great."
Gen. xlviii. 19.

(CUT OF THE OBVERSE SIDE OF OUR NATIONAL SEAL.)

fact, that when Manasseh separated from Ephraim— when the people who have become *a great nation* separated from those who have become a *company of nations,* because their branches have continued to run over the wall—he, Manasseh, or America, had just thirteen states, and that thirteen is the prominent number in all the emblems and heraldry of the land.

The first national flag of those original United States had thirteen *Stars* and thirteen *Bars*. The bars symbolize the Union, and the constellation of thirteen stars was intended to symbolize the nation formed of thirteen independent states.

In this, the Great Seal of our country, as represented above, we have the arms and crest of the United States of America. We would first call your attention to the fact that the eagle is holding in what is called the "Dexter" talon an Olive Branch. In the fourteenth chapter of Hosea, that prophet, who has so much to say about lost Ephraim-Israel, we have the following: "O Israel, return unto the Lord thy God; I will heal their backslidings; I will love them freely; for mine anger is turned away from him...I will be as the dew to Israel; he shall grow like the lily (the national flower of Egypt), and cast forth his roots as Lebanon (royal cedar). His *branches shall spread,* and his beauty shall be as the Olive tree. Ephraim will say, What have I to do any more with idols?" Ephraim is the representative of the house of Joseph, and we have placed this Scripture before our readers that they may see that the *Olive* tree is among the insignia of the birthright family, and that it is here represented as belonging to one of the *Branches* of the birthright kingdom, and since the birthright is Joseph's, it is *the Olive Branch of Joseph* which has been placed in the "Coat of Arms" of Manasseh, the thirteenth tribe in Israel, who has now fulfilled the prophecy of becoming a *great nation.*

Still this fact, if it stood alone, might not mean so much, but in the other talon, which is called the "Sinister," is a "Bundle of thirteen *Arrows*," which represents the nation individually and collectively prepared for war.   It is marvelous that the *Olive Branch* should have been made our official insignum of *Peace,* and that the *Arrows* should have been made by law to represent the War Power of the country, for the *Arrows* were in the heraldry of Israel, as well as the Unicorn and Lion, when Balaam was compelled to bless instead of curse them.   Also, the Josephites were *Bow*-men, and Jacob, after speaking of Joseph and his branches, said, "The archers have sorely grieved him, and shot at him, and hated him. But his Bow (munitions of war) abode in strength, and the *Arms* of his hands were made strong by the hands of the mighty God of Jacob."— Gen. 49:23-24.   It is a well-known, and much-rejoiced-over fact that the *Bow* of the United States, which has sent her *Arrows* into the ranks of her enemies, has always *abode in strength,* and that both her chief men and people have always said: *"God has helped us."*

When Israel marched through the wilderness, she had four standards that were called "Camp Standards." One of these was on the north, one on the east, one on the south, and one on the west. But there were, besides these, a family standard or ensign for each tribe. Hence the Lord commanded saying: "Every man of the children of Israel shall pitch by his own standard, with the ensign of their father's house; afar off about the tabernacle shall they pitch."—Num. 2: 2. The object of the camp standards was, that when the time came to camp or pitch their tents for the night, the three tribes which belonged to each of these four camp standards might gather to them. The compilers of our reference Bibles understood this, hence they have given the references to the four living creatures of Ezekiel 1:10 as follows: "As for the likeness of their faces, they four had the face of a *Man* (Num. 2:10) and the face of a *Lion* (Num. 2:3), on the right side; and they four had the face of an *Ox* (Num. 2:18) on the left side; they four also had the face of an *Eagle*. (Num. 2:25.)"

The reference to the Lion reads: "And on the east side, toward the rising of the sun, shall they of the standard of the camp of Judah pitch throughout their armies." It was dying Jacob who gave the Lion to Judah as the ensign of his royal house, in the following: "Judah is a lion's whelp; from the prey, my son, thou art gone up; he stooped down, he crouched as a lion, and as an old (Lawbee-old, great, stout) lion, who shall rouse him up?" Oh! this is truly wonderful, for, mark this, when his race was young Judah as a *Lion's Whelp* took a leap with Dan from Palestine to the isles, and now he is there as an *Old Lion*, and the question is, "Who shall rouse him up?"

The fact that we find Judah's Lion with the Unicorn of Ephraim-Israel in the national seal of the Brith-ish, or covenant, people is another evidence that the royal remnant of the Judo-Davidic house found their way to Ephraim-Israel at the time of the uprooting of the Pharez line, who was then, as now, living in the isles of the northwest. And it is also another evidence that the Saxon nations are the nations of Israel upon whom "lighted" the Divine word, who is also *"The Lion of the Tribe of Judah."*

The reference from the *Ox* in Ezekiel is as follows: "On the west side shall be the standard of the camp of Ephraim according to their armies." Here again we have the representative of Joseph, the birthright holder, of whom Moses said: "His glory is like the firstling of his *Bullock*." The Hebrew word that is here translated *bullock* is the same as that in Ezekiel 1 : 10, which is rendered *Ox*. In fact, there is but one word in the Hebrew (shur, or shour) for ox, bull, or cow. But the above shows us that the family ensign of Joseph was a bovine. This is the reason for such expressions as, "Ephraim is an heifer that is taught," and "Israel slideth back as a backsliding heifer." It was also because of this fact that, when Jeroboam, of the house of Joseph, wanted to make idols which would be attractive to Ephraim-Israel, he made two calves; i. e., a bullock and a heifer. The Unicorn of Israel is now in the national insignia of that people, but the family ensign still clings to them as a national nickname; i. e., *"John Bull."*

Thus far it is clear that the *Lion* of Ezekiel's vision was the camp standard of Judah, which was on the east; and that the *Ox* of his vision was the ensign of the family of Joseph, which was with Ephraim in the west. As we continue to investigate the signification of these four living creatures we find that the reference to the *Eagle* reads as follows: "The standard of the camp of Dan shall be on the north side of their armies." We have already shown, while explaining

Ezekiel's riddle concerning the pulling down of *him that was high,* and the exaltation of *him that was low,* that the *Eagle* was, at that time, the ensign of the tribe of Dan ; but since that time they have used the *Leaping Lion's Whelp, with the serpent's tail,* and the *Eagle,* like everything else that pertains to national Israel, has fallen to the birthright family, and is now the national ensign of the thirteenth tribe of Israel, the people of which are not only the descendants of Manasseh, the first-born of Joseph, but they also compose the first-born nation out of the "MANY NATIONS," which were promised to Abraham, Isaac, Jacob, and Joseph, and whose ensign Eagle holds in his beak a scroll upon which is written their national motto, "*E Pluribus Unum,*" which has thirteen letters, and means "One out of MANY."

Therefore, concerning a certain land which is indwelt by a portion of Israel, we have the following: "Ho (or Hail, not *Woe,* as in the King James version of the Scriptures) to the land shadowing with wings, which is beyond the rivers of Ethiopia : that sendeth ambassadors by the sea, even in vessels of bulrushes upon the waters, saying: Go, ye swift messengers, to a nation scattered and peeled, to *a people terrible from their beginning* [note that] ; hitherto a nation meted out [measured out by a time of prophecy, which is called *the times of the Gentiles*] and trodden down, whose [home, or ancient] land the RIVERS [*Now, therefore, behold the Lord bringeth upon them* (Israel) *the* WATERS *of the* RIVER, *strong and many, even the king of Assyria, and all his glory; and he shall come up over all his* (Israel's) *channels, and go over all his* banks."—Isa. 18:8-7] have spoiled! All ye inhabitants of the world, and dwellers on the earth, see ye, when he (that nation shadowed with wings) lifteth up an ensign." We have thus parenthesized Isa. 18:8-7 with Isa. 18:1-3, that our readers may know that this land which had set up an ensign of outstretched wings was a land in which Israelites were dwelling, for it was the king of Assyria, who came up against Ephraim-Israel, overflowed his land, and led him into captivity. Prior to this, Moab had once held Israel in derision, and the Lord, in condemning their arrogance, said: "He (Israel) shall fly as an Eagle, and *spread his wings* over Moab."—Jer. 48: 40. No wings except those which are spread out can be shadowing wings, and the *Shadowing wings* of Israel's *Spread Eagle* are in the ensign of the United States of America. Hence, America is the land shadowed by wings of which Isaiah wrote, whose ambassadors cross the sea in vessels of bulrushes, or, literally, of *caldrons which absorb water;* i. e., the modern steamship.

The *Shield,* or escutcheon, which is borne on the breast of the Spread Eagle, has thirteen pieces, called pales, or paleways, which comes from the same word as palings or pickets. These thirteen paleways are united by one at the top. The Lord said to Abraham: "I am thy *Shield.*"

On the national seal of America, the "Great People," above the shadowing wings and the scroll, is a *Cloud* emitting rays of *Glory.* "Aaron spake unto the whole congregation of the children of Israel,...and behold the *Glory* of the Lord appeared in the *Cloud.*" To our fathers that glory *Cloud* was significant of the presence of Jehovah.   That Glory Cloud, which hung over Israel, guided those who had but just escaped from the Egyptian bondage, and it stood between them and their enemies.   But this is not all, for this Cloud of our American heraldry surrounds what is called "The Constellation."

THE GREAT PYRAMID.

THE REVERSE SIDE OF AMERICA'S NATIONAL SEAL.

This constellation is a group of thriteen stars, or planets, on a field of azure sky, which is exactly the same number of planets that appeared on the azure sky in the dream of Joseph, which drove him into separation from his brethren.

Any one of these features in the blazonry of our nation might have been a coincidence, but when we see that there is not a single feature, but that which is Josephic and Israelitish, it is simply astounding. But when we turn our face upon the reverse side of that great national seal we are overwhelmed, for there stands the Great Pyramid of Egypt, which is one of the two great monuments of Egypt, the birthplace of Ephraim and Manasseh, the Egypto-Israelitish sons of Joseph, the son of Jacob, the son of Isaac, the son of Abraham. And, marvel of marvels! The national Crest of England has that other great monument of Egypt, the Sphinx, on its reverse side. Thus do the people of Great Britain and the United States of America, the Brother nations, by that which speaks louder than words, for signs are arbitrary, say that they are the offsprings of the Egypto-Israelitish holders of the Abrahamic birthright.

The people of the United States made this declaration by that which was made a law on Thursday, June 20, 1782, for on that day the ensign which bears those shadowing wings of Israel, together with the Heraldry of Joseph, became a law among us. Also over the pyramid on the reverse side of the Great Seal of America is another thirteen-lettered motto, which, of course is not only lawful, but also national; i. e., "Annuit Coeptis,"—"*He* (the Lord) hath *prospered* our undertakings." This also is Josephic, for we read, "The Lord was with Joseph, and he was a *prosperous* man." "The Lord was with him (Joseph), and that which he did the Lord made it to *prosper*."—Gen. 39: 3-23.

To those who understand the Cabala and the arithmography of the Scriptures, it is known that the number thirteen is significant of *Rebellion,* but all that we can say about it here is that the first time this number occurs in the Bible it is with reference to *Rebellion* (Gen. 14: 4). Surely that people whose characteristic number is *thirteen* did rebel in 1776, and *prospered* in it, too. They also prospered in 1814, in another little affair concerning the acquisition of a vast stretch of territory known as Louisiana.

This people have also had rebellion within their own borders, and it is a remarkable fact that, although thirteen was not the number of states in the Confederacy, the Confederate Congress, in 1863, formally adopted a battle flag for the Confederacy, and also a Confederate flag. The *Battle Flag* was a white field with a blue cross of this (✖) shape, in which there were thirteen stars. The flag for the Confederacy was white, with a red field in the Dexter chief corner, bearing this same (✖) cross with its thirteen stars. Here again is both rebellion and the birthright cross of the house of Joseph. In this struggle the government also prospered, and it was essential that it should thus prosper, not only in this case, but also in the others of which we have spoken, in order to fulfill a prophecy concerning one feature of their history, namely: "Shew my people their transgression, and the house of Jacob their sins. Is not this the fast that I have chosen? to undo the heavy burdens, and let the OPPRESSED GO FREE, and that YE break every yoke?" These are the reasons for which *Our Race* go to war. England freed her slaves in 1838 and America freed hers in 1861.

It has often been said that brothers would quarrel.

Judah and Ephraim did, and so have Ephraim and Manasseh; and the troubles to which we have thus far alluded have been family affairs. When it comes to these family difficulties, that one will always conquer which must do so in order to fulfill the word of God. But when it comes to war with non-Israelitish nations, whether it be to *undo heavy burdens,* to let the *oppressed go free,* to *break the yoke* of slavery, or for whatever reason, then the Israel of which we speak will always succeed. For it is of literal, fleshly, Joseph Israel, of whom also is spiritual Israel, of whom it is said: "No weapon that is formed against thee shall prosper." And also the following: "The remnant of Jacob shall be among the Gentiles in the midst of many people as a lion among the beasts of the forest, as a young lion among the sheep (marg. goats); who, if he go through, both treadeth down, and teareth in pieces, and none can deliver. Thine hand shall be lifted up upon thine adversaries, and all thine enemies shall be cut off."—Mich. 5: 8-9.

It was in fulfillment of these promises that Napoleon, the hitherto victor, bit the dust at Waterloo. It was in fulfillment of these promises that the American fleet entered Manila Bay, and destroyed the enemy's fleet with the loss of only seven men. It was in fulfillment of these words of Divine truth that the American fleet destroyed the Spanish fleet in Cuban waters and lost only one man. It was that these promises might be fulfilled that Sam Houston, with only seven hundred and fifty raw recruits, fought the decisive battle against the Mexican army at San Jacinto, April 21st, 1836, in which he annihilated the Mexicans at one blow, killing six hundred and fifty, capturing three hundred and fifty, and putting the rest to flight, and yet losing only eight men and twenty-five wounded. But space forbids to tell of the many similar cases.

When the children of Israel were singing unto the Lord over the victory he had given them by destroying the armies of Pharaoh, they said: *"Thou didst blow with thy wind,* the sea covered them: they sank as lead in the mighty waters. Who is like unto thee, O Lord, among the mighty ones? Who is like thee, glorious in holiness, fearful in praise, doing wonders?" In the forty-first chapter of Isaiah, where the Lord says to Israel in the isles, "They that WAR against thee shall be as nothing, and as a thing of naught," he also says: "Thou shalt fan them, and the wind shall carry them away, and the whirlwind shall scatter them." One fulfillment of this promise was the destruction of the "Invincible Spanish Armada," when they went against the English in 1588, concerning which the American Cyclopedia gives the following: "The Spanish Armada sailed May 29, *but a storm compelled it to return;* and it was not till the end of July that the two fleets met and joined in battle near the English coast. After a series of actions that lasted several days, the Spaniards were utterly routed, *the elements assisting the English."* The underscores are ours, as we wish to call your attention to how the Lord helped. This Armada consisted of 130 vessels all told, and was unequaled in its time. Israel in the isles had not yet fully renewed their strength. The history continues, "Having left Lisbon for Corunna for stores, May 29, 1588, *the fleet was dispersed by a violent* storm, and, though all the ships joined at Corunna with the exception of four, they were considerably shattered, and had to be repaired. Reports having reached England that the armament was completely disabled, the government ordered its own ships to be laid up; but Lord Howard, the admiral, opposed this order, set sail for Corunna, learned the truth, and on his return continued warlike preparations. Soon after, being informed that the Armada had hove in sight, he weighed anchor, and as it passed Plymouth, July 31, stood out in its rear and opened a destructive fire. Having the windward position, and being greatly superior in speed, he was able to inflict serious damage without loss to himself. All the way along the channel the English followed the Armada with the same tactics, taking advantage of the *changing winds,* harassing the Spaniards, capturing two or three of their best vessels, and yet keeping all the while virtually out of reach. The Spaniards proceeded toward the coast of Flanders, keeping as close together as possible . . . Off Calais the Armada cast anchor, waiting for the Duke of Parma's fleet to come out of the Flemish harbors; but Parma had nothing but unarmed barges, and could not come out until the Armada had beaten off the Anglo-Dutch blockading squadron. Driving the Spaniards out of Calais roads by means of fire ships, Aug. 8, Howard and Drake now forced them toward the Flemish coast, with the purpose of getting them into the North Sea and cutting off their communications with Dunkirk. The battle began at daybreak off Gravelines, and lasted till dark. The Spaniards were completely defeated. Several of their largest ships were lost, and 40,000 men were killed, and probably at least as many were wounded. It was impossible either to return to Calais or to reach the Duke of Parma. Their provisions were nearly exhausted, and the English fleet, *apparently little injured,* still hovered on their weather beam. It was imperative that they should return to Spain for fresh stores. The passage through the channel being closed by the English fleet, the Spaniards, now counting 120 vessels, undertook to round Scotland and Ireland. *But in the neighborhood of the Orkneys they were dispersed by a storm. Some of them foundered. About thirty were afterward wrecked on the west coast of Ireland. Those of the crews who escaped to shore were generally killed, and it was calculated that about 14,000 thus perished."*

Remember, these historic and cyclopædic writers are not supposed to know that God has said that, in order to defend his birthright people, he would send a wind to carry away this so-called "Invincible Armada," and a whirlwind to scatter them. Hence their testimony is all the more striking. Surely the people of modern Israel, who dwell in the Isles, might also sing unto the Lord, saying: "Thou didst blow with thy wind, and carried them (their enemies) away, and the whirlwind did scatter them. Who is like the Lord, glorious in holiness, fearful in praise, doing wonders?" Truly, Jesus has well said: *"If I have told you of earthly things, and ye believe not, how shall ye believe if I tell you of heavenly* (spiritual) *things?"*

CONCESSIONAL.

Still we call to our God of old;
  God of the *"far off"* Isaac line;

Our God, whose word doth make us bold
  To claim *our* heritage divine.
The Lord of hosts is with us yet,
Doth He forget? Doth He forget?

It cannot be that *Isaac* dies;
  His people and his kings depart;
Before his God the *Saxon* lies,
  Glad and brave, but with contrite heart.
The Lord of hosts is with him yet,
Doth He forget? Doth He forget?

Called in Him we are today
  No longer passing through the fire;
Altho' we were but yesterday
  As one of Nineveh and Tyre.
The Lord of *nations* guides us yet.
Doth He forget? Doth He forget?

When battles rage we *cannot* lose,
  God makes all men to stand in awe
Of Saxons, now that He doth use
  The race to whom He gave his law.
His *"Battle ax"* we are, as yet,
Doth He forget? Doth He forget?

Our fathers once did idols trust,
  Also their strength and iron shard;
Now, though we number as the dust,
  We call on thee, Lord God, to guard!
For Thou hast proved Thy holy word,
Shown mercy to Thy people, Lord!

CHAPTER IX.

THE TWO-FOLD ASPECT OF PROPHETIC ISRAEL.

The multitude of people which was predicted for the house of Joseph never was realized while they dwelt in Samaria, their **Palestinean** home; but the increase of the Saxon race is acknowledged to be phenomenal. National statistics show that Russia doubles her population in 140 years, Spain in 142 years, France in 150 years, Turkey in 555 years; but that England doubles her population every 45 years, and that the United States doubles theirs in 25 years. This is a wonderful vindication of the truth which we are bringing, for the word of truth declares: "Thou hast increased the nation, O Lord, thou hast increased the nation: thou hast removed it far unto all the ends of the earth."—Isa. 26:15. The fulfillment of this prophecy is today called "Imperialism."

One of the first national characteristics mentioned in prophecy concerning Isaac's seed is, that *they shall possess the gates of those that hate them*. Gates are entrances. National gates are now called "*ports*." Since the acquisition of the Sandwich Isles, Porto Rico and the Philippines by the United States, the Saxons control nearly all the national gateways of the world. For, prior to that time, England and America controlled all the ports of the North American continent, and England possessed, not only all the ports of the British Isles and those in Australian waters, but also Gibraltar, Suez Canal, Malta, Alexandria, Cyprus Island, gates into China, the German Ocean, the Cape gate into the Indian Ocean, and all the gates of India, gates along the east and west coasts of Africa, and the Cape Horn gate from the Atlantic into the Pacific Ocean.   In the face of such foretold facts as these for the house of Joseph, need we be surprised that God, who declareth the end from the beginning, should include in the blessings of his birthright man, *"the deep that croucheth beneath"* his vessels?

The Lord also says of Joseph, "He shall push the people *together,* to the ends of the earth: and they (who together are doing the pushing) are the ten thousands of Ephraim, and they are the thousands of Manasseh."   This seems to imply an alliance, offensive and defensive, on the part of these brother nations, the outcome of which will be that they together shall push the rest of the nations to the ends of the earth.   This alliance would be but natural, for while it is true that brothers are apt to quarrel and fight among themselves, it is also true that one of these brothers is not going to stand by and allow a stranger to jump on his brother and thresh him.   And while we write, the talk of just such an alliance is in the air, and we are sure the result will be as God hath said.

God also further says, "Behold, the people of Israel shall rise up as a great Lion, and lift himself as a young lion; he shall not lie down until he eat of the prey, and drink of the blood of the slain.   He hath as it were the strength of an Unicorn: he shall eat up the nations his enemies, and shall break their bones, and pierce them through with his ARROWS." We have requoted this Scripture, concerning the eating up of the nations, so that our readers may see that, when this time of the destruction of the nations comes, the Lion of Judah, which is with Ephraim, the *Unicorn* of Ephraim, and the *Arrows* of Manasseh are together, i. e., England and America.

The Lord also says of this same people, "The portion of Jacob is not like them (destroyed); for he (God) is the former of all things: Israel is the rod of his inheritance: the Lord of hosts is his name. Thou art my BATTLE AX and WEAPONS OF WAR: *for with thee will I break in pieces the nations, and with thee will I destroy kingdoms.*"—Jer. 51: 19-20. "There is none like unto the God of Jeshurun (symbol name for Israel), who rideth upon the heaven in thy help, and in his excellency on the sky. The eternal God is thy refuge, and underneath are the everlasting arms: and he shall thrust out the enemy from before thee; and shall say, *Destroy them.* Israel then shall dwell in safety alone."—Deut. 33: 26-27.

This is undoubtedly to be the final outcome of Israel's history, and yet, prior to this, and while they are dwelling in the midst of other nations, it is said of them: "The remnant of Jacob shall be in the midst of many people *as a dew from the Lord,* as the showers upon the grass." And yet it is in the very next verse that the prophet says of this same people, that they are the strongest power on earth, "Who, if he go through, both treadeth down, and teareth in pieces, and none can deliver."—Micah 5: 7-8.

Here, to say the least, is a two-fold aspect, or two characteristics of the same race; that is, a people who are as the refreshing and fruitful showers, and as dew from the Lord to the nations around them; and yet they are a people whom none of those nations who go to war with them can conquer. This double phase of character is due to the fact that they are that portion of the *elect race* with whom are those who also belong to the *election of grace*. This is both the national and the spiritual character of the Christianized house of Joseph, for the Lord does say of Ephraim-Israel, whom he says is *in the isles afar off*, whom he also calls the *nations*, of whom he says, *"Thou shalt yet plant vines upon the mountains of Samaria,"* that they "FOUND GRACE *in the wilderness; even Israel."*— Jer. 31. We are told that the *law* was given by Moses, but that *grace* and truth came by Jesus Christ, and since the Divine word which was sent to Jacob lighted upon Israel, even Ephraim, we know that the grace which they received in their far away home was the Grace of the Gospel of the Son of God. The wilderness where these people received the grace of God is that country whither they went when they were cast out of the land of their fathers, which at that time was unknown and uninhabited, hence a wilderness. The fact that this people received the Gospel, while cast out and lost, is also a fulfillment of the prophecy by Jeremiah in which the Lord says that he will send many fishers, Gospel fishers, *and they shall fish them.* This is also why we are told that "Ephraim shall say, What have I to do any more with idols?"

"But," questions one, "are there no Gentiles who have become Christians except these nations which are of the birthright kingdom of Israel?" Our answer is, Yes; but each of these also, like Ephraim and Manasseh, needed to be adopted. This is why we are told, "As many of you as have been baptized into Christ have put on Christ. And if ye be Christ's, *then are ye Abraham's seed, and heirs according to* THE PROMISE." This adoption is necessary in all cases where the persons are of non-Israelitish nations, for the covenants, the promises, and the adoption are Israelitish, and belong to none who are not of the seed of Abraham. Those who are thus adopted become flesh of his flesh and bone of his bone. It is for this reason that Jesus took on himself the seed of Abraham, for it behooved him to be made like unto his brethren. This involves many questions which cannot be discussed here, but we take time to say that, in order to belong to the election of grace, the adopted son is BORN of the spirit, and the home-born must also be born of the spirit. It is the conquering, literal, fleshly Israel that is a type of the conquering, literal, spiritual Israel. It is the literal, fleshly adoption into national Israel, which is the earthly family of God, that is a type of the literal spiritual adoption into the heavenly family of God, of whom Jesus Christ was the first-born among many brethren, both in the flesh and in the spirit, and who is also the first-born among many brethren in a two-fold sense, for he was not only the first among those who are both sons of God and sons of Abraham, but he was also the first out of the many who shall yet be *"the children of the resurrection."*

The fact that Joseph-Israel becomes Christianized while cast out of their land is the reason for the following: "Loose thyself from the bands of thy neck, O captive daughter of Zion. For thus saith the Lord, Ye sold yourselves for naught, and ye shall be redeemed without money. For thus saith the Lord God, My people went down aforetime into Egypt to sojourn there, and then Assyrian oppressed them without cause." To be *redeemed without money* is certainly a new covenant truth, and one that is heralded from our pulpits everywhere. On Mt. Zion, inside the walls of Jerusalem, the city of David, were the royal dwellings; hence, Zion becomes one of the generic names for the seed of Abraham, Isaac, Jacob, Joseph or Judah. This captive daughter of Zion, who the Lord declares shall be redeemed without money, went first to Egypt, and was also oppressed by the Assyrian. It was the Birthright people who were led captive into Assyria.

It is the *barren* woman, the *desolate,* the woman *forsaken,* the one who knew the *reproach of widowhood,* the *wife of youth,* who had been divorced, of whom the Lord declares, that she had more children than when married, and to whom the Lord says: "Enlarge the place of thy tent (dwelling) and let them stretch forth the curtains of thine habitations, spare not, lengthen thy cords, and strengthen thy stakes; for thou shalt break forth on the right hand and on the left; and thy seed shall inherit the Gentiles." "Imperialism" again. But it is this same woman to whom the Lord says, "Thy maker is thine husband . . . for a small moment have I forsaken thee; . . . In a little wrath I hid my face from thee for a moment; but with everlasting kindness will I have mercy on thee, saith the Lord thy *Redeemer*. . . . In righteousness shalt thou be established; and great shall be the peace of thy children. . . . Whosoever shall gather against thee shall fall for thy sake. . . . No weapon that is formed against thee shall prosper (be this weapon against either the election of grace or against their nation); and every tongue that shall rise against thee in judgment thou shalt condemn. This is the heritage (national and spiritual) of the servants of the Lord, and *their righteousness is of me,* saith the Lord."—Isa. 54th chapter. "For the transgressions of MY PEOPLE was he (he is brought as a LAMB to the slaughter) stricken."

Jesus said, concerning his Church, "I will never leave thee nor forsake thee"; and concerning this one-time cast-off and forsaken people, this promise is given: "Thou shalt no more be termed forsaken." Why? Because "the Redeemer shall come to Zion, and unto them that turn from transgression in Jacob, saith the Lord. As for me, this is my covenant with them, saith the Lord; My spirit that is upon thee, and the words which I have put in thy mouth, shall not depart out of thy mouth, nor out of the mouth of thy seed, nor out of the mouth of thy seed's seed, saith the Lord, from henceforth and forever."—Isa. 59:20-21.

The failure, hitherto, to identify the Gospel promise as belonging to that branch of the Abrahamic posterity which has the accompanying national characteristics, has been the cause of untold confusion, untold harm, untold skepticism, as well as much loudly-told infidelity, both within the pale of Christian denominations and out of them.

Tom Paine boldly asserted that he was led into infidelity because he saw that the Jewish people never had fulfilled and never could fulfill the prophecies of the Old Testament. In 1898 B. Fay Mills, the one-time Spirit-filled evangelist, said, "In the fourth place, the prophecies of the Old Testament (to Israel) have not been realized. Today," he says, "the Bible is no more inspired than the Koran."

"The Lord of Hosts hath sworn, saying, Surely as I have thought, so shall it come to pass; and as I have proposed, so shall it stand."—Isa. 14: 24.

Prof. Rawlinson, in his Homiletics on the above text, says: "It is weakness on the part of man to need any confirmation of a promise which God makes. When He condescends to swear that his promise shall hold good, it does not really add to the certainty of the thing promised, since the certainty was absolute from the first. But man is so accustomed to mistrust his fellows that he will even mistrust God, as though with him were 'variableness or shadow of turning.'" And yet this same Prof. Rawlinson when writing of the ten-tribed Kingdom of Israel, says: *"They ceased to exist."* It is painful to find men who will speak so highly of God at one time and so belittle him in regard to his promises to Israel. Well may the Lord say, "Thus have they despised my people, that they should be no more a nation before them."

The Rev. Baring Gould tells us that "God's first purpose has been partially frustrated. The church has taken Israel's place as the body."

Dr. Ladd, in The Doctrine of Scripture, Vol. 1, page 442, says: "The Christian church has taken the place of the Jew to receive in different form the substance of the salvation which they expected for themselves. The Christian church is the true Israel, the seed of Abraham, the inheritor and recipient of the Messianic prophecies."

Opinions, similar to these, are held generally throughout the Christian church; while others hold that we are a sort of modern Israel of whom the Bible is silent, and yet both schools appropriate to Christianity all the good things which are promised to the Lord's chosen people, and pile all the evil things upon the Jews. As if the Lord were guilty of making promises to one people and fulfilling them to another.

To be in harmony with the facts, Dr. Ladd should have defined the situation as follows: "The Christian church is the true Israel of God which has received, in the same form and substance, that salvation which the Jews refused, for it is composed of men who are born of the spirit and who belong to the material Israel, the seed of Abraham, the inheritors and recipients of the Messianic prophecies, upon whom lighted the Divine *word*—he whom the Jews rejected."

In the chapter on the heraldry of Israel and the Saxons, we explained that the Lion, the young Ox, and the Eagle were the camp standards of Israel. But we gave no explanation concerning "The Man," which was also one of these four camp standards. The reference to the man in Ezekiel 1:10 cites us to Numbers, 2:10, which reads: "On the south side shall be the standard of the camp of Reuben." Concerning these symbols, Dr. Seiss says: "Jewish writers tell us that the standard of each tribe of Israel took the color of the stone which represented it in the High Priest's breastplate, and that there was wrought upon each a particular figure—a lion for Judah, a young ox for Ephraim, a man for Reuben, and an eagle for Dan. These were the representative tribes, and all the rest were marshaled under these four standards (Num. 11);—Judah, on the east, with Issachar and Zebulon; Reuben, on the south, with Simeon and Gad; Ephraim, on the west, with Manasseh and Benjamin; and Dan, on the north, with Asher and Naphtali. In the center of this quadrangular encampment was the tabernacle of God, with four divisions of Levites forming an inner encampment around it. It was thus that Israel was marched through the wilderness, under the four banners of the lion, the young ox, the man, and the flying eagle. These were their ensigns, their guards, their coverings, the symbols of power by which they were protected and guided. They were parts of that divine and heavenly administration which led them forth from bondage, preserved them in the wilderness, and finally settled them in the promised land." These facts were undoubtedly known to the compilers of our reference Bibles, hence the references from Ezekiel's vision to the outward, material and earthly aspect of the people to whom Ezekiel was sent, for he was sent to the ten-tribed kingdom, and remained among them seven days. (See former chapter.)

We know of no Old Testament Scriptures which will show why the ensign of *Reuben* was a man except that the name Reuben means "Behold a son," or "See ye a son." Genesis 29:32 settles that forever. A son presupposes a man. The sons of *Benjamin* were the men of Benjamin, as we have shown. Also, *a son* of Israel is *a man* of Israel. It is certainly fitting that the ensign of Reuben should have been *a man,* for he was the first-born of Israel. An expression like this: "Who raised up this righteous *man* from the east?" as applied to the nation of Israel, may have had some reference to the ensign of *the man* of Reuben. But, if this be so, it would be next to an impossibility to trace it positively, for the word man is in such general use that, should we undertake it, we should soon get lost in the mazes.

But we are sure of this one thing, namely: that the ensign of that first-born of Israel was a type of another first-born, of whom the prophet declares, "Unto us A SON is born, and my people Israel, even Ephraim, shall know." Also, when this son of Abraham was led out to be slain for the sins of that people, Pilate said: "Behold *the* MAN."

Joseph inherited the first-born blessing which Reuben forfeited and the ensign of the cross in the hands of the people who are the inheritors of the blessings of the Gospel of the grace of the Son of God, declared, in the arbitrary language of signs, "Behold the man." Thus it seems that the "Double Portion" of Joseph was a type of his double blessing, i. e., the blessing of the Abrahamic Birthright and the Gospel of Grace, for they certainly are the recipients of both.

It is for this reason that the Lord says: "They," Joseph-Israel, "shall rejoice in their portion: therefore in their land they shall possess the *Double* (i. e., two portions in the land): everlasting joy shall be unto them. . . . And their seed shall be known among the Gentiles, and their offspring among the people; all that see them shall acknowledge them, that *they are the seed which the Lord hath blessed.*"—Isa. 61:7-9.

This word *double* gives that whole prophecy in the context to Joseph. The next verse is as follows: *"I will greatly rejoice in the Lord; my soul shall be joyful in my God for he hath clothed me with the garments of salvation, he hath covered me with the robe of righteousness, and as a bridegroom decketh himself with ornaments, and as a bride adorneth herself with her jewels."*

Truly "God is good to Israel, even to such as are of a clean heart." Among that people who received "grace in the wilderness" none may have a clean heart except those who trust the blood of atonement; i. e., the blood of Jesus Christ, the Lamb of God, who taketh away the sin of the world.

Prior to the crucifixion of this man, this first-born Son of God, Caiaphas, in the heat of discussion concerning the interests of their nation, said: "Ye know nothing at all, nor consider that it is expedient for us, that one man should die for the people, and that the whole nation perish not. And *thus spake he not of himself*: but being high priest that year, he (unconsciously) prophesied that Jesus should die for that nation; and *not for that nation only, but that also he should gather together in one the children of God that were scattered abroad."* The children of God that were scattered abroad at that time were the ten tribes of the Birthright kingdom of Israel, and we say, without the possibility of being successfully contradicted, that *the restoration of Israel is in the atonement,* and that Jesus not only died to fulfill Isa. 53:8, but also that he might perform that good thing which he had promised unto the house of Israel and to the house of Judah; i. e., the gathering, the return, the restoration of his chosen people, with all its glorious results.

This is why Paul said, "And now I stand and am judged for the hope of the promise made of God unto our fathers: unto which promise our *twelve tribes,* instantly serving God day and night, HOPE TO COME. For which hope's sake, King Agrippa, I am accused of the Jews." (Acts 26:6-7.) This is also why he says, "Now we beseech you, brethren, by the coming of the Lord Jesus Christ, and by our *gathering together* unto HIM." It was because this restoration is all through the words of Moses and the prophets, and because Jesus had died to accomplish it, that, after his resurrection, and just before his ascension, the last question which his apostles ask is, "Lord, wilt thou at this time restore again the kingdom to Israel?" He did not tell them that there was to be no restoration. He simply told them that they were not to know the times or seasons which the Father hath put in his own power. Later they understood that it was to come, with the second coming of Christ, at which time he is to gather Israel, and reign over the house of Jacob forever.

Thus, on the day of Pentecost, when men out of every nation under heaven were assembled together,

Peter said: "Men and brethren, let me freely speak unto you of the patriarch David, that he is both dead and buried, and his sepulchre is with us unto this day. Therefore, being a prophet, and knowing that God had sworn with an oath unto him that of the fruit of his loins, according to the flesh, he would RAISE UP Christ to sit on his throne; he, seeing this before, spake of the *resurrection of Christ."* (Acts 2: 29-31.)

According to this reasoning, David did not expect Christ to sit on his throne until after he shall have been raised from the dead, and we know that he is not on David's throne now. He is sitting at the right hand of God on his throne, for "Him hath God exalted with his right hand to be a Prince (a Prince is a coming king) and a Saviour, for to give repentance to Israel, and forgiveness of sins." (Acts 5:31.) Hence, Peter, after telling the Jews that this Prince whom they had killed, was both Lord and Christ, very kindly says, "And now, brethren, I wot that through ignorance ye did it (God help Christians of today to be thus, or even more charitable), as did also your rulers. But those things, which God before had shewed by the mouth of all his prophets, that Christ should SUFFER, he hath so fulfilled." Thus we see, that the apostles only claimed, for others of them were with Peter, that those things which were written concerning the sufferings of Christ were fulfilled. So, Peter continues his discourse, saying, "And he (God) shall send Jesus Christ, which before was preached unto you: Whom the heaven must retain until the times of restitution of all things, which God hath spoken by the mouth of all his holy prophets since the world began." (Acts 3:17-21.)

Mark that, please! "All things which God hath spoken by the mouth of all his holy prophets," and nothing else, but surely *all* that which God hath spoken. Just that, nothing more, nothing less, can vindicate. Nothing more is necessary, but it is absolutely essential for the complete vindication of God and his Christ that all which God hath spoken be *so* fulfilled.

All the suffering phases concerning this rejected one, as recorded by all the prophets, have in like manner been fulfilled. The despised and rejected Man of Sorrows came. The oppressed, afflicted and grief-stricken man with the marred visage has been smitten. The stripe-beaten back has been bared and has borne its heavy load. The prison, the judgment hall, the trial, the mocking, jeering, insulting, spitting, raging mob are come and gone. The dumb Lamb, whose heart broke and melted like wax within him, has been led to the slaughter. In company with criminals, he has poured out his soul unto death, and the mutilated body has been laid away in its foretold rich man's grave. But that grave could not hold its holy treasure, for his prophet Father had said, "Neither wilt thou suffer thine Holy One to see corruption."

These and many other things which were foretold by the prophets he hath *so* fulfilled; but Jesus, himself, said: "Think not that I am come to destroy the law (word), or the prophets: I am *not come* to destroy, but to fulfill (these). For verily I say unto you, Till heaven and earth pass, one jot or one tittle shall in no wise pass from the *law* ("to the law and to the testimony, if they speak not according to thy *word*, it is because there is no light in them"), *till all be fulfilled.*"

The heaven and the earth are still held in their places, all that is written in the prophets has not yet been fulfilled, but IT SHALL BE. For Gabriel said to Mary, "Thou shalt conceive in thy womb (she did), and bring forth A SON (she did), and shalt call his name JESUS (that was his name). He shall be great (Prophet, High Priest, Prince, and Saviour), and shall be called the Son of the Highest (God, himself, opened heaven, and said, *This is my beloved Son*); and the Lord God shall give unto him the throne of his father David [that throne has not yet been given to him], and he shall reign ["Upon the throne of David, and upon his kingdom, *to order it*, and to establish it with judgment and justice (elements which it now lacks) from henceforth even forever (the zeal of the Lord of hosts will perform this)] over the house of Jacob forever and of his kingdom there shall be no end." Thus we see that these promises concerning David's greater Son were fulfilled only in part at his first coming. When Jesus comes the second time, he will come as SHILOH. Unto him shall the people gather, and he will then sit on the throne of his father David, and reign over the house of Jacob forever. For it is written: "Behold, the days come, saith the Lord, that I will raise unto David a righteous Branch, and a King shall reign and prosper, and shall execute judgment and justice in THE EARTH."

It is of the fact of this coming King for the kingdom of David that, when the apostles and elders of the newly founded church were in counsel, James spoke: "Men and brethren, hearken unto me: Simeon hath declared how God at first did visit the Gentiles, to take out of them a people (the remnant of grace) for his name (i. e., that they might become his bride).   And to this agree the words of the prophets; as it is written, After this I will return, and will build again the tabernacle (royal dwellings, and palaces) of David, which are fallen down (those on 'Mt. Zion); and I will build again the ruins thereof, and I will set it up."   (Acts 15:13-16.)

Jesus died to confirm the promises made to the fathers, not to transfer them.   "He that keepeth thee will not slumber.   Behold, he that keepeth Israel shall neither slumber nor sleep."   (Ps. 121:3-4.)

CHAPTER X.

THE COMING EXODUS.

"Therefore, behold, the days come, saith the Lord, that it shall no more be said, The Lord liveth, that brought up the children of Israel out of the land of Egypt; but, The Lord liveth, that brought up the children of Israel from the land of the north, and from all the lands whither he had driven them: and I will bring them again into their land that I gave unto their fathers." (Jer. 16:14-15.)

Here is a promised exodus which is based upon the exodus of Israel out of Egypt, and which, because of its magnitude, is to so eclipse the one upon which it is based that the former will cease to be remembered.

The blindest of the blind leaders of the blind claim that this prophecy was fulfilled when the Jewish people returned from the Babylon captivity. But such could not have been the case, for the Jews went only to Babylon, and from Babylon they returned! but this oncoming exodus includes *the children of Israel,* who are to come *from all lands* whither the Lord has driven them.

When Israel came up out of Egypt they numbered about two and a half millions. This estimate is made from the fact that there were six hundred thousand men of war beside the young men, who were too young for war, and the old men, who were too old for war, and also women and children. This great company was taken out of Egypt in a body by the Lord himself with the greatest manifestations of Divine power the world has ever known—will ever know, until the exodus in question takes place. But the Jews returned from Babylon in two small companies, without any supernatural manifestation as to their leaving Babylon, while they were en route, or when they arrived at Jerusalem; and the Divinest authority of this earth declares, "The whole congregation together was forty and two thousand three hundred and threescore, beside their servants and their maids, of whom there were seven thousand three hundred thirty and seven; and there were among them two hundred singing men and singing women." (Ezra 2: 64-65.)

But "it shall come to pass in that day, when the Lord shall set his hand again the second time to recover the remnant of his people, which shall be left, from Assyria, and from Egypt, and from Cush, and from Elam, and from Shinar, and from Hamath, and from the islands of the sea. And he shall set up an ensign (the ensign of one who is "a *root of Jesse*") for the nations (i. e., *the nations* into which the Birthright people have developed), and shall assemble the outcasts of Israel (or the outcast Israel), and gather the dispersed of Judah from the four corners of the earth. The envy also of Ephraim shall depart, and the adversaries of Judah shall be cut off (Russia, beware! Roumania, beware! France, beware!): Ephraim shall not envy Judah, and Judah shall not vex Ephraim. . . . And the Lord shall utterly destroy the tongue of the Egyptian Sea; and with his mighty wind shall he shake his hand over the river, and shall smite it in the seven streams,* and make men go over dry shod. And there shall be an highway for the remnant of his people which shall be left from Assyria, like as it was to Israel in the day that he came up out of the land of Egypt." (Isa. 11:12-16.)

Ephraim-Israel is that portion of the Lord's people which is left from the Assyrian captivity, and Judah is the Jewish portion of the Lord's people which has been scattered to the four corners (or wings) of the earth. These are to return together, and for that reason one shall not vex the other. At one stage of this return, or while they are returning, the Lord is not only to destroy utterly the tongue of the Egyptian Sea, but is also to dry up the seven mouths, or delta, of the river Nile. This was not done, nor could it have been done, when the Jews returned from Babylon, for these places are in diametrically opposite directions.

Another feature of this returning is that "In those days, and in that time, saith the Lord, the children of Israel shall come, they and the children of Judah together, going and weeping; they shall go, and seek the Lord their God. They shall ask the way to Zion with their faces thitherward, saying, Come, and let us join ourselves to the Lord in a perpetual covenant that shall not be forgotten." This people did forget, and did break the law covenant, but now they are going back to Zion to make an everlasting covenant with the Lord.

Other features of this returning are given as follows: "Behold, I will bring them from the north country, and gather them from the coasts of the earth, and with them the blind and the lame, the women with

*See frontispiece.

child and her that travaileth with child together: a *great company* shall return thither. They shall come with weeping, and with supplications will I lead them; I will cause them to walk by the rivers of waters in a straight way, wherein they shall not stumble: for I am a father to Israel, and Ephraim is my first-born.

"Hear the word of the Lord, O ye nations (Ephraim, the Birthright people, who, prior to this return, have become many nations), and declare it in the isles afar off (Ephraim now living in the British Isles) and say, He that scattered Israel will gather him and keep him, as a shepherd doth his flock.

"For the Lord hath redeemed Jacob, and ransomed him from the hand of him that was stronger than he. Therefore they shall come and sing in the height of Zion, shall flow together to the goodness of the Lord, for wheat, and for wine, and for oil, and for the young of the flock and of the herd; and their soul shall be as a watered garden; and they shall not sorrow any more at all." (Jer. 31:8-13.)

When this return is consummated, the Lord will keep his people, as a shepherd keepeth his flock. When the Jews returned from Babylon, they were not thus kept. Also, after this return has been accomplished both Israel and Judah are to sorrow no more. But when the Jews returned from Babylon they had more sorrow than before. This great company sorrows while returning, but when once there they are to "sing in the heights of Zion." The Jews returned from Babylon to "cry from sorrow of heart, and with vexation of spirit."

Furthermore, Babylonia, or Chaldea, of which the city of Babylon was the capital, was an inland empire, and was not in possession of any island territory; neither did they possess the "coasts of the earth." Hence the Jews could have come neither from the coasts of the earth, nor from the isles of the sea, when they came from Babylon.

This return is taught in that wonderful forty-ninth chapter of Isaiah, in which there is so much of the history of Israel since they went to the isles, and in which is the following: "Listen, O isles, unto me: hearken, ye people, from far; . . . thou art my servant, Israel, in whom I will be glorified. . . . *Behold, these shall come from the north and west," i. e., Northwest. But when the Jews returned from the Chaldean empire they came from the east.†

Still other incidents of this exodus are, that these people shall come "upon horses, and in chariots (wheeled vehicles), and in litters (marg. coaches), and upon mules, and upon swift beasts, and to my holy mountain Jerusalem, saith the Lord." (Isa. 66:20.) Also the following: "Surely the isles shall wait for me, and the ships of Tarshish first to bring my sons from far, their silver and their gold with them, unto the name of the Lord thy God, and to the Holy One of Israel."

One of the results of this return is given as follows: "I will bring again the captivity of my people Israel, and they shall build the waste cities, and inhabit them; and they shall plant vineyards, and drink the wine thereof; they shall also make gardens, and eat the fruit of them. And I will plant them upon their land, and they shall no more be pulled up out of their land which I have given them, saith the Lord thy God." (Amos

*See frontispiece.
†See frontispiece.

9:14-15.) After the Jews returned from Babylon they were pulled up; but after this return has taken place, both Israel and Judah shall remain in their land forever.

But it is also certain that this return cannot take place until Israel has been lost, increased to a multitude, and then been found. For it is written: "Yet the number of the children of Israel (Joseph-Ephraim) shall be as the sands of the sea, which cannot be measured nor numbered; and it shall come to pass, that in the place where it was said unto them, Ye are not my people (lost), there it shall be said unto them, Ye are (found) the sons of the living God. "Then"—yes, THEN, and not until *then*—"shall the children of Judah (the Jews) and the children of Israel (the Joseph-Ephraim Birthright) be gathered together, and appoint themselves one head, and they shall come up out of the land: for great shall be the day of Jezreel." (Hosea 1:11.)

Zara, or Zera, is the root of this word *Jezreel*, and means, not only *the seed*, but also *to sow* (the seed), to plant, to fructify. But the word Jezreel means *"God will sow"* (see Strong's Exhaustive Concordance). Hence the day of Jezreel is God's time to fulfill the prophecy given by Amos, which we have quoted above, i. e., "I will plant them upon their land, and they shall no more be pulled up," etc

It is because this day of Jezreel was in prospect that the Lord gave the following to the prophet Ezekiel: "Prophesy therefore concerning the land of Israel.... But ye, O mountains of Israel, ye shall shoot forth your branches, and yield your fruit to my people of Israel; for they are at hand to come. For, behold, I am for you, and I will turn unto you all the house of Israel, even all of it; and the cities shall be inhabited, and the wastes shall be builded. And I will multiply upon you man and beast, and they shall increase and bring fruit; and I will settle you after your old estates, and will do better unto you than at your beginnings: and ye shall know that I am the Lord. Yea, I will cause men to walk upon you, even my people Israel! and they shall possess thee, and thou shalt be their inheritance, and thou shalt no more henceforth be bereaved of them." (Ezek. 36:8-12.)

When this return has been accomplished, Israel, "*all of it,*" shall *do better* than at the first. But after the Jews returned from Babylon, although they returned cured of idolatry, they suffered more and did worse than they did before; for they said, concerning that royal Prince of the house of David, "*Let his blood be upon us, and upon our children.*"

Also, when the day of Jezreel comes, Judah and Israel are to appoint themselves one head (rosh—chief ruler). It is at that time that the Lord will take the two sticks, the stick of Joseph and the stick of Judah, put them together, and they shall be one in his hand. At that time the Lord says, "I will make them one nation in the land upon the mountains of Israel; and one king shall be king of them all; and they shall be no more two nations, neither shall they be divided into two kingdoms any more at all. Neither shall they defile themselves any more with their idols, nor their detestable things, nor with any of their transgressions; but I will save them out of all their dwelling places, wherein they have sinned, and will cleanse them: so shall they be my people, and I will be their God. And David (the royal line) my servant shall be king over them; and they all shall have one shepherd: they shall also walk in my judgments, and observe my statutes, and do them. And they shall dwell in the land that I have given unto Jacob my servant, wherein your fathers have dwelt; and they shall dwell therein, even they, and their children, and their children's children, *forever*: and my servant David (they are to gather to an ensign of a root of Jesse) shall be their prince FOREVER.

"Moreover, I will make a covenant of peace with them (the remnant according to the election of grace have, already, found peace through Jesus Christ, the son of David, the son of Abraham, the son of God); it shall be an everlasting covenant with them ("They shall ask the way to Zion with their faces thitherward, saying, Come, and let us join ourselves to the Lord in a perpetual covenant that shall not be forgotten"), and I will place them, and multiply them, and I will set my sanctuary in the midst of them forevermore. My tabernacle (dwelling place) also shall be with them. Yea, I will be their God, and they shall be my people. And the heathen shall know that I, the Lord, do sanctify Israel (the remnant, according to the election of grace, may, by meeting the conditions, be sanctified now through the blood of the slain Prince of David, i. e., the Lamb of God that taketh away the sin of the world), when my sanctuary shall be in the midst of them forevermore." (Ezek. 37:22-28.)

This is to be the time of the everlasting possession of the land which God gave to our fathers. Prior to this time it is declared: "The people of thy holiness have possessed it (the land) but a little while." But in the thirty-seventh chapter of Ezekiel, prior to the giving of that part of the chapter which we have quoted, the Lord told the prophet that the valley of dry bones was the whole house of Israel, and told him to say unto them: "Behold my people, I will open your graves, and cause you to come out of your graves, and bring you into the land of Israel. And ye shall know that I am the Lord, when I have opened your graves, O my people, and brought you up out of your graves, and shall put my spirit in you, and ye shall live, and I shall place you in your own land. Then shall ye know that I the Lord have spoken it, and performed it, saith the Lord."

This is to be the time of which the Lord has spoken, saying, "The nation and kingdom that will not serve thee shall perish; yea, those nations shall be utterly wasted. The glory of Lebanon shall come unto thee, the fir tree, the pine tree, and the box together, to beautify the place of my sanctuary; and I will make the place of my feet glorious. The sons also of them that afflicted thee shall come bending unto thee; and all they that despised thee shall bow down at the soles of thy feet; and they shall call thee, The city of the Lord, The Zion of the Holy One of Israel. Whereas thou hast been forsaken and hated, so that no man went through thee, I will make thee an *eternal* excellency. * * * Thy sun shall no more go down; neither shall thy moon withdraw itself; for the Lord shall be thine everlasting light, and the days of thy mourning shall be ended. Thy people also shall be righteous; they shall inhabit the *land forever; the branch of my*

planting, the work of my hands; that I MAY BE GLORI-
FIED." (Isa. 60; 12-13-14-15 and 20-21.)

Great violence has been done to the truth of God
by those who have tried to spiritualize these prophecies,
instead of seeing in them a time foretold, during which
this earth is to see its most spiritual, hence its most
glorious, age; for this is but the climax of the Gospel
era, which, in the New Testament, is often called "The
Day of the Lord." This is the time long foretold
when, "the wolf also shall dwell with the kid; and
the calf and the young lion and the fatling together;
and a little child shall lead them. And the cow and
the bear shall feed; their young ones shall lie down
together; and the lion shall eat straw like the ox. And
the sucking child shall play on the hole of the asp,
and the weaned child shall put his hand on the cocka-
trice's den. They shall not hurt nor destroy in all my
holy mountain; for the earth shall be full of the knowledge of the Lord, as the waters cover the sea. And
in that day there shall be a root of Jesse, which shall
stand for an ensign of the peoples." This is in harmony with Zech. 3:10, which reads as follows: "I
will remove the iniquity of that land in one day. In
that day, saith the Lord of Hosts, shall ye call every
man his neighbor under the vine and under the fig
tree."

Now, these facts are in perfect accord with the outcome of the new covenant, as declared in the New Testament, of which Christ is the mediator, and which
could not begin to come into effect until the death of the
testator. So it is recorded in the book of Hebrews as
follows: "But now hath he (Christ) obtained a more

excellent ministry, by how much also is he the mediator of a better covenant, which was established upon better promises. For if that first covenant had been faultless, then should no place have been sought for the second. For, finding fault with them, he saith, Behold the days come, saith the Lord, when I will make a new covenant with the house of Israel and the house of Judah (the two houses); not according to the covenant that I made with their fathers in the day when I took them by the hand to lead them out of the land of Egypt; because they continued not in my covenant, and I regarded them not, saith the Lord. For this is the covenant that I will make with the house of Israel after those days, saith the Lord; I will put my laws into their mind, and write them in their hearts; and I will be to them a God, and they shall be my people. And they shall not teach every man his neighbor, and every man his brother, saying, Know the Lord: for all shall know me, from the least to the greatest."

Thus we find that both houses, Israel and Judah—Joseph and Judah, the Sceptre and the Birthright—are included in this new covenant, which, when it reaches its climax, must be in fulfillment of that foretold condition, in which every man from the least to the greatest shall know the Lord; together with all spiritual and glorious results, which are described as following such a blessed and holy condition among men. Also, according to this explanation of the Gospel or New Testament covenant, it is understood that our Jewish brother of the house of Judah must come into this covenant before the doors of grace and mercy are closed. That part of the new covenant promises which is quoted by the writer of the Epistle to the Hebrews was given to the prophet Jeremiah, who also says, in addition to that which is quoted in Hebrews, "I will cause the captivity of *Judah* and the captivity of *Israel* to return, and will build them, as at the first. And I will cleanse them from all their iniquity, whereby they have sinned against me; and I will pardon all their iniquities, whereby they have sinned, and whereby they have transgressed against me. . . . Behold the days come, saith the Lord, that I will perform that *good thing* which I have promised unto the house of Israel and to the house of Judah. In those days, and at that time, will I cause the Branch of Righteousness to grow up unto David; *and he* (the Branch) *shall execute judgment and righteousness* IN THE LAND."

"*In those days shall Judah be saved,* and Jerusalem shall dwell safely; and this is the name wherewith she shall be called THE LORD OUR RIGHTEOUSNESS." (Jer. 33:7-14-16.)

Still Jeremiah prophesies concerning this time as follows: "Behold, the days come, saith the Lord, that I will raise unto David a righteous Branch, and a King shall reign and prosper, and execute judgment and justice in the earth. In his days Judah shall be saved, and Israel shall dwell safely: and this is his name whereby he shall be called THE LORD OUR RIGHTEOUSNESS."

Meanwhile Paul asks "What then?" and answers, "Israel hath not obtained that for which he seeketh; but the election (of grace) hath obtained it and the rest were blinded." It seems that the reason that Jeremiah is careful in these prophecies to say that Judah shall be saved in those days when David's son is king, is that Israel is having her opportunity now, and that all in Israel who will turn to God and serve him are doing so in this the dispensation of the Spirit. Excepting, of course, those out of all Israel who will turn to God in the time of the great tribulation, which is also called the time of Jacob's trouble. For that is the time of which it is written, "They shall look upon me whom they have pierced (prior to this the *whole* house of Israel will have been brought up out of their graves), and they shall mourn for him, as one mourneth for his only son, as one that is in bitterness for his firstborn. In that day there shall be great mourning in Jerusa·· lem." (Zech. 12:10-11.)

It was because of this time that Jesus Christ, the Son of God, said to the house of Judah, "Your house is left unto you desolate, and ye shall see me no more until ye say, Blessed is he that cometh in the name of the Lord." They had said this when he made his triumphal entry into the holy city, for they thought that the promised restoration, and its attendant kingdom *"should immediately come,"* but our Lord gave them the parable of the nobleman's son going to a far country to receive a kingdom and return, and gave the command "Occupy *till* I COME." Thus we see that that glad hosannah which went up from Jerusalem was but a type. Its great prototype is ahead. Just ahead, as we verily believe.

This work of planting Israel in their own land and keeping them there forever, that the Lord might be glorified, is in harmony with the following: "When the house of Israel dwelt in their own land they defiled it by their own way and by their doings. . . . I poured my fury upon them. . . . I scatttered them among the heathen and they were dispersed among the countries. . . . When they entered unto the heathen, whither they went, they profaned my holy name, when they (the heathen) said of them, These are the people of the Lord, and are gone out of his land. But I had pity for mine holy name, which the house of Israel had profaned among the heathen, whither they went. Therefore say unto the house of Israel, Thus saith the Lord God: I do this *not for your sakes,* but for MINE HOLY NAME'S SAKE, which ye have profaned among the heathen, whither ye went. And I will sanctify my great name, which was profaned among the heathen, which ye have profaned in the midst of them; and *the heathen* SHALL KNOW that I am the Lord God, when I shall be sanctified in you before their eyes. For I will take you from among the heathen and GATHER YOU out of all countries, and will BRING YOU INTO YOUR OWN LAND . . . I, THE LORD, HAVE SPOKEN IT AND I WILL DO IT." (Ezek. 36.)

When this exodus takes place, and the gathering to Shiloh is completed—concerning which there are many things that we dare not mention because we cannot deal with them conclusively—it will be on such a stupendous, glorious, and supernatural scale, that the Lord called John up into the etherial heaven to give him a revelation of it, the description of which is found in the fourth chapter of Revelation.

Before John was taken up a voice said to him: "I will show thee things which must be hereafter." After he was taken up the first thing which John saw was *a throne set in heaven.* This signifies a kingdom. Around this throne there was a *rainbow,* which is **a** symbol of *the promise.* "And round about the throne were four and twenty seats (thrones) and upon the seats I saw four and twenty elders sitting, clothed in white raiment; and they had on their heads crowns of gold." In Christianized Israel there are twenty-four elders, i. e., the twelve patriarchal sons of Jacob, and the twelve apostles of Jesus Christ. "Out of the throne proceeded lightnings and thunderings and voices." These are the symbols of the judgment and in connection with these scenes, we are told that *the judgment was set.*

Around about the throne were four beasts, or living creatures. The first of these was like a LION; the second like a Calf, or young ox; the third had the face of A MAN; and the fourth was like a FLYING EAGLE. These, as we have learned, are the national ensigns of the nations of Israel. Some writers oppose the translation of the original word into *beasts,* and others oppose the translation of *living creatures,* but both are correct; for beasts are the symbols of human governments, and these governments are made up of living creatures. These living creatures are said to be in the midst of the throne, and also round and about the throne. Hence they represent the nations and the people of Israel, under whose insignia they gather.

Jehovah, by the mighty power of his own right arm, took Israel out of Egypt; and by his own glorious presence guided, protected, and led them through forty years of wandering in the wilderness. But it is written, "With many of them God was not well pleased."

Still he withdrew neither his protection nor his manifest presence from them as a nation. Today it might also be written, "With the greater portion of Joseph-Israel God is not well pleased, and yet they are manifestly the people, nationally speaking, whom he has blessed, and to whom he has remembered the word of his oath. On the other hand it is written, "And many of the Jews believed on him"; and yet, nationally speaking, the Jews are the enemies of the Gospel of grace. But when this greater exodus takes place the Jews will join with Christian Israel in shouting the glad acclaim, "Blessed is he that cometh in the name of the Lord!" even as Jesus foretold, when he was weeping over Jerusalem. For it is also in fulfillment of the following: "The stone which the builders rejected is become the head of the corner. This is the Lord's doing; it is marvelous in our eyes. This is the day which the Lord hath made; we will rejoice and be glad in it. Save now, I beseech thee, O Lord: O Lord, I beseech thee, send now prosperity. Blessed is he that cometh in the name of the Lord." (Psa. 118: 22-26.)

Thus we see that it is the *rejected stone* unto whom they will cry, "O Lord, save!" and concerning whom they will say, "Blessed is he that cometh in the name of the Lord," for this is the time when the Lord himself *shall appear the second time in power and great glory.* At which time he will have SET HIS HAND AGAIN, *the* SECOND TIME to recover his people and his manifest presence shall once again be among them.

When Israel was led through the wilderness under the protection of God with those four ensigns flying in

the breeze, there were only three wings, or encamp-
ments on each of the four sides of the great hollow
square, because there were only three tribes on each of
the four sides, but in the revelation given to Saint John
for each of these four *Living Creature*s there were *six
wings*. We should expect this, for it is an enlarged
view of the double portion of Joseph-Israel. This is
the gathering of the *House of God*, in which also there
is the *House of God*, for it is Bethel, the stone kingdom
which the Lord set up in the days of the kings of Chaldea, Medo-Persia, Greece, and Pagan Rome. It is the
kingdom which shall smite the image of empire on its
feet *"and break in pieces and consume all these kingdoms; and it shall stand forever."*

In this kingdom are the *living stones* that are builded
together for a habitation of God through the Spirit, of
which Jesus Christ himself is the chief corner stone.
"This is a great mystery, but I speak concerning Christ
and the Church"—his wife—who are to be the inhabitants of the New Jerusalem, which is to come down
from God out of heaven, and which has twelve gates
of pearl, each of which has upon it the name of one
of the twelve sons of Jacob. But in the foundations of
this city are the names of the *twelve apostles* of the
Lamb, and thus in it also is the double everlasting portion, or the twenty-four elders in Christianized Israel,
to whose care was committed the shepherd stone
of Israel, who still have it with them, and who will
carry it back; for it must yet become the headstone
of the temple, of which Ezekiel gives the plan. For
in Ezekiel's city there is a temple, but in the city which
comes down from God there is no temple.

It seems that one of these cities, Ezekiel's, is to be on the earth, and the other is to remain in the air. Then the following words of Jesus to Nathaniel will be fulfilled: "Verily, verily, I say unto you, Hereafter ye shall see heaven open and the angels of God ascending and descending upon the Son of man." Then also will be fulfilled that of which Jacob's ladder was a type.

There is also, in the book of Revelation, the description of a company which is composed of one hundred and forty-four thousand persons who were redeemed from the earth, and who, insofar as their nationality is concerned, are Israelites; for there are twelve thousand out of each of the twelve tribes of Israel. But insofar as the moral character of this company is concerned, "They are without fault before the throne of God." Since he alone who brought grace to their race has power to present men faultless before the throne of God, it must be through the atonement of Jesus Christ that these are made pure.

When this gathering, which is not only the hope of Israel, but also the hope of the Church of Israel, takes place, then the Zarah and Zedekiah branches of the royal family of the Abrahamic people will need to abdicate in favor of "He whose right it is," for he will have come. Prior to the time when the kingdom over Israel was given to David and his sons, the Lord was King of Israel, and after the enthronement of Solomon, we are told that, "Solomon sat on the THRONE OF THE LORD as king instead of David his father." Hence when the Lord returns he will have a twofold right to that throne, i. e., as the *Son of David* and THE SON

OF GOD, who, when he comes, will not only be the Christ for whom the Christians are looking, but will also be the long expected MESSIAH for whom the faithful ones among the Jewish people are looking.

This present age is the dispensation of the Spirit. The dispensation which shall follow this gathering will be THE DAY OF THE LORD.

APPENDIX.

We find a minister of the Gospel who, in his homily
on Jer. 33:17-18, asks, "Do the prophets prophesy
falsely?" He answers his question as follows: "If the
statements of these verses be taken literally it would
seem as if they did. The house of Israel never, since
its exile, has had a throne at all, nor has any descendant of David been acknowledged as its prince. Yet
these verses say 'David shall never want a man to sit
upon the throne of the house of Israel (not the house
of Judah), etc.' And literally, it never came to pass,
for in the lapse and confusion of the ages their genealogical tables have been utterly lost, so that none can
certainly say who is of the house of David or who is
of the house of Levi. The Asmonean princes who occupied the throne of Judah were of the tribe of Levi,
and Herod was no Jew at all (Herod belonged to the
house of Esau). Now, the promise of these verses
is one that is repeated (2 Sam. 7,16; 1 Kings 2, 4; Psa.
89, 4-29, 36; Num. 25, 12, etc). How, then, are they
to be understood, since events have most surely false-
fied them if understood in any literal way? And so the
prophet Hosea cheered the ten tribes of Israel—those
of whom we speak now as the lost ten tribes—by promises of their restoration; and Jeremiah does the same
* * * But in spite of all these prophecies, the ten
tribes never were restored and never, as a whole, received any favors from God after they went into cap-

369

tivity. Our own belief is that, in regard to this world, these promises were illusions, but in regard to the world to come, they shall in substance and reality be fulfilled there. Meanwhile let us have faith in God, who, in ways better than we think, will fulfill that which now sometimes seems as if it will be never fulfilled at all." (Rev. S. B. Conway, B. A.).

It is a marvel that this man has any faith at all, and yet he not only has faith in God, but can exhort others also to have faith; even though the case seems hopeless. This is as it should be, and it gives us joy; but we are sure, if this brother, and thousands like him, had these truths which we bring, they would be giants in faith. This entire work is intended as a guide to all such bewildered believers. For their further encouragement, and also to show that *the genealogical tables have not been utterly lost,* we append a genealogical table which begins with Adam and passes down through the royal family of Israel to the present generation.

The publisher of this table says: "The possible descent of Queen Victoria from King David was first entered upon in the present day by the Rev. F. R. A. Glover, M. A. He did not, however, attempt to give the genealogy link by link, nor enter into the proofs in detail. Since then the whole subject of her Majesty's Jewish ancestry has been further examined by various students and writers on our Israelitish origin. Mr. J. C. Stephens has compiled a 'Genealogical Chart,' showing the connection between the House of David and the Royal Family of Britain."

One of the workers in this cause, says: "The difficulty heretofore has been to supply the line from Queen Tephi to King Fergus of Scotland. This we now supply through the valuable researches of the Rev. A. B. GRIMALDI, M. A."

Rev. A. B. Grimaldi says: "The descent of our Royal Family from the royal line of Judah is, however, no new discovery. The Saxon kings traced themselves back to Odin, who traced back his descent to David, as may be seen in a very ancient MS. in the Heralds' College, London, and in Sharon Turner. ('History of the Anglo-Saxons', Vol. I.) The full and complete genealogy of Victoria from David does not appear ever to have been printed; and it has, therefore, been thought that it would be useful, as well as interesting, to put it on record, both for reference and testimony. In its compilation reliable works of reference have been used —such as Anderson ('Royal Genealogies,' London, 1732), Keating ('History or Ireland,' Dublin, 1733), Lavoisne ('Genealogical and Historical Atlas.' London, 1814), and others. Perfect accuracy is hardly to be expected in such an attempt; but it is believed that the genealogy is as correct as our present knowledge of this obscure and intricate subject will permit."

Another worker in this cause, says: "From the tables we are able to furnish a complete list of the royal line from David and Zedekiah to Queen Victoria. We believe the account here given is very nearly correct. If any error be detected we should be happy to be informed. Dates after private names refer to births and deaths; those after sovereigns' to their accession, and death; and b and d stand for born and died (vide, Talmud, London, 1887)."

GENERATIONS.

1. Adam (B. C. 4000-3070), Eve.
2. Seth (B. C. 3869-2957).
3. Enos (B. C. 3764-2859).
4. Canaan (B. C. 3674-2895).
5. Mahalaleel (B. C. 3604-2709).
6. Jared (B. C. 3539-2577).
7. Enoch (B. C. 3377-3012).
8. Methusaleh (B. C. 3312-2344).
9. Lamech (B. C. 3125-2349).
10. Noah (B. C. 2943-2007), Naamah.
11. Shem (B. C. 2441-1841).
12. Arphaxad (B. C. 2341-1903).
13. Salah (B. C. 2306-1873).
14. Heber (B. C. 2276-1812).
15. Peleg (B. C. 2241-2003).
16. Reu (B. C. 2212-1973).
17. Serug (B. C. 2180-2049).
18. Nahor (B. C. 2050-2002).
19. Terah (B. C. 2221-1992), Amtheta.
20. Abraham (B. C. 1992-1817), Sarah.
21. Isaac (B. C. 1896-1716), Rebekah.
22. Jacob (B. C. 1837-1690), Leah.
23. Judah (b. B. C. 1752), Tamar.
24. Hezron.
25. Aram.
26. Aminadab.
27. Naasson.
28. Salmon.
29. Boaz (B. C. 1312), Ruth.
30. Obed.
31. Jesse.

KINGS IN PALESTINE.

32. K. David (B. C. 1085-1015), Bathsheba.
33. K. Solomon (B. C. 1033-975), Naamah.
34. K. Rehoboam (B. C. b. 1016, d. 958), Maacah.
35. K. Abijah (B. C. 958-955).
36. K. Asa (B. C. 955-914), Azubah.
37. K. Jehoshaphat (B. C. 914-889).
38. K. Jehoram (B. C. 889-885), Athaliah.
39. K. Ahaziah (B. C. 906-884), Zibiah.
40. K. Joash (B. C. 885-839), Jehoaddan.
41. K. Amaziah (B. C. b. 864, d. 810), Jecholiah.
42. K. Uzziah (B. C. b. 826, d. 758), Jerusha.
43. K. Jotham (B. C. b. 783, d. 742).
44. K. Ahaz (B. C. b. 787, d. 726), Abi.
45. K. Hezekiah (B. C. b. 751, d. 698), Hephzibah.
46. K. Manasseh (B. C. b. 710, d. 643), Meshulle-meth.
47. K. Amon (B. C. b. 621, d. 641), Jedidiah.
48. K. Josiah (B. C. b. 649,, d. 610), Mamutah.
49. K. Zedekiah (B. C. 599-578).

KINGS OF IRELAND.

50. Q. Tea Tephi (b. B. C. 565), marries Herre-mon, a Prince of the scarlet thread.
51. K. Irial Faidh (reigned 10 years).
52. K. Eithriall (reigned 20 years).
53. Follain.
54. K. Tighernmas (reigned 50 years).
55. Eanbotha.
56. Smiorguil.
57. K. Fiachadh Labhriane (reigned 24 years).

58. K. Aongus Ollmuchaidh (reigned 21 years).
59. Maoin.
60. K. Rotheachta (reigned 25 years).
61. Dein.
62. K. Siorna Saoghalach (reigned 21 years).
63. Oholla Olchaoin.
64. K. Giallchadh (reigned 9 years).
65. K. Aodhain Glas (reigned 20 years).
66. K. Simeon Breac (reigned 7 years).
67. K. Muirteadach Bolgrach (reigned 4 years).
68. K. Fiachadh Tolgrach (reigned 7 years).
69. K. Duach Laidhrach (reigned 10 years).
70. Eochaidh Buailgllerg.
71. K. Ugaine More the Great (reigned 30 years).
72. K. Cobhthach Coalbreag (reigned 30 years).
73. Meilage.
74. K. Jaran Gleofathach (reigned 7 years).
75. K. Coula Cruaidh Cealgach (reigned 25 years).
76. K. Oiliolla Caisfhiachach (reigned 28 years).
77. K. Eochaidh Foltleathan (reigned 11 years).
78. K. Aongus Tuirmheach Teamharch (reigned 30 years).
79. K. Eana Aighneach (reigned 28 years).
80. Labhra Suire.
81. Blathucha.
82. Easamhuin Eamhua.
83. Roighnein Ruadh.
84. Finlogha.
85. Fian.
86. K. Eodchaidh Feidhlioch (reigned 12 years).

87. Fineamhuas.
88. K. Lughaidh Raidhdearg.
89. K. Criomhthan Niadhnar (reigned 16 years).
90. Fearaidhach Fion Feachtnuigh.
91. K. Fiachadh Fionoluidh (reigned 20 years).
92. K. Tuathal Teachtmar (reigned 40 years).
93. K. Coun Ceadchathach (reigned 20 years).
94. K. Arb Aonflier (reigned 30 years).
95. K. Cormae Usada (reigned 40 years).
96. K. Caibre Liffeachair (reigned 27 years).
97. K. Fiachadh Sreabthuine (reigned 30 years.)
98. K. Muireadhach Tireach (reigned 30 years).
99. K. Eochaidh Moigmeodhin (reigned 7 years.)
100. K. Nail of the Nine Hostages.
101. Eogan.
102. K. Murireadhach.
103. Earca.

KINGS OF ARGYLESHIRE.

104. K. Fergus More (A. D. 487).
105. K. Dongard (d. 457).
106. K. Conran (d. 535).
107. K. Aidan (d. 604).
108. K. Eugene IV. (d. 622).
109. K. Donald IV. (d. 650).
110. Dongard.
111. K. Eugene V. (d. 692).
112. Findan.
113. K. Eugene VII. (d. A. D. 721), Spondan.
114. K. Etfinus (d. A. D. 761), Fergina.
115. K. Achaius (d. A. D. 819), Fergusia.
116. K. Alpin (d. A. D. 834).

SOVEREIGNS OF SCOTLAND.

117. K. Kenneth II. (d. A. D. 854).

118. K. Constantin II. (d. A. D. 874).

119. K. Donald VI. (d. A. D. 903).

120. K. Malcolm I. (d. A. D. 958).

121. K. Kenneth III. (d. A. D. 994).

122. K. Malcolm II. (d. A. D. 1033).

123. Beatrix m. Thane Albanach.

124. K. Duncan I. (d. A. D. 1040).

125. K. Malcolm III. Canmore (A. D. 1055-1093). Margaret of England.

126 K. David I. (d. A. D. 1153), Maud of North-umberland (i. e., North-Kumbri-land).

127. Prince Henry (d. A. D. 1152), Adama of Surrey.

128. Earl David (d. A. D. 1219), Maud of Chester.

129. Isobel m. Robert Bruce III.

130. Robert Bruce IV. m. Isobel of Gloucester.

131. Robert Bruce V. m. Martha of Carrick.

132. K. Robert I. Bruce (A. D. 1306-1329), Mary of Burke.

133. Margary Bruce m. Walter Stewart III.

134. K. Robert II. (d. A. D. 1390), Euphemia of Ross (d. A. D. 1376).

135. K. Robert III. (d. A. D. 1406), Arabella Drummond (d. A. D. 1401).

136. K. James I. (A. D. 1424-1437), Joan Beaufort.

137. K. James II. (d. A. D. 1460), Margaret of Gueldres (d. A. D. 1463).

138. K. James III. (d. A. D. 1488), Margaret of Denmark (d. A. D. 1484).

139. K. James IV. (d. A. D. 1543), Margaret of England (d. A. D. 1539).

140. K. James V. (d. A. D. 1542), Mary of Lorraine (d. A. D. 1560).

141. Q. Mary (d. A. D. 1587), Lord Henry Darnley.

SOVEREIGNS OF GREAT BRITAIN.

142. K. James VI. and I. (A. D. 1603-1625), Ann of Denmark.

143. Princess Elizabeth (1596-1613), K. Frederic of Bohemia (1632).

144. Princess Sophia, m. Duke Ernest of Brunswick.

145. K. George I. (1698-1727), Sophia Dorothea of Zelle (1667-1726).

146. K. George II. (1727-1760), Princess Caroline of Anspach (1683-1737).

147. Prince Frederick of Wales (1707-1751), Princess Augusta of Saxe-Gotha.

148. K. George III. (1760-1820), Princess Sophia of Mecklenburgh-Strelitz (1744-1818).

149. Duke Edward of Kent (1767-1820), Princess Victoria of Leiningen.

150. Q. Victoria (b. 1819, Crowned 1838, d. 1901), Prince Albert of Saxe-Coburg-Gotha.

151. K. Edward VII.

152. K. George V.

153. K. George VI.